D0216262

COMMUNITY CARE FOR NURSES AND THE CARING PROFESSIONS

Nigel Malin,
Jill Manthorpe,
David Race and
Stephen Wilmot

OPEN UNIVERSITY PRESS
Buckingham • Philadelphia

Open University Press
Celtic Court
22 Ballmoor
Buckingham
MK18 1XW

email: enquiries@openup.co.uk
world wide web: http://www.openup.co.uk

and
325 Chestnut Street
Philadelphia, PA 19106, USA

First Published 1999

Copyright © Nigel Malin, Jill Manthorpe, David Race and Stephen Wilmot 1999

All rights reserved. Except for the quotation of short passages for the purpose of criticism and review, no part of this publication may be reproduced, stored in a retrieval system, or transmitted, in any form or by any means, electronic, mechanical, photocopying, recording or otherwise, without the prior written permission of the publisher or a licence from the Copyright Licensing Agency Limited. Details of such licences (for reprographic reproduction) may be obtained from the Copyright Licensing Agency Ltd of 90 Tottenham Court Road, London, W1P 9HE.

A catalogue record of this book is available from the British Library

ISBN 0 335 19670 5 (pbk)   0 335 19671 3 (hbk)

Library of Congress Cataloging-in-Publication Data
   Community care for nurses and the caring professions / Nigel Malin . . .
[*et al.*].
      p.   cm. — (Social science for nurses and the caring professions)
   Includes bibliographical references and index.
   ISBN 0-335-19671-3. — ISBN 0-335-19670-5 (pbk.)
   1. Community health services.   2. Community health nursing.
3. Human services.   I. Malin, Nigel.   II. Series.
RA427.C614   1999
362.1′2—dc21
                                                                98–40515
                                                                CIP

Typeset by Graphicraft Limited, Hong Kong
Printed in Great Britain by Redwood Books, Trowbridge

CONTENTS

SERIES EDITOR'S PREFACE

Community care is central to British social policy and the work of those employed by the National Health Service. Since the Second World War successive governments have advocated a community care policy, which is best understood as providing care for those with high levels of care need, in the community rather than in residential accommodation – homes and hospitals. The impact of these policies has not been the same for all client groups, however, and informal carers often have to provide high levels of support.

An understanding of the debates surrounding the policy and of the role of nurses and other caring professionals, as well as informal carers, is essential for all nurses, not just those working in the community. This book provides a detailed analysis of the development and contemporary implementation of the policy. It will enable nurses and other caring professionals to understand it and its implications for different client groups and for informal and formal carers. The Labour government elected to power in May 1997 is unlikely to change the emphasis on community as opposed to residential care, although it has indicated that it agrees that care in the community may not be appropriate for all those with mental health problems. This follows a number of campaigns by groups concerned that some people with mental health problems receiving community care are a danger to themselves and/or other people and need more surveillance and support than is available in the community. The Labour government has also emphasized the need for 'joined-up care' – for the recipients of services to experience them as seamless. Community care is a key area in which services provided by a number of state, private and voluntary sector agencies are experienced as uncoordinated. An understanding of the experiences of recipients of services and of their expectations should enable caring professionals to meet clients'/patients' needs more effectively and efficiently.

This book will enable nurses and other caring professionals to reflect critically on their roles and the roles of other service providers in meeting the needs of those being cared for in the community. It will also enable them to consider the extent to which community care can and does meet the needs of diverse groups of people with diverse care requirements and the needs of informal carers. Community care is often seen as a humanitarian policy, enabling people to continue to live in the community. However, not everyone being cared for in the community receives the level and kind of care they need, and often a heavy, or indeed intolerable, burden is placed on informal carers. This book will inform nurses and other caring professionals and faciliate reflexive practice and evidence-based care.

Pamela Abbott

NOTES ABOUT THE AUTHORS

Nigel Malin is Professor of Community Care and Divisional Research Coordinator at the University of Derby. He is editor of *Implementing Community Care, Services for People with Learning Disabilities* and *Reassessing Community Care*. His main teaching has been social policy on health and social work programmes and he is currently undertaking research on clinical supervision and practice ethics in learning disabilities' services, as well as leading the planning of the Southern Derbyshire Community and Social Care Research Forum.

Jill Manthorpe is Senior Lecturer in Community Care at the University of Hull. She has wide research interests including the relationships between health and social services and private, voluntary and family networks. She has been a recent co-grant holder (both ESRC and ENB) conducting research under the Risk and Welfare Initiative and on Risk and the Nursing Curriculum.

David Race is Lecturer in the School of Social Work, Education and Counselling at Stockport College, teaching mainly on the BA Professional Studies: Learning Difficulties degree. He has studied health and social services in Hong Kong, the USA, Canada and Sweden and has been involved in various forms of training and evaluation, both in the UK and abroad. He is currently preparing a book on social role valorization.

Stephen Wilmot is Senior Lecturer in Health Care at the University of Derby, teaching mainly on health-related courses. He is currently Programme Leader for the M.Sc. General Practice Medicine and recent author of *The Ethics of Community Care* (Cassell 1997). His research interests include ethical dimensions of clinical practice, professional dilemmas and interprofessional issues in community care.

SECTION A

THE POLICY CONTEXT

BACKGROUND DEVELOPMENTS, 1957–88

Introduction

What is community care?

Problems in the use of the term 'community care' lie in the fact that it can mean quite different things. Official usage has not distinguished consistently between these meanings with the result that the term when used has lacked clarity and specificity. Originally the term referred to care outside of large institutions and it has retained this meaning in the areas of mental health and learning disabilities. This chapter will look at landmarks in legislation, progress, consolidation and retreat in policy and how changes in meaning have altered the perceptions and actions of main parties involved – for example, professionals, **user** groups and politicians.

One perspective on community care policy is to view it as a campaign without a target – not as a continuum or sequence of legislative events but as a series of distinct occurrences loosely welded together. It has been stated that the beginnings of the term 'community care' are obscure – see for example, Walker (1982), Bulmer (1987), Means and Smith (1994), Payne (1995), Lewis and Glennerster (1996). Bulmer argues that part of the responsibility for this lies with the lack of definition of '**community**' and of 'care'.

Early developments in community care

The National Health Service Act (1946) and the National Assistance Act (1948) set in the context of the post-Second World War welfare state period gave responsibilities to health and local authorities to provide residential accommodation for the elderly and the training and occupation of mental defectives over the age of 16. The Acts also identified a role for Medical Officers of Health in mental health work. This was followed by official reports, mainly on care of the elderly, addressing the need for small units, increased family care and domestic support (Walker 1982: 14; Lewis and Glennerster 1996: 1). But the publication of the *Report of the Royal Commission on Mental Illness and Mental Deficiency* (the Percy Report (Percy 1957) which led to the 1959 Mental Health Act) is viewed justifiably as the commencement of an era when the term community care became employed regularly. The World Health Organization's (WHO) Third Expert Committee on Mental Health (convened in 1953) suggested an open-door policy and a recognition of the importance of 'ward atmosphere', following the new practice of the therapeutic community developed by Dr Maxwell Jones at the Henderson Hospital, Claybury.

Since this period community care has attained a degree of prominence following a spate of developments and a refocusing of its aims. However, the relationship between 'policy' and '**ideology**' has remained nebulous despite the fact that both have engaged a continuing interest from academics and policy makers. Means and Smith (1994: 2) state that the 1959 Act referred to 'a policy shift away from hospitals and towards community-based provision for mentally handicapped people and for people with mental health problems'. The Act signified the emergence of local authorities in providing residential accommodation in order to reduce the need for hospital admission. It drew a distinction between mental illness, subnormality, severe subnormality and psychopathic disorder and the Percy Report (Percy 1957) entitled one of its chapters 'The Development of Community Care'. The chapter states: 'Community care covers all forms of care (including residential care) which it is appropriate for local health or welfare authorities to provide' (Percy 1957: 208).

The Commission was asked to consider and make recommendations on the statutory possibility of voluntary patient status, which would allow treatment without the necessity for certification. There was a clear directive to the Commission to consider means for reducing formalities of admission, discharge and community care. It considered a mass of evidence and its recommendations aimed to treat mental health in a comprehensive manner. The Commission proposed a new social work service for mentally ill and handicapped people to be provided by local councils (Younghusband Working Party 1959). As a result the 1960s saw a growth in residential homes and day centres and the beginnings of deinstitutionalization. Between 1955 and 1974 the number of patients resident in mental hospitals in Britain was reduced by some 30 per cent, although many of those released were old people (Giddens 1990).

Community care arising from deinstitutionalization

There exists no clear consensus regarding the forces driving the **deinstitutionalization** movement. The theme of the intellectual attack on institutional care is one in which other themes inevitably become interwoven. Supporting evidence was gathered from theoretical work covering institutions, notably that of Goffman (see Box 1.1), Foucault, Szasz and British empiricists such as Russell Barton and Peter Townsend.

By the beginning of the 1960s there was a serious questioning of the place of the subnormality hospital in the care of mentally handicapped

---

Box 1.1 Goffman's critique of community care

To take Goffman as an example, his critique focused upon 'role dispossession'. He invented the concept of the 'total institution' contending that such institutions have four main characteristics: batch living, binary management, the inmate role and the institutional perspective. 'Batch living' describes a situation where 'each phase of the member's daily activity is carried on in the immediate company of a large batch of others, all of whom are treated alike, and required to do the same thing together' (Goffman 1961: 6). His contention was that institutions have features in common. Not all features are specific to each institution, but residing in an institution is the 'antithesis of individual living', contrasted with: 'a basic arrangement in modern society [where] the individual tends to sleep, play and work in different places, with different co-participants under different authorities, and without an overall rational plan' (Goffman 1961: 13).

How do ordinary people, with their own way of life and personal networks and round of activities become inmates? Goffman thought that this was not a process of 'acculturation' that involved moving from one culture to another, but of 'disculturation' or 'role-stripping' – a process so powerful that the individual who was subjected to it would be rendered incapable of normal living when returned to the community. The individual was reduced from a person with many roles to a cypher with one: the 'inmate role'. The central feature of a total institution was said to be a 'breakdown of the barriers' found in ordinary life normally separating the place to live, the place to work and the place for recreation.

people (hereafter referred to as people with **learning difficulties**). Some hospital reformists saw a new role for the hospitals as centres of excellence where people with learning difficulties could come, from the community, for various periods of intensive training to prepare them to return to life outside. The debate grew throughout the 1960s, and was given urgency towards the end of the decade by a series of official and unofficial reports which revealed to the public for the first time the sordid results of public neglect and under-finance in many hospitals. Needless to say this had effectively influenced the hospital staff's understanding of the proper role of the organization, and of their own role towards the patients. A consequence of the hospital's ambivalent role was that the dilemma had spread elsewhere – to other organizations that ostensibly catered for people with learning difficulties, such as occupation centres and special schools.

Bayley (1973: 5) alleged that 'community care as a positive principle' and 'the genesis of the policy as a political fact' stemmed from the 1961 Annual Conference of the National Association for Mental Health where Enoch Powell, then minister of health radically supported deinstitutionalization: 'In fifteen years time there may well be needed not more than half as many places in hospitals for mental illness as there are today. Expressed in numerical terms, this would represent a redundancy of no fewer than 75,000 hospital beds' (National Association for Mental Health 1961: 8).

The subsequent Hospital Plan of 1962 (revised in 1966) and the complementary 'blue book' entitled *Health and Welfare: The Development of Community Care* (Ministry of Health 1963) confirmed this administratively and stressed a comparison between existing and planned local authority services needed to care for more people in the community, who otherwise might need care out of the community, generally in hospital. The plans referred more specifically to the mentally ill (hereafter referred to as people with mental health problems) and intended to reduce beds from 3.3 per 1000 population to 1.8 per 1000 population. Walker (1982: 16) quotes from the blue book regarding its intentions to expand community care for the elderly:

> Elderly people living at home may need special support to enable them to cope with their infirmities and to prevent their isolation from society. As their capabilities diminish, they will more often require such services as home help, laundry services, meals cooked ready for eating, and chiropody. Loss of mobility brings the need for friendly visiting, transport to social clubs and occupation centres, and arrangements for holidays. When illness is added to other infirmities, they need more home nursing, night care and help generally in the home. In terminal illness, an elderly person may for a limited period need considerable help from many of the domiciliary services.

The Hospital Plan of 1962 was born out of pressure to reduce the in-patient population in mental hospitals due to overcrowding in run-down, decaying, Victorian institutions (Scull 1977). Townsend (1971) suggested that the very existence of the long-stay hospital shaped our ideas about mental handicap (learning disability) and mental health, and affected our values, our fears and even our willingness to assume that the problem was one primarily for medicine and nursing. In his introduction to Pauline Morris's book *Put Away* (1969: iv), Townsend had asserted:

the mentally handicapped are not a distinct and identifiable group in themselves, their condition is defined by society, and the definitions are often highly suspect . . . if people are treated as mentally subnormal they often conform to expectations and appear subnormal. They can be stunted by their environment, particularly in an institutional setting. In fact there is a continuum from very high intelligence to very low intelligence and our places on it are not fixed; within limits we can move up and down.

The general public, Townsend argued, has an emotional investment in continuing to treat people with learning difficulties as a separate and definable group: 'it cannot admit its closeness to them, because it is afraid of them' (Morris 1969).

The idea of community care was not advanced as a principle during the 1960s chiefly because of lack of attention from central government and poor – almost invisible – coordination of services at local level. An impetus was provided by a series of revelations over conditions in long-stay institutions. *Sans Everything* (Robb 1967) was concerned mostly with mental health and elderly patients but it was followed shortly by reports of ill treatment of patients with learning difficulties at Ely Hospital, Cardiff (this particular **inquiry** into allegations of cruelty and neglect was published as the Howe Report (Howe 1969)).

Race (1995: 62) states that this report had little immediate effect in practice but that it won the support of Richard Crossman (then the Department of Health and Social Security (DHSS) minister). Crossman's diaries (1977) revealed how the DHSS had been reluctant to publish the *Howe Report* even though officials in the department had been aware of conditions at Ely Hospital for some time before the inquiry was instigated. However, the *Howe Report* helped to bring about the setting up of the Hospital Advisory Service, which reported directly to the minister.

This may have been a turning point but prevailing evidence does not seem to indicate any significant policy advances in line with findings from academic studies that were being conducted. Such studies during the 1960s highlighted two principal concerns: the poor and inappropriate treatment found in hospitals serving people with long-term care needs and how better quality of care could be achieved in smaller (community) units (see, for example, Townsend 1962; Tizard 1964; Morris 1969).

Barham's (1992) book covering mental health policy states that: 'the declarations of government policy in this period represented not so much a new departure as an assertive formulation of trends that were already taking place' (p. 11). Community care was unspecified 'simply because the character of the ex-mental patient in the community remained to a large degree unspecified' (p. 12). Community care facilities at this time were envisaged as transitional stepping-stones between a brief period of hospitalization and full reintegration into the community. A transitional period in a rehabilitation hostel or day centre, it was believed, would accomplish the mutation of former mental health patients into ordinary citizens, distinguishable from their associates only by their occasional attendances at out-patient clinics to renew their prescriptions. The new-found psychiatric optimism about the major tranquillizers coupled with protest about the indignities of mental hospital regimes converged to suggest that the concept of community care did not require elaborate specification or commitment (Bennett and Morris 1983). In truth the community came to possess a null value (Barham 1992: 14); it was not seen as a therapeutic site or as the arena for an interrogation of the moral crisis in the relations between people with mental health problems and the larger society, but just as the place to which people were to be returned after medicine had cured them.

It was never really the case that the critiques of institutions made a great impact on policy formation. However, they did shed light on the future meaning of community care through what they implied it should *not* represent: loss of liberty, social stigma, loss of autonomy, depersonalization and low material standards. The questioning of standards in such institutions created the suggestion that a culturally valued analogue, a different almost oppositional quality of lifestyle, was needed for patients. This was not articulated effectively at the political level. Had it been, it probably would have uncovered a myriad of issues relating to the civil and legal rights and freedoms of those in society being cared for in institutions or those living at home with similar infirmities or disabilities. A decade or more later such concerns gradually unfolded.

Goffman's book *Asylums* (1961) identified four 'interrelated characteristics' of the hospital pattern of care: rigidity, block treatment, depersonalization and social distance between staff and patients. Findings from British studies of the 1950s and 1960s deserve mention because they service the anti-institutional side of the argument and because of their interrelatedness (see Boxes 1.2–1.5).

Box 1.2 *Institutional Neurosis* (Barton 1959)

This book, amounting to only 63 pages, was written by a consultant psychiatrist based at a large mental hospital near London. His thesis was that patients came into mental hospitals with one form of illness, and the hospitals themselves could give them another. Institutional neurosis was a distinct condition which could be diagnosed and treated, clinical features being: apathy, lack of initiative, loss of interest in the outside world, submissiveness and resignation.

Barton pointed to 'clusters of factors' in the mental health environment which cause institutional neurosis to develop and which can be tackled at ward level: loss of contact with the outside world; enforced idleness; bossiness of medical and nursing staff; loss of personal friends, personal possessions and personal events; and drugs – the use of sedatives to produce apathy. The 'clusters of factors' also included ward atmosphere – poor furniture, decoration and lighting, dirt, noise, smell and the appearance of other patients all produce a general environment of drabness and depression; loss of overall prospects – the difficulties of taking up the patterns of family life again; loss of job prospects; problems of accommodation and making friends; and fears of loneliness in the outside world.

Box 1.3   *The Last Refuge: A Survey of Residential Institutions and Homes for the Aged in England and Wales* (Townsend 1962)

This was based on a national survey undertaken in the preceding four years. Jones and Fowles (1984: 79) state: 'The facts were amassed with a sense of moral outrage, and intended for practical action rather than for intellectual understanding; the style was distinctive . . . and set a fashion for social research'. The evidence of lack of privacy, loss of occupation, isolation, inability to form new relationships and the collapse of self-determination closely parallels institutional neurosis. Townsend developed scales for the measurement of the quality of homes and the capacities or incapacities of residents.

  He advocated at political level for the development of a 'family help service' to provide care for old people in their own homes. He also advocated the extension of services in the community such as better medical attention, sheltered housing, periodic inspection and small homes with a maximum capacity of 20–25 beds. Townsend used the argument that people living in institutions do not form a community in any accepted or meaningful sense of the word.

Box 1.4   *Put Away* (Morris 1969)

This was a sociological survey of 35 'subnormality hospitals' in England and Wales, which interpreted findings in terms of 'concepts of care'. Principal findings were poor physical conditions, staff shortages, poor communications between staff, lack of patient assessment and the isolation of 'subnormality hospitals', with lack of any identity with a local community felt by the patients. Similar in methodology to *The Last Refuge*, *Put Away* provided a wealth of material on actual living conditions:

> over one third of the patients sleep in dormitories of 60 or more, often with only a few inches between the beds and with no room for any other furniture. Patients are not encouraged to have personal possessions; there is nowhere to keep or display them. Physically the day rooms are in rather better condition, but most are too large to be 'homely' and do not have sufficient armchairs or settees to enable all patients to sit comfortably at the same time. Provisions in sanitary annexes are often extremely rudimentary, being deficient in lavatories and baths, as well as totally lacking in opportunities for privacy.
>
> (Morris 1969: 86)

Only a minority of residents seemed to need hospital care: 65 per cent of the patients had no physical handicap, 65 per cent were able to dress and feed themselves and only 12 per cent were severely incontinent. Emphasis was placed on the contrast between life led in hospitals and the rest of society: a loss of family contact, lack of activity for many of the patients, crowded living conditions, treatment of residents by staff as if they were children and the sheer emptiness of patients' lives.

Box 1.5 *Community Services for the Mentally Handicapped* (Tizard 1964) and *Patterns of Residential Care* (King *et al.* 1971)

The work of Professor Tizard and colleagues at the MRC Social Psychiatry Unit at the Maudsley Hospital, London had produced influential studies affecting the Percy Report (Percy 1957) and subsequent thinking about family care of children with learning disabilities (see, for example, O'Connor and Tizard 1956; Tizard and Grad 1961). Tizard's 1964 work furthered the social care planning argument by illustrating the divergence between 'ascertained' and 'administrative' prevalence (showing the gap between those receiving services and those that *ought* to be receiving services).

Community Services for the Mentally Handicapped was an account of the Brooklands Unit, a small experimental children's unit for 16 children of 'imbecile grade' run for two years (1958–60) where the children were treated according to principles developed in residential services rather than on medical and nursing lines. In *Patterns of Residential Care* the research progressed, utilizing quality of care scales devised by Tizard's colleagues at the Institute of Education in London (King and Raynes 1968). *Patterns of Residential Care* employed Goffman's (1961) ideas (rigidity, block treatment, depersonalization and social distance between staff and children) and compared hospital wards with local authority and voluntary homes. Findings showed that on all four dimensions there was considerable evidence of the negative criteria but that 'the hostel pattern of care involved these characteristics to a much lesser degree or else they were absent altogether' (King *et al.* 1971: 286). This lent weight to those on the 'community' side of the general argument over care (Race 1995) which continued as hospital boards began to come under heavy attack for depriving 'subnormality hospitals' of the facilities to carry out effective rehabilitation and for the hospital boards failing to accept their responsibilities as a training environment.

Community care arising from the 'planning for priority groups' movement in the 1970s

This period introduced a degree of serious planning in health and social care provision. Community care was an underlying goal of many of the plans but its presence was unremarkable and its objectives still rather vague. Yet the 1970s heralded a fundamental landmark in terms of reassessment with a different style of relationship between central and local government. Central plans on health and social care began to articulate service 'principles', ways forward and numerical targets. Walker (1982: 16) describes community care during this period as 'one of painfully slow progress towards timid goals' and having a precarious foundation. In truth the absence of strategy necessary to translate policy into practice, lack of earmarking central funds and wide ranging local autonomy in deciding how money was to be spent proved a frustrating barrier in moving services forward significantly.

Most of the (central government) health and social services master plans published in the 1970s for client groups such as mental health, learning difficulties and the elderly took the view that community care could be planned rationally and incrementally through 'local agency collaboration' following general objectives and principles laid down by central government. In retrospect this seems naive and ephemeral.

Other 'planning' assumptions were that there existed some kind of geographical groupings of people who were both able and willing to take on active caring on a consistent and reliable basis. This was despite the fact that the Seebohm Report (Seebohm Committee 1968), which set up social service departments at that time, recognized the force of the argument that links between individuals who form a non-geographical 'community of interest' may be stronger than relationships made on the basis of locality.

In a study of the 1974 Labour government's attempts to redirect local health and social service resources to priority groups the authors concluded that plans had not succeeded above all because 'the intellectual model for achieving change was simply inappropriate' (Lewis and Glennerster 1996: 20). The government had tried to adopt centralized, rational, comprehensive planning. It had produced a national budget and planning guidelines, and local districts and social service departments were intended to plan jointly to implement these guidelines. In practice, power in the National Health Service (NHS) and local authorities was so diverse and the competing bureaucratic interests so entrenched that such a model had little hope of success.

To take learning difficulties as an example, the central government plan (DHSS 1971a) was gradually to decant hospitals over a 20-year period and place people in suitable smaller units in the community from where they would commute daily to various day-care centres. Between 1971 and 1991 around 1100 new places were to be provided in the community per annum as hospitals narrowed down. Table 1.1 provides compelling evidence of the scale of such events.

Table 1.1 Residential places for adults with learning difficulties

	1969	1979	1985	1991* Projected number	1991* Actual number	1995
NHS hospital beds/places	52,100	45,400	41,000	27,000	20,074	11,400
Private nursing homes, hospitals			790		3,961	3,100
Local authority homes		11,400 (staffed and unstaffed)	11,100 (staffed)	29,400	12,978	9,670
Voluntary sector homes	4,300	3,800 registered	3,180		16,181	13,960 (staffed)
Private residential homes			2,950			12,730 (staffed)
Lodgings, foster homes	550			7,400		
Local authority unstaffed group homes			1,650			2,700
Small registered residential homes (less than 4 places, voluntary/private)						2,470
						Total: 56,030

* This column includes data on projected numbers taken from DHSS 1971a.

Change towards community care: Myths and realities

Although there is an approximate displacement from the health to the community sector numberswise, shown in Table 1.1, (i.e. around 38,000 fewer places in hospital and an equivalent increase in the community) three things stand out:

- the pace of change became more rapid during the last decade;
- care in the private sector opened up: there was a sevenfold increase in places between 1979 and 1995 (it is not only in provision for the elderly that the independent sector became the dominant partner);
- around 26,000 places (roughly 65 per cent) are still in facilities of over 20 places (Emerson *et al.* 1996) – i.e. 'institutional' or at least not an ordinary home, albeit 'in the community'. In other words, moving to a community home from a large hospital does not recessarily mean home-like accommodation.

The above example (Table 1.1) illustrates the point regarding residential services that real change in the number and range of places available 'in the community' (albeit in various types of residential home) did not take place until the latter part of the 1980s. The 1970s saw relatively slow progress in this type of provision despite the fact that the bulk of services fell under the heading of capital spending with more emphasis on constructing residential and day-care establishments rather than extending domiciliary care or in supporting a family-based service (of the kind advocated in the original terms of reference which underlay the creation of social service departments in 1971). The absence of clear policy and detailed planning was demonstrated in the extension of 'community care' to include some residential institutions and hospitals (Ministry of Health

1963: p. 24; DHSS 1976a: 38, 45, 49; Plank, 1978) rather than remaining as an alternative to institutional forms of care.

The Seebohm Report (Seebohm Committee 1968) which commenced the planning era of social care has a chapter on 'The Community':

> The term 'community' is usually understood to cover both the physical location and the common activity of a group of people. The definition of a community, however, or even of a neighbourhood, is increasingly difficult as society becomes more mobile and people belong to 'communities' of common interest, influenced by their work, education or social activities, as well as where they live. Thus, although traditionally the idea of a community has rested upon geographical locality, and this remains an important aspect of many communities, today different members of a family may belong to different communities of interest, as well as the same local neighbourhood. The notion of a community implies the existence of a network of reciprocal social relationships, which among other things ensure mutual aid and give those who experience it a sense of wellbeing.
>
> (Seebohm Committee 1968: para. 476)

This is a rather quaint, distant, verging upon patriarchal view of community care drawing some of its potency from an imagined past in which aged, handicapped and sick people were cared for in family or neighbourhood groupings. Its theoretical roots lie in earlier 'community studies' such as *The Family Life of Old People* (Townsend 1957), a survey of working-class life in Bethnal Green, East London and the new housing estates to which families were being moved. In a similar vein *Family and Kinship in East London* (Young and Willmott 1957) had examined the extended family concept and *Family and Class in a London Suburb* (Young and Willmott 1960) had discussed the emotionally impoverished life of nuclear families on a housing estate, where the loss of the extended family was compensated for by the acquisition of consumer goods.

'Planning' becomes localized

Community care in the 1970s was not an official policy; it was still not clear what did constitute such. The newly-created DHSS was involved in a massive realignment and reorganization of health and social services agencies, creating social service departments and area health authorities who were co-terminous and respectively responsible for separate 'social care' and 'health' functions. This did not signify an extensive resourcing of community care, or the researching of community care needs, but a consolidation of professional interests where the extension of bureaucratic organizational control and empire-building stood largely apart from the spectre of unmet needs in the community.

Government **White Papers** (for example, DHSS 1971a, 1975) spelled out planning targets and a series of largely uncoordinated principles and recommendations but these failed to be developed satisfactorily at local level. There was no real political force nor central lobby and left to their own devices local statutory agencies began to redefine their role and extend their expertise. They were rather less preoccupied with appraising the measure of unmet needs empirically, both at an individual and population level. Cooperation and coordination between separate services became a dominant policy theme, rather than the committed and imaginative expansion of domiciliary services and the closure of institutions (DHSS 1971a: 9–10, 1974: 35, 1976a: 1, 1981a). The White Paper *Better Services for the Mentally Handicapped* (DHSS 1971a) offered the first comprehensive guidance to be issued for any client group by a central department (Malin *et al.* 1980: 67; Korman and Glennerster 1990: 21) and it became a model for subsequent White Papers on the mentally ill (DHSS 1975) and the elderly (DHSS 1981b).

Better Services for the Mentally Handicapped stated that health, social services and education agencies should *jointly* plan, develop and operate services which are situated close to the people they are designed to serve (those with learning difficulties and their relatives). Local authority social services departments should provide residential places for people categorized as 'low dependency' (who constituted slightly more than half those needing residential care and who were inappropriately living in hospitals – (see DHSS 1971a, Table 5). The health authorities should provide the rest of the places needed and should concentrate on developing improved residential services for people with learning difficulties categorized as 'high dependency' – the most severely handicapped. The White Paper stated that 'when local authority services are fully developed fewer hospital beds for mentally handicapped in-patients will be needed than we have now' (DHSS 1971a: 47, para. 221). In discussing residential care in the community, it suggested the need for 'various forms':

> Residential care may be with foster parents, in lodgings, ordinary housing or a group of flatlets with social work support, a children's home, a home for the elderly mentally infirm, or a home (local authority or voluntary) specifically for mentally handicapped children or adults. The choice depends on the age, handicap and degree of social independence of each handicapped person.
>
> (DHSS 1971a: 35, para. 159)

The situation was perceived not simply as a case of 'running down' hospitals and building up community hostels or homes. Declarations of intent were made on the hospital situation and guidelines offered to cover the introduction of new provision: 'New assessment and treatment facilities will be needed for out-patients, day-patients and in-patients. Staff, buildings, equipment, furnishings and other essentials must be sufficient in quantity and quality to provide all patients with good treatment and good living conditions' (DHSS 1971a: 47, para. 221). Each health authority was expected to produce a 'development programme'; the key component in hospital improvement was 'domesticity' so as to allow for 'the possibility of rehabilitating institutionalised patients' who could be 'assessed in more normal living conditions' (p. 47). A cornerstone of the White Paper philosophy in the provision of any type of service for both children and adults of whatever level of ability was the need to develop their skills through educational and training methods: 'Each handicapped person needs stimulation, social training and education, and purposeful occupation or employment in order to develop to his maximum capacity and to exercise all the skills he acquires, however limited they may be' (9, para. 40(v)).

The influence of government White Papers

Better Services for the Mentally Handicapped (DHSS 1971a) began a debate over *what type* of care should be provided within the community and *for whom* this should be provided. Discussion became hindered by confusion over grading and packaging 'levels of ability' and matching these up with what were then considered alternative living environments – for example, hostel, hospital or group home. Typologies were presented (DHSS 1971b; Development Team for the Mentally Handicapped 1978) which sought to distinguish those needing hospital care from others, but no broadly acceptable basis for distinctions of this kind was ever created (Malin *et al.* 1980: 79).

The government White Paper *Better Services for the Mentally Ill* (DHSS 1975) produced a similar type of commitment to reduce the number of available psychiatric hospital beds and extend community treatment. It was based upon norms for service provision and envisaged local planning allowing for size of the population, their age, sex, ethnicity, length of hospitalization, diagnosis, chronic physical disabilities, and including rating of dependency. It drew a distinction between treatment function and the long-term supportive function of day services to be run by local authorities which was fundamental to the advancement of community care (although the fine details on day-care treatment were not set out precisely). It symbolized a planning vision of community care, essentially service-led, based upon the 'primary care team' consisting of the general medical practitioner (GP), the health visitor, the home nurse and the social worker: 'We believe that the philosophy of integration rather than isolation which has been the underlying theme of development still holds good; and that for the future, the main aims must continue to be the development of more locally-based services and a shift in the balance between hospital and social services care' (DHSS 1975: 2, para. 2.17).

The emphasis again was upon moving the main responsibility of care away from hospitals. The White Paper talked about what an ideal service would look like: the 'specialist therapeutic team' would be hospital-based, and would cover out-patient clinics, hostel provision and day care as well as in-patient work. There would be a crisis service, a mobile team on call 24 hours a day for emergencies. Kathleen Jones (1988: 39) was one critic later to express reservations and states of the 1975 White Paper:

> an outline was presented of what an ideal service would look like: the basis would be the 'primary care team', consisting of the general medical practitioner, the health visitor, the home nurse and the social worker . . . [then she refers to the] specialist therapeutic team [etc, and goes on to state]. This outline begged several questions. It assumed that a medical-nursing team based on general practice and trained in general medicine was capable of diagnosing and treating psychiatric conditions; that social workers would be available in sufficient numbers to be attached to medical teams, and would wish to work in such teams rather than in social services departments, organized around their

own professional skills; and that the administrative split between health and social services was unimportant – it could be dealt with by that trinity of graces co-ordination, collaboration and co-operation.

This lack of clarity over purpose, to equate function with setting, was neither practical nor desirable. Omitting to distinguish between different functions, as in the list of functions set out for day services, would continue to impede progress (Pilling 1991: 101). For example, the first three of the following day service functions were viewed by the White Paper as treatment functions to be provided by day hospitals:

1 As an alternative to hospital admission when an individual cannot be supported by out-patient services.
2 As a transitional phase between in-patient care and community residence.
3 As a venue for a period of intensive treatment or rehabilitation for limited periods.
4 As a source of long-term support and rehabilitation.

Coordination and collaboration

How to achieve coordination in the absence of a central coordinator became an issue taken up by the DHSS. Wistow and Whittingham (1988) diagnosed the difficulty as couched within the simultaneous reorganizations of the NHS and local government which came into effect in 1974. Here the distribution of functions between the reorganized services was based on a single fundamental principle: that their responsibilities should be demarcated according to the skills of providers rather than the needs of the individuals they served (DHSS 1970). The major consequence to flow from the application of this principle was the transfer of community health services from local government to new area health authorities, where they were managed alongside hospital services.

The separation of health and social services (each intended as independent and internally unified) was contrary to central government policies for service development and to the care needs of individuals served by both professions. In both these latter respects, the case presented was for greater integration in the planning and provision of care. Wistow and Whittingham (1988: 15) concur that at this time objectives of community care were 'shrouded in ambiguity'. They admit however, that community care recognizably implied a shift in the balance of responsibilities from the NHS to other agencies, as well as the ability and willingness of such agencies to assume proportionately greater responsibilities for providing care, and also that service planning and delivery processes needed to be more effectively integrated across agency boundaries.

Having created administrative, organizational and professional obstacles to achieving a needs-based approach (were that ever to have been an intention) the DHSS somewhat ironically then began to urge both agency and grass roots collaboration. Bachrach and Baratz (1962) have employed the expression 'mobilization of bias' to describe the characteristic of non-decision making resulting from the practice of limiting the scope of actual decision making to 'safe' issues. This may occur 'when the dominant values, the accepted rules of the game, the existing power relations among groups, and the instruments of force, singly or in combination, effectively prevent certain grievances from developing into fully fledged issues which call for decisions' (Bachrach and Baratz 1962: 642). Against a background of shadowy centralized leadership the prescribed remedy was to legislate for a process of localized collaboration.

This was to be facilitated through two means: drawing the boundaries of area health authorities to coincide with those of the local authorities responsible for personal social services ('one-to-one coterminosity'); and placing on both sets of authority a statutory duty to collaborate through a joint consultative committee (or JCC), a body which also had a statutory basis.

Joint planning

Whatever the real or alleged intentions of this, JCCs were viewed as largely stillborn (DHSS 1976b) and were supplemented in 1976 with the joint planning and joint finance initiatives. Joint planning was intended to be a more specific and strategic concept than the generalized notion of collaboration which it superseded. Accordingly, each health authority was required to establish with its matching social services authority a joint care planning team (JCPT) which would report to the JCC but be composed of officers with sufficient skills and authority to drive forward joint planning at a strategic level. Each JCPT could be supported by specialist subteams for specific client groups or issues.

Research on joint planning (in support of community care) showed that most agencies worked separately and at best only in parallel with each other (Booth 1981; Glennerster *et al.* 1983; Challis *et al.* 1988). An incrementalist rather than rational model predominated with joint objectives surfacing only when there was agreement of interests. A systems-wide view of need and service interdependencies contrasted with a perspective limited by the boundaries of a single organization or its subsections. Lindblom (1965, 1979) termed such an approach 'successive limited comparisons' where planning starts from basic issues (of agreement) and builds up, changing incrementally. He used the phrase 'partisan mutual adjustment' to describe coordination based on independent decision makers simply adapting to decisions around them, rather than focusing upon end goals. Whereas much joint planning might agree on service principles (of community care), the interpretation, prioritization and means of achieving such were frequently locked in combat.

A survey conducted by the Campaign for Mentally Handicapped People (CMH 1984) involving 79 district health authorities (DHAs) showed an apparently promising picture of 88 per cent of DHAs reporting the existence of JCPTs, but disparities in function and range of membership were wide. In this survey very few health districts saw themselves as being involved in the planning of comprehensive local services and joint planning remained dominated by health professionals with the likely, though not inescapable, implication that a medical model remained influential.

Joint finance

Joint finance was an earmarked sum of money allocated annually by the DHSS to health authorities in England (different arrangements existed in Scotland and Wales: see Hunter and Wistow 1987). The joint finance programme was designed to enable short-term financial support to be provided to projects in the personal social services which were of demonstrable benefit to the health service. From 1977 it was extended to include voluntary organizations, housing, education, community health and primary health services. Most of the money was allocated to the personal social services, though evidence existed that at least a significant minority of health authorities allocated substantial sums to the support of community health services (National Audit Office 1987).

At its inception, ministers identified the primary purpose of joint finance as being 'to reduce dependence on long-stay hospitals' (Castle 1975) by providing the personal social services with a tangible incentive to engage with the health service in the development of community care. The programme provided short-term pump priming support which many local authorities used to deal with growing demands for care from individuals living in the community rather than to discharge patients from long-stay hospitals. By the early 1980s central government wished to speed up the discharge of long-stay patients to the community and new solutions needed to be found.

Community care arising from the continuum of formal and informal care

Research studies rather than policy achieved recognition of the view, during the 1980s, that most caring was provided by family members, mainly women. Pressure to demonstrate this was supplied through a buoyant central government ideology to disestablish welfare planning and substitute it with a notion that 'care in the community must increasingly mean care by the community' (DHSS 1981a: 4). Community care policy was re-examined in response to an increasingly ubiquitous **carers**' lobby. The nature of care and who provided it became issues subject to frequent, rigorous analysis.

In its original form, community care policy had envisaged a significant role for public services in maintaining highly dependent people outside large institutions. By the early 1980s this was less clearly the case (Baldwin and Twigg 1991). Under the twin pressures of fiscal crisis and an ideologically driven commitment to reducing the role of the state in service provision, the original vision was replaced by a much stronger emphasis on the provision of care by 'the community' itself (Parker 1990).

The 'emergence' of gender

At this point, gender emerged for the first time as a key variable in the analysis of community care policy in a paper presented by Janet Finch and Dulcie Groves to the Annual Conference of the Social Administration

Association, and subsequently published in the *Journal of Social Policy* (Finch and Groves 1980). Influential studies from feminist writers began to play a key part in community care developments (for example, Pahl 1980; Nissel and Bonnerjea 1982; Graham 1983; Baldwin 1985; Green 1988; Arber *et al.* 1988; Qureshi and Walker 1989; see also Box 1.6).

Box 1.6 Key community care studies

Arber, S. and Gilbert, N. (1989) *Men: The Forgotten Carers.* London: Sage.
Arber, S., Gilbert, N. and Evandrou, M. (1988) Gender, household composition and receipt of domiciliary services by the elderly disabled. *Journal of Social Policy*, 17 (2): 153–76.
Audit Commission (1986) *Making a Reality of Community Care.* London: HMSO.
Baldwin, S. (1985) *The Costs of Caring: Families with Disabled Children.* London: RKP.
Finch, J. and Groves, D. (1983) *A Labour of Love: Women, Work and Caring.* London: Routledge and Kegan Paul.
Green, H. (1988) *Informal Carers: A Study.* London: OPCS, HMSO.
Nissel, M. and Bonnerjea, L. (1982) *Family Care of the Handicapped Elderly: Who Pays?* London: PSI.
Parker, G. (1990) *With Due Care and Attention: A Review of Research on Informal Care.* London: Family Policy Studies Centre.
Qureshi, H. and Walker, A. (1989) *The Caring Relationship: Elderly People and their Families.* London: Macmillan.
Ungerson, C. (1987) *Policy is Personal: Sex, Gender and Informal Care.* London: Tavistock.

Such studies showed how carers formed the bedrock of policy and that they were exploited. At the root of all community care policies seemed to be the firm belief that the family was the appropriate unit and location of care. Privacy and independence, both regarded as being goals to be prized and achieved, could best be secured by remaining in one's own home. Finch's critique (1984) questioned whether a non-sexist version of community care was possible, suggesting that continued reliance upon the family primarily would ensure women's exploitation. One of the most significant developments in carer literature was the trend to disaggregate the category of carer and explore how its dynamics operated differentially in regard to different relationships (Baldwin and Twigg 1991).

The unequal burdens on women in the care of elderly relatives, disabled offspring and family members with mental health problems appeared throughout, particularly in the heavy end of caring involving more intimate tasks of personal care (Green, 1988). Genuine shared care was rare. Studies (for example Parker 1990), pointed to the effects of these responsibilities on the psychological and physical health of women carers and to the failure by service providers to develop the kind of help women carers were likely to perceive as useful (Parker 1989). There was also evidence that male carers received more help from statutory services than female carers did.

The association of caring with femaleness was explored by writers such as Ungerson (1981, 1987), Graham (1983) and Dalley (1988). Caring for and caring about (according to Dalley) were deemed to form a unitary, integral part of a woman's nature. She suggested that 'this blurring of the boundaries between functions typif[ied] a woman's universe ... [that] the menial tasks of family servicing [were] wrapped up and presented as part and parcel of her role as a mother' (Dalley 1988: 8). The root of the confusion – to identify femaleness with motherhood, and hence caring – lies, Dalley alleges, in 'the nature of women's psychological make-up' (p. 9) which is characterized as being about 'being' rather than about 'doing'. The argument continues with respect to the public sphere, where the same forces are said to be at work; women go into the caring occupations because their natures and their overlapping capacities for caring for and caring about are thought to suit them well for those types of jobs.

A policy of reliance on the family

Policies during the 1980s, such as the House of Commons Select Committee Report (House of Commons 1985) talked of the failure of central government to show leadership in developing community care. The 1985 report criticized the slow movement of people being discharged into the community, stressing that community-based services cannot be established on a cost-neutral proposition. Yet it also tacitly furthered the status quo, confirming the salience of the family as prime carer (these issues are discussed in greater depth in Chapter 6). Policies in the 1980s rarely included carers and merely referred to 'supporting families', interweaving statutory formal with **informal care**, working in partnership or complementing the role of the family (for example, DHSS 1986). In short, policies in the 1980s took 'family care' for granted.

For example, a DHSS review of services for people with learning difficulties (DHSS 1971a) stated that 'services for people living at home are central to a successful policy of community-orientated care' (para. 2.32), and 'that little is known about such services and consideration ought to be given to the part volunteers can play'. A chapter on the role of the voluntary sector was typically the penultimate section of government reports produced during this period, urging a commitment towards co-ordinating volunteer labour in the development of the concept of community care depending upon local interests and resources. The **Audit Commission**'s *Making a Reality of Community Care* (1986), while admitting that 'policies place[d] an additional burden on relatives at a time when the whole concept of a supporting community is breaking down' (para. 9) still took the view that support from relatives and even neighbours remained at high levels (in the form of 'dispersed extended families') and – by implication – that this was not necessarily a source of concern. As Twigg and Atkin (1994: 6) have remarked 'supporting carers represented a highly cost-effective strategy'. Social care agencies only needed to put in small amounts of formal resources to ensure extensive **inputs** from the informal sector.

However, the carer issue did emerge significantly at one (pressure group) level during the 1980s with the creation of what is now the Carers National Association. Twigg and Atkin (1994) claim that studies exploring the daily grind of care giving and the costs it imposes – emotional, physical and financial – played a large part in this creative activity by pushing the carer issue onto the policy agenda. In the background, research such as that by Wenger (1984) on networks among the elderly was showing how support for care givers was 'too little and too late'. The study by the University of Kent's Personal Social Services Research Unit (PSSRU) (Davies and Challis 1986) indicated how the use of residential homes to relieve relatives for short periods consumed only a small proportion of the resources of that service, and how 'at least 85 per cent of domestic help, the biggest home care service, is largely allocated to those living alone or with their elderly spouses' (Davies and Challis 1986: 46). Bayley's Dinnington study (1982) showed furthermore that resources allocated to the cared-for person were not often used in a way that would complement and encourage the efforts of informal carers and those who could potentially be informal carers (illustrated for example through 'wardens' contacting informal carers so rarely).

The policy of increased reliance upon the family to provide care (through reducing the proportion of public expenditure going to personal social services) was set, as Qureshi and Walker later claimed (1989), against a panoply of the Conservative government's own economic and social policies which were undermining the ability of families to shoulder such responsibilities (policies that increased the poverty divide and which contributed to mass unemployment). It was not until the publication of Sir Roy Griffiths' seminal report in 1988 (*Community Care: An Agenda for Action*) that a measure or semblance of recognition emerged (in policy-speak) towards unpaid carers, noting that the delivery of community care had, to date, depended largely on their goodwill.

Community care arising from the Conservative government's 'care in the community' initiative

The intention of the community care initiative was to help long-stay hospital patients unnecessarily kept in hospital to return to the community. The 1981 Care in the Community consultative document (DHSS 1981c) began with the phrase: 'most people who need long-term care can and should be looked after in the community. This is what most of them want for themselves and what those responsible for their care believe to be best' (para. 1.1). It continued: 'There are many people in hospital who would not need to be there if appropriate community services were available. But the legal, administrative and financial framework within which health and local authorities operate presents obstacles to their transfer' (para. 1.2).

The real motive of government was to cut the formidable expense of long-term hospital care and later to promote more cost-effective, cost-efficient varieties of care through separating the purchaser of care from the provider. The emphasis would be upon altering the means rather than the **outcomes** (unless cutting the overall state financial contribution counted as an outcome). In a 1983 Circular, the government established a number of pilot projects to investigate ways of moving long-stay patients out of hospital (DHSS 1983). Twenty-eight demonstration projects were centrally funded for three years (13 in the first round which began in April 1984, and 15 in the second which commenced a year later). Most of the projects represented models of care for people with mental illness or learning difficulties, and for elderly or elderly mentally infirm people. Together these pilot projects expected to provide services which would enable about 900 hospital patients to move into the community (Renshaw et al. 1988). As the PSSRU evaluation indicates, by March 1987 456 people (only) had moved out to the community, from a planned total of 896 (Renshaw et al. 1988). The main problems concerned finance (for example, 'double funding' – transitional costs required to put a new service in place before the old one can be removed); timescales (nearly all projects found that every step took far longer than had been anticipated); and professional resistance.

Initiatives and incentives

The policy of the Conservative government was not to fund deinstitutional-ization nationwide but to set up initiatives such as care in the community where lessons could be learned, particularly with respect to managing joint finance and monitoring the health/local authority partnership. There occurred no decisive intervention by government in the activities of 'locals' apart from a range of relatively small-scale financial incentives. Hence the shape of what emerged was set by the character of competing local actors. For example, the authors of the PSSRU evaluation state how projects characterized by innovation and enterprise were outnumbered 'by others exhibiting a singular blend of confusion and inertia' (Renshaw et al. 1988: 186). It was not until the funding issue became public knowledge through publication of the Audit Commission report in 1986 that a more robust lead was taken by government.

Cambridge et al. (1994), in discussing the government's 'care in the community programme' drew attention to the fact that the purpose was not simply relocation of care for a group of vulnerable people but an 'opportunity to improve individual quality of life and also an opportunity to test the feasibility and quality of community care under carefully mon-itored circumstances' (p. 7). The intention was for both good and bad experiences from the pilot services to be disseminated. In addition, those agencies receiving DHSS pump-priming grants needed to evidence a com-mitment to 'carefully coordinated, needs-led care planning' (Cambridge et al. 1994). In truth the pilot projects of the mid-1980s were early attempts to do many of the things later demanded or encouraged by the 1990 National Health Service and Community Care Act (such as **care manage-ment** in consultation with users, commissioning with voluntary sector providers etc.).

The care in the community programme did not lay down a single model of community care, and as a result different 'care technologies' and mixtures of provision emerged. For example, in learning disabilities much experimental and development work was set around housing-based community services. Studies continued to claim that significant gains in skill acquisition were found together with improvements in user and family satisfaction and other aspects of service delivery (Hemming 1982; Malin 1983; Felce *et al.* 1986; Flynn 1986; Mansell *et al.* 1987). Yet it was argued that the results of these 'first generation' or demonstration projects became difficult to sustain as later similar evaluations produced mixed results:

> although most other aspects of service quality have been found to be better in staffed housing, the persistence of low levels of service **user involvement** in meaningful activity and low levels of staff-client interaction in some services represents a failure to fully realise the opportunities created by the abandonment of institutions.
>
> (Mansell *et al.* 1994: 70)

A critique of the institutional nature of community-based day care led similarly to development work seeking to improve the relationship between service organization and client experience (Dalgleish and Matthews 1980, 1981). In most of the demonstration projects, however, segregated services such as social education centres and adult training centres still pervaded – few people had found employment and few centres provided a working routine (Cambridge *et al.* 1994: 67).

A further aspect of the Conservative government's initiative was to publish the Second Report from the House of Commons Social Services Select Committee Report 1984–5 entitled *Community Care* (House of Commons 1985) Volumes I and II. This was a weighty document and included verbatim evidence from a wide ranging number of organizations and individuals. It concluded that the DHSS '[was] not in every respect living up to its duties of central management' but generally endorsed the overall policy. Nicholas Bosanquet (who earlier as a member of a previous government's working group into training of nursing staff – the Jay Enquiry 1979 – had been responsible for a critical minority report) wrote in an article that the Select Committee failed to deal with the central question: can the system actually be tuned to deliver community care? (Bosanquet 1985). It was difficult to disagree with this conclusion: the Report lamented the failure (or rather slow pace and commitment) of efforts to bring about major change in hospital closure, in using joint finance, and in meeting housing and employment needs. Nevertheless it did not recommend a viable alternative approach.

The Report commended the achievements of schemes to improve the lives of vulnerable and disabled people around the country, and stated how government expenditure on residential and day care for people with mental health needs and people with learning difficulties had been rising three times as rapidly as the average overall increase in all social services spending. Its main concern was with the hospital discharge mechanism and preventing people from being moved into the community without a practical individual care plan devised by all concerned. Whereas the indicators seemed to show that social security funding would form the basis of future community care, this, the Select Committee remarked, did not seem to be 'widely appreciated' by either central or local government.

Others (for example MIND (National Association for Mental Health) 1984) said that there was no alternative to the government making available annually substantial extra resources.

Conclusions

The remainder of this book explores many of the issues raised here in more depth. The following chapter looks at the policy reforms which impacted upon community care and which occurred during the late 1980s, introducing a mixed-economy approach. Subsequent sections consider the relationship between theory and practice, and policy and practice. Section B explores concepts and values in policy and service delivery, whereas Section C examines the position of both users of services and carers. It questions whether services support carers adequately and how their needs and interests are incorporated. The section considers the empowerment of service users and the principles supposedly inherent in government policies (like accessibility, choice, redress and representation). The final section, Section D, looks at the professional side of community care and how this has been organized and presented. It analyses consensus and conflict among professional groups, values, knowledge and the viability of working in teams. A central part of this book is a concern with evaluating continuing themes in community care: the search for meaning, purpose and long-term strategy.

Summary

- The beginnings of community care policies are obscure although the 1957 Royal Commission relating to mental health and mental deficiency is usually regarded as a key symbolic landmark.
- Policies have arisen from a combination of loosely welded together activities and events, for example, closure of long-stay hospitals, social care planning during the 1970s, activities of pressure groups, and various government health initiatives.
- Critiques of institutional care had the greatest impact on the future direction of community care through what they implied it should *not* represent: loss of liberty and autonomy, social stigma and low material standards.
- Government plans during the 1970s were based upon norms for service provision and identifying principles and targets relying somewhat ambitiously for their success on coordinating advice and finance from central government with local developments.
- Policies consistently appeared to take for granted the family as unpaid carer, particularly exploiting women. Mainstream literature on carers during the 1980s re-examined policies in response to an increasingly ubiquitous carers' lobby.

- The government-led 'care in the community' project demonstrated nationwide the need for individual care plans, service flexibility and the removal of structural, professional barriers. It also demonstrated the salience of leadership and of government taking more responsibility if practice was to change radically.

Further reading

Bean, P. and Mounser, P. (1993) *Discharged from Mental Hospitals*. Basingstoke: Macmillan.

Bulmer, M. (1987) *The Social Basis of Community Care*. London: Unwin Hyman.

Malin, N. (ed.) (1987) *Reassessing Community Care*. London: Croom Helm.

Mansell, J. and Ericsson, K. (eds) (1996) *Deinstitutionalization and Community Living*. London: Chapman & Hall.

Ottewill, R. and Wall, A. (1990) *The Growth and Development of the Community Health Services*. Sunderland: Business Education Publishers.

Renshaw, J., Hampson, R., Thomason, C., Darton, R., Judge, K. and Knapp, M. (1988) *Care in the Community: The First Steps*. Aldershot: Gower/PSSRU, University of Kent.

Seebohm Committee (1968) *Report of the Committee on Local Authority and Allied Personal Social Services*, Cmnd. 3703. London: HMSO.

Walker, A. (ed.) (1982) *Community Care: The Family, the State and Social Policy*. Oxford: Blackwell.

References

Arber, S., Gilbert, N. and Evandrou, M. (1988) Gender, household composition and receipt of domiciliary services by the elderly disabled. *Journal of Social Policy*, 17 (2): 153–76.

Audit Commission (1986) *Making a Reality of Community Care*. London: HMSO.

Bachrach, P. and Baratz, M. (1962) Two faces of power. *American Political Science Review*, 56: 664–79.

Baldwin, S. (1985) *The Costs of Caring: Families with Disabled Children*. London: RKP.

Baldwin, S. and Twigg, J. (1991) Women and community care: reflections on a debate, in M. McLean and D. Groves (eds) *Women's Issues in Social Policy*. London: Routledge.

Barham, P. (1992) *Closing the Asylum: The Mental Patient in Modern Society*. London: Penguin.

Barton, R. (1959) *Institutional Neurosis*. Bristol: John Wright & Sons.

Bayley, M. (1973) *Mental Handicap and Community Care*. London: Routledge.

Bayley, M. (1982) *What Resources Does the Informal Sector Require to Fulfil its Role?* Sheffield: Department of Social Studies, University of Sheffield.

Bennett, D. and Morris, I. (1983) Deinstitutionalization in the UK. *International Journal of Mental Health*, 11 (4): 5–23.

Booth, T. (1981) Collaboration between the health service and social services. *Policy and Politics*, 9 (1): 23–9.

Bosanquet, N. (1985) Failure to identify opportunities. *Health and Social Services Journal*, 18 (April): 16–19.

Bulmer, M. (1987) *The Social Basis of Community Care*. London: Unwin Hyman.

Cambridge, P., Hayes, L. and Knapp, M. (1994) *Care in the Community: Five Years On*. Aldershot: Gower.

CMH (1984) *A Survey of District Health Authorities Planning Groups for Services to People with a Mental Handicap*. London: CMH.

Castle, B. (1975) Speech to the National Association of Health Authorities, 11 July. London: NAHA.

Challis, L., Fuller, S., Henwood, M., Klein, R., Plowden, W., Webb, A., Whittingham, P. and Wistow, G. (1988) *Joint Approaches to Social Policy*. Cambridge: Cambridge University Press.

Crossman, R. (1977) *The Diaries of a Cabinet Minister*, vol. 3. London: Hamish Hamilton.

Dalgleish, M. and Matthews, R. (1980) Some effects of environmental design on the quality of day care for severely mentally handicapped adults. *British Journal of Mental Subnormality*, 26: 94–102.

Dalgleish, M. and Matthews, R. (1981) Some effects of staffing levels and group size on the quality of day care for severely mentally handicapped adults. *British Journal of Mental Subnormality*, 27: 30–5.

Dalley, G. (1988) *Ideologies of Caring: Rethinking Community and Collectivism*. London: Macmillan.

Davies, B. and Challis, D. (1986) *Matching Resources to Needs in Community Care*. Aldershot: Gower.

Development Team for the Mentally Handicapped (1978) *First Report 1976–7*. London: HMSO.

DHSS (1970) *National Health Service: The Future Structure of the NHS*. London, HMSO.

DHSS (1971a) *Better Services for the Mentally Handicapped*, Cmnd. 4683. London: HMSO.

DHSS (1971b) *MO (MS) 46 Development Project: Feasibility Study Report Proposing a New Pattern of Service for the Mentally Handicapped in Sheffield County Borough*. London: HMSO.

DHSS (1974) *Report of the Committee of Enquiry into South Ockenden Hospital*. London: HMSO.

DHSS (1975) *Better Services for the Mentally Ill*, Cmnd. 6233. London: HMSO.

DHSS (1976a) *Priorities for Health and Social Services in England*. London: HMSO.

DHSS (1976b) *Joint consultative committee review: 31 March, report 2*. London: DHSS.

DHSS (1981a) *Care in Action*. London: HMSO.

DHSS (1981b) *Growing Older*, Cmnd. 8173. London: HMSO.

DHSS (1981c) *Care in the Community: A Consultative Document for Moving Resources for Care in England*, HC (81) 9, LAC (81) 9, LAC (81) 5. London: HMSO.

DHSS (1983) *Care in the Community*, HC (83) 6, LAC (83) 5. London: HMSO.

DHSS (1986) Neighbourhood Nursing: A Focus for Care (Report of the Community Nursing Review). London: HMSO.

Emerson, E., Cullen, C., Hatton, C. and Cross, B. (1996) *Residential Provision for People with Learning Disabilities: Summary Report*. Manchester: University of Manchester, HARC.

Felce, D., de Kock, V., Thomas, M. and Saxby, H. (1986) Change in adaptive behaviour of severely and profoundly mentally handicapped adults in different residential settings. *British Journal of Psychology*, 77: 489–501.

Finch, J. (1984) Community care: developing non-sexist alternatives. *Critical Social Policy*, 9: 6–18.

Finch, J. and Groves, D. (1980) Community care and the family: a case for equal opportunities? *Journal of Social Policy*, 9 (4): 486–511.

Flynn, M. (1986) *A Study of Prediction in the Community Placements of Adults who are Mentally Handicapped (1983–86)* (final report submitted to the ESRC). London: Economic and Social Research Council.

Giddens, A. (1990) *Sociology*. Cambridge: Polity Press.

Glennerster, H., Korman, N. and Marslen-Wilson, F. (1983) *Planning for priority groups*. Oxford: Martin Robertson.

Goffman, E. (1961) *Asylums: Essays on the Social Situation of Mental Patients and Other Inmates*. Harmondsworth: Penguin.

Graham, H. (1983) Caring: a labour of love, in J. Finch and D. Groves (eds) *A Labour of Love: Women, Work and Caring*. London: Routledge.

Green, H. (1988) *Informal Carers: A Study*. London: OPCS, HMSO.

Griffiths, R. (1988) *Community Care: An Agenda for Action. A report to the Secretary of State for Social Services*. London: HMSO.

Hemming, H. (1982) Mentally handicapped adults returned to large institutions after transfers to new small units. *British Journal of Mental Subnormality*, 28: 13–28.

House of Commons (1985) *2nd Report from the Social Services Committee Session (1984–85), Community Care: With Special Reference to Adult Mentally Ill and Mentally Handicapped People*, vols I–II. London: HMSO.

Howe, G. (1969) *Report of the Committee of Inquiry into Allegations of Illtreatment of Patients and Other Irregularities at the Ely Hospital, Cardiff (the Howe Report)*, Cmnd. 3795. London: HMSO.

Hunter, D. and Wistow, G. (1987) *Community Care in Britain: Variations on a Theme*. London: King's Fund.

Jones, K. (1988) *Experience in Mental Health: Community Care and Social Policy*. London: Sage.

Jones, K. and Fowles, A. (1984) *Ideas on Institutions – Analysing the Literature on Long-term Care and Custody*. London: Routledge.

King, R. and Raynes, N. (1968) An operational measure of inmate management in residential institutions. *Social Science and Medicine*, 2: 41–53.

King, R., Raynes, N. and Tizard, J. (1971) *Patterns of Residential Care: Sociological Studies in Institutions for Handicapped Children*. London: Routledge.

Korman, N. and Glennerster, H. (1990) *Hospital closure*. Buckingham: Open University Press.

Lewis, J. and Glennerster, H. (1996) *Implementing the New Community Care*. Buckingham: Open University Press.

Lindblom, C. (1965) *The Intelligence of Democracy*. New York: The Free Press.

Lindblom, C. (1979) Still muddling, not yet through. *Public Administration Review*, 39: 151–68.

Malin, N. (1983) *Group Homes for Mentally Handicapped People*. London: HMSO.

Malin, N., Race, D. and Jones, G. (1980) *Services for the Mentally Handicapped in Britain*. London: Croom Helm.

Mansell, J., Felce, D., Jenkins, J., de Kock, U. and Toogood, A. (1987) *Developing Staffed Housing for People with Mental Handicaps*, Tunbridge Wells: Costello.

Mansell, J., McGill, P. and Emerson, E. (1994) Conceptualising service provision, in E. Emerson, P. McGill and J. Mansell (eds) *Severe Learning Disabilities and Challenging Behaviours*. London: Chapman & Hall.

Means, R. and Smith, R. (1994) *Community Care: Policy and Practice*. Basingstoke: Macmillan.

MIND (1984) *Common Concern*. London: MIND.

Ministry of Health (1963) *Health and Welfare: The Development of Community Care*, Cmnd. 1973. London: HMSO.

Morris, P. (1969) *Put Away: A Sociological Study of Institutions for the Mentally Retarded*. London: Routledge.

National Association for Mental Health (1961) *Annual Report for 1960–61*, London: NAMH.

National Audit Office (1987) *Community Care Developments, Report by the Comptroller and Auditor General, HC 108*. London: HMSO.

Nissel, M. and Bonnerjea, L. (1982) *Family Care of the Handicapped Elderly: Who Pays?* London: PSI.

O'Connor, N. and Tizard, J. (1956) *The Social Problem of Mental Deficiency*. London: Pergamon.

Pahl, J. (1980) Patterns of money management. *Journal of Social Policy*, 9 (3): 313–35.

Parker, G. (1989) 'A study of non-elderly spouse carers', unpublished research report. University of York, SPRU.

Parker, G. (1990) *With Due Care and Attention: A Review of Research on Informal Care*. London: Family Policy Studies Centre.

Payne, M. (1995) *Social Work and Community Care*. Basingstoke: Macmillan.

Percy, N. (1957) *Report of the Royal Commission on Mental Illness and Mental Deficiency* (the Percy Report), Cmnd. 169. London: HMSO.

Pilling, S. (1991) *Rehabilitation and Community Care*. London: Routledge.

Plank, D. (1978) *Caring for the Elderly: Report of a Study of Various Means of Caring for Dependent Elderly People in 8 London Boroughs*. London: GLC.

Qureshi, H. and Walker, A. (1989) *The Caring Relationship: Elderly People and their Families*. London: Macmillan.

Race, D. (1995) Historical development of service provision, in N. Malin (ed.) *Services for People with Learning Disabilities*, pp. 62–3. London: Routledge.

Renshaw, J., Hampson, R., Thomason, C., Darton, R., Judge, K. and Knapp, M. (1988) *Care in the Community: The First Steps*. Aldershot: Gower.

Robb, B. (ed.) (1967) *Sans Everything: A Case to Answer*. London: Nelson.

Scull, A. (1977) *Decarceration: Community Treatment and the Deviant; a Radical View*. Englewood Cliffs, NJ: Prentice Hall.

Seebohm Committee (1968) *Report of the Committee on Local Authority and Allied Personal Social Services*, Cmnd. 3703. London: HMSO.

Tizard, J. (1964) *Community Services for the Mentally Handicapped*. Oxford: Oxford University Press.

Tizard, J. and Grad, J. (1961) *The Mentally Handicapped and their Families*. Oxford: Oxford University Press.

Townsend, P. (1957) *The Family of Old People*. Harmondsworth: Penguin.

Townsend, P. (1962) *The Last Refuge: A Survey of Residential Institutions and Homes for the Aged in England and Wales*. London: Routledge.

Townsend, P. (1971) Limiting factors in policy making, in *Action for the Retarded*, NSMHC, Conference papers, March/April. London: NSMHC.

Twigg, J. and Atkin, K. (1994) *Carers Perceived: Policy and Practice in Informal Care*. Buckingham: Open University Press.

Ungerson, C. (1981) Women and caring: skills, tasks and taboos, in E. Gamarnikow, D. Morgan, J. Purvis and D. Taylorson (eds) *The Public and the Private*. London: Heinemann.

Ungerson, C. (1987) *Policy is Personal: Sex, Gender and Informal Care*. London: Tavistock.

Walker, A. (ed.) (1982) *Community Care: The Family, the State and Social Policy*. Oxford: Blackwell.

Wenger, C. (1984) *The Supportive Network: Coping with Old Age*. London: George Allen and Unwin.

Wistow, G. and Whittingham, D. (1988) Policy and research into practice, in D. Stockford (ed.) *Integrating Care Systems: Practical Perspectives*. Harlow: Longman.

Young, M. and Willmott, P. (1957) *Family and Kinship in East London*. London: Routledge.

Young, M. and Willmott, P. (1960) *Family and Class in a London Suburb*. London: Routledge and Kegan Paul.

Younghusband Working Party (1959) *Report of the Working Party on Social Workers in the Local Authority and Welfare Services*. London: HMSO.

THE REFORMS AND THE MIXED ECONOMY

Introduction

This chapter examines the reforms introduced at the end of the 1980s which led to the National Health Service and Community Care Act 1990. It discusses how the reforms unfolded and their impact, expanding on the idea of needs-based planning, taking *Caring for People* (Department of Health 1989) and allied documents as a foundation. It describes briefly the crisis in funding and the curtailment of local financial autonomy, as well as how policy has created opportunities to shift the burden of responsibility for care from the state to the individual. It finally discusses some dilemmas that have faced practitioners and their organizations charged with implementing community care.

Background to the reforms

The build-up to the reforms was described in the previous chapter. The argument has been made that somehow policies became overtaken by events and that there was now a need to do something. Community care had never been installed as a main political cause. There had been criticism of the effects of what was happening at local level but lack of leadership became a buzz-phrase following the House of Commons (1985) Select Committee Report. Lewis and Glennerster (1996) argue (and many have agreed with the conclusion) that it was the funding issue, or rather the unchallenged financing of private residential and nursing home care which made the enormous claim upon the social security budget, that caused the Thatcher government to act:

> From November 1980 the rules under which people could claim board and lodging expenses were regulated by statute under Parliamentary statutory instruments. These allowed someone who was a boarder to claim the full board and lodging charge plus an amount to cover personal expenses. A 'lodger' included not only those lodging with a landlady, say, in the normal sense of the word, but also those living in hostels and residential homes for the elderly and disabled and in nursing homes. A maximum sum for fee reimbursement was set, which had to be a reasonable charge for a facility 'of no more than a suitable standard' for the purpose in hand. It was fixed in relation to the normal levels of residential home fees in operation in a supplementary benefit office's area and became known as the 'local limit'.
>
> (Lewis and Glennerster 1996: 3)

If personal income of a home resident ran out, then the social security system would pay. Local authority treasurers and politicians began to ask why they should go on providing old people's homes if individuals could seek a home for themselves in the private sector and get the social security system to pay. Unlike health and local authority budgets, social security payments were not cash limited. In December 1979, supplementary benefit paid to support individuals in residential and nursing home care provided by the independent sector amounted to £10 million (12,000 claimants). By May 1991 the level of income support for such people was estimated to be £1872 million (231,000 claimants), and the total amount was estimated to reach £2480 million (270,000 claimants) by April 1993 (House of Commons Social Security Committee 1991: para. 4). These substantial increases in expenditure took place despite successive attempts by central government to restrict their rate of growth.

The Audit Commission report *Making a Reality of Community Care* (1986) focused upon the central problem that people were receiving care but not in the right place (that is, not being supported in their own homes but mainly within private residential care). It proved embarrassing to central government to be seen publicly to be on the one hand arguing for community-based care but to be found, on the other, to be funding arbitrarily alternative types of independent sector residential-home care. The escalating costs proved a driving incentive. Under the heading 'Perverse effects of social security policies', the Audit Commission documented the rise in spending and argued that the government was being wholly inconsistent (Lewis and Glennerster 1996: 5). The outcome was claimed as a 'policy failure' (Wistow *et al*. 1994): the Audit Commission report outlined the contradictions and ineffectiveness of previous policies. These underlying problems are outlined in Box 2.1.

Box 2.1   The Audit Commission's policy critique

- disincentives for local authorities to invest in community care caused by a mismatch between policy objectives and funding systems;
- lack of bridging finance to support the shift from hospitals to care in the community;
- perverse incentives from an income support system which supported care in residential and nursing homes but not in other settings;
- organisational fragmentation and confusion in the responsibilities of agencies at all levels; and
- staffing problems resulting from the absence of workforce planning and effective staff training for community care.

Source: Wistow *et al*. (1994: 4).

The Conservative government responded by setting up an enquiry led by Sir Roy Griffiths who had previously led a review of NHS management in 1983. The expectation of the enquiry was to establish a mechanism for managing public funding of community care more satisfactorily and which would justify the purpose of public fund allocation. Griffiths's terms of reference were: 'To review the way in which public funds are used to support community care policy and to advise me [the secretary of state] on options which would improve the use of these funds' (Griffiths 1988:). This occurred within the context of a government drive to 'reform' and overhaul public sector services (for example, health and education) so as to make professionals employed there more accountable for the work they had undertaken. The method sought after was one of improving, and by necessity increasing, overall management as this was perceived as the essential solution.

The Griffiths Report: *Community Care: An Agenda for Action* (1988)

Griffiths did not address levels of resources for community care but acknowledged that having ambitious policy goals without the means to implement them was the worst of all possible worlds. Modernizing the management of community care was seen as more important than changing the organization: 'If community care means anything it is that responsibility is placed as near to the individual and his carers as possible' (Griffiths 1988: para. 30).

At the centre of the framework, Griffiths proposed a minister for community care who would link national policy more clearly to resources and timetables. The minister would be responsible for monitoring local and national policies, ensuring that they were consistent and up to standard. But social services' authorities would be left responsible for deciding the content of the plans themselves. The report stressed the **mixed economy of care**, arguing that it was not necessary for social services' authorities to provide all services themselves, but simply to ensure that they were provided. They should act: 'as the designers, organisers and purchasers of non-healthcare services and not primarily as direct service providers, making the maximum possible use of voluntary and private sector bodies to widen **consumer choice**, stimulate innovation and encourage efficiency (Griffiths 1988: para. 1.3.4).

Griffiths argued that the role of social services would become one of case management, assessing the gap between resources and individual needs, targeting funds to devise cost-effective care packages and regularly reviewing priorities. The role of 'health' care (as opposed to social care) was never defined satisfactorily but complementarity of purpose was nevertheless desired. Radical changes in the workforce were needed, involving significant changes in role for a number of professional and occupational groups. There was a further argument taken up from the earlier Audit Commission report (1986), namely the creation of a new occupation of 'community carer' to undertake 'the front-line personal and social support of dependent people' (Griffiths 1988: para. 8.4). This provided a case for developing new skills among existing staff to enable them to tackle the new tasks proposed, developing completely new roles and replacing those that no longer appeared to be necessary.

Griffiths's report lamented the fact that such a gap existed between policy and reality on the ground. Why, given all the 'essential facts' were contained in the reports of the Social Services Committee (House of Commons Select Committee 1985), the Audit Commission (1986) and the National Audit Office (1987), was 'the gap between political rhetoric and policy on the one hand, or between policy and reality in the field ... so great' (Griffiths 1988: iv). Griffiths's report strove in the main not to dismiss this question but to seek an acceptable solution. His terms of reference precluded his examining the adequacy of the resources allocated to community care but he appeared to be not entirely unsympathetic with the views of those critical of the adequacy of funding. Briefly his recommendations fell under two headings: changes to the strategic management of community care (macro level) and improving services to the individual client or service user (micro level). Harrison *et al.* (1990: 63) summarized the report in ten points, shown in Box 2.2.

The Griffiths Report sought to eliminate the perverse incentive towards residential care which the system had created by making both local authorities and social security responsible for funding residential and domiciliary care in an ad hoc manner. Griffiths's solution was that a unified community care budget be allocated to local social services authorities in the form of a specific grant, principally composed of resources transferred from the social security system. This principle was adopted by the government and formed the basis for the financial arrangements ultimately introduced in 1993.

Box 2.2 The Griffiths Report: A ten-point summary

The Griffiths Report recommended:

- a clearer strategic role for central government including the appointment of a Minister for Community Care;
- a more facilitative and enabling role for social services departments as lead agencies;
- the continuing need for collaboration at local level between different agencies, including the development of case management;
- new methods of financing community care, including a specific community care grant to local authorities;
- a single gateway to publicly-financed residential care;
- greater encouragement of experiments to promote new forms of more pluralist provision;
- encouragement of joint or shared training between different professions;
- facilitation of greater consumer choice;
- clarification of the respective responsibilities of health and social care agencies; and
- the establishment of a better balance between policy aspirations and the availability of resources.

Source: (Harrison *et al.* (1990: 63–4).

Residential and nursing home residents in the public, private and voluntary sectors should receive public financial support only following separate assessments of the financial means of the applicant and of the need for care. The process should start with an assessment of whether residential care is the most appropriate way of meeting care needs. The social security system should then contribute a financial assessment but the resultant benefit (the residential allowance) would be set in the light of the average total of income support and housing benefit to which someone living other than in residential care would be entitled. This system would 'leave the social services authority to pay the balance of the costs' (Griffiths 1988: 19).

Finally there was the suggestion that local authorities should have a lead in strategic management of community care and because of the Conservative government's known antipathy towards such bodies, it was expected that this recommendation would be problematic. It was partly 'resolved' by insistence that local authorities should be merely 'enablers' and not direct providers of services (with the later condition added that 64 per cent of the total grant received by each one of them would be spent on the independent sector). A further compromise was a 'watering down' of proposals to earmark funds delivered to local authorities – by only including specific grants under this heading and by 'slow-timing' transfer of funds to local authorities in three annual stages. (For more detailed discussion of the proposals of the Griffiths Report and their implications for those involved in community care at all levels of government and outside government, see Hunter and Judge 1988; Hunter *et al.* 1988.)

The White Paper *Caring for People* (1989)

The 1989 White Paper constitutes the government's response to Griffiths and this was followed by enactment of the 1990 legislation. This White Paper was revealed as the partner to another: *Working for Patients* (Department of Health 1988) covering reforms in the NHS. Both sets of advice recommended a mixed economy approach to health and social welfare and led to the setting up of an internal market in care (where one agency – for community care being the local authority – would buy care from others who would provide it). Means and Smith (1994: 56) describe the aftermath of Griffiths as having '(a) lack of positive spirit of implementation, especially at central government level'.

Caring for People had an underlying purpose of promoting *choice* and *independence*, with a consequential emphasis on home-based care, personal development and a greater consumer voice (Wistow *et al.* 1994: 8). There were six key objectives, shown in Box 2.3.

Box 2.3   The six key objectives of *Caring for People*

1 To promote the development of domiciliary, day and respite services to enable people to live in their own homes wherever feasible and sensible.
2 To ensure service providers make practical support for carers a high priority.
3 To make the proper assessment of need and good case management the cornerstone of high-quality care.
4 To promote the development of a flourishing independent sector alongside quality public services.
5 To clarify the responsibilities of agencies and so make it easier to hold them to account for their performance.
6 To serve better value for taxpayers' money by introducing a funding structure for social care.

The third objective (to properly assess case management, later called care management) was seen as the most significant for practising professionals. The main responsibilities for social services authorities were presented as a three-pronged process of creating care packages for clients, shown in Box 2.4.

The main differences from the Griffiths proposals were the omission of the role of minister for community care, who would set national objectives

Box 2.4 The role of social services

1 To carry out an appropriate *assessment of an individual's need* for social care (including residential and nursing home care) in collaboration as necessary with medical, nursing and other caring agencies, before deciding what services should be provided.
2 To *design packages of services* tailored to meet the assessed needs of individuals and their carers. The appointment of a 'case manager' may facilitate this.
3 To *secure the delivery of services*, not simply by acting as direct providers, but by developing their purchasing and contracting role to become **enabling** authorities.

and priorities, and the rejection of specific earmarked **community care grants** to local authorities. Apart from a limited scheme to fund community services for those with severe mental health problems and another to fund alcohol and drug services, extra funds to meet the increased social care responsibilities of local authorities were to be channelled through the revenue support grant system. Innovations included the introduction of a new system of complaints and a new system of inspection for residential care, 'at arm's length' from the management of services.

Wistow (1990) described the purpose of the White Paper as operating at three levels: the macro (or service system) level; the micro (or individual user) level; and the inter-agency level. Encouraging local authorities to focus upon a needs approach was to be achieved through linking *planning* for the whole community with *planning* at individual client level. Wistow's model implies:

• the organization of service systems based on the separation of purchaser and provider functions, the promotion of a mixed economy and the creation of new providers operating in an external market;
• the organization of service delivery through systematic arrangements for assessment, care management, devolved budgeting and, hence, some degree of **decentralized** purchasing; and
• a re-emphasis on joint working through the clearer allocation of responsibilities for health and social care, combined with strengthened financial incentives for collaboration and a focus on planning outcomes rather than structures or processes.

The Community Care Act (as part of the National Health Service and Community Care Act 1990)

When the National Health Service and Community Care Act (NHSCC) went through Parliament, there was considerable – but unsuccessful – pressure to provide ring-fenced funding. The reforms were delayed because of government fears that they would add 30 pence per week to poll tax bills (Massie 1992).

A duty to assess

Essentially, the Act replicates the framework of the White Paper but is short on its commitments, mainly confined to user rights to assessment. The legislation states that if a person appears to be in need of community care services which a local social services authority can provide, then there is a duty to assess that person. However if a person does not appear to be in such need, social services can refuse to make the assessment.

Section 47 states that: 'where it appears to a local authority that any person for whom they may provide or arrange for the provision of community care services may be in need of any such services, the authority – (a) shall carry out an assessment of his needs for those services' (National Health Service and Community Care Act 1990, Section 47 (1) (a)).

What is meant by 'need'?

Mandelstam and Schwehr (1995) state that it would be difficult to challenge authorities on the principle of a restrictive definition of need (for example, a policy which stated that only people who appear to be a high risk would be deemed to appear to be in need). Further difficulty arises because community care services are provided under different pieces of legislation. If 'need' is identified under some (e.g. the Chronically Sick and Disabled Persons Act 1970), but not all, of this legislation, then authorities do, it has been argued, automatically have legal obligations to provide services to meet that need. However government guidance had been issued suggesting that local authorities could avoid such obligations by distinguishing between people's 'preferences' and their 'needs' (Department of Health and Social Service Inspectorate 1991).

Other aspects of the Act

Legislation was silent about care plans, user **empowerment** and increased choice for users (Mandelstam and Schwehr 1995: 163, 171). Section 47 (1) of the Act stated that after assessment: 'having regard to the results of that assessment, [the local authority] shall then decide whether his needs call for the provision by them of any such services' (National Health Service and Community Care Act 1990).

Policy guidance for the 1990 Act none the less stated that care plans should follow assessments, and listed, in order of preference, a number of types of care packages, from support for people in their own homes to institutional long-term care. Only the Department of Health practice guidance stated explicitly that users should receive copies of their care plans (SSI/SWSG 1991: 61). Also advocacy, promoted by community care guidance, remained lacking the statutory basis which the unimplemented

Section 3 of the earlier Disabled Persons Act 1986 had supplied. The NHSCC Act did not mention carers, although policy guidance stated that carers were able to request assessments (and that in practice, local authorities might assess carers).

Lewis and Glennerster (1996: 19) in their discussion of the implementation of the reforms distinguished between the deep normative core of a policy, the near-core and secondary aspects. The last can be changed by local acts with the policy still achieving its basic objectives. Reducing the growth of state social security spending, Lewis and Glennerster allege, was the normative core, the real heart of the government's policy. Creating a mixed market where the local authorities moved from their dominant provider role to an enabling role and encouraging collaboration between health and social services were near-core policies in the sense that the government could be somewhat relaxed about the way they were implemented. Forms of assessment and individual client care management and care planning were secondary to the government's main purposes.

Rhetoric versus reality

The rhetoric of the reforms package proved confusing to professional carers – for example, the notion of 'seamlessness' found in practice guidelines (SSI/SWSG 1991: 81–99), whereby the user should not be aware of any divisions between health and social services. Indeed it was claimed that working within either a health or social services agency which was beginning to base its practice upon values of the internal market appeared to urge professionals to reorientate their roles away from expertise and towards facilitation (Fox 1993). The legislation itself gave rise to uncertain areas of responsibility between health and social care: it imposed statutory duties relating to inter-agency working both at policy and planning level and at individual assessment level (although it did not mention 'seamless' services as such).

Yet it proved difficult to specify which agency had responsibility for providing a particular service for an individual, as few specific services were mentioned in the legislation. Even where they were mentioned, they were not well-defined. Services occupying such 'grey' areas might include, for example, disability equipment, incontinence laundry, washing, dressing, bathing, lifting, mobility rehabilitation and respite care (Mandelstam and Schwehr 1995: 193). The accompanying practice guidance explained that these could all be viewed as either health care or as social care. The House of Commons Health Committee (1993b) itself pointed out that even if the boundaries of health and social care could be agreed in principle, 'funding arrangements between authorities do not always match those arrangements' (1993b: 26). One reason for this had been the existence of further 'perverse incentives'. For example, since April 1993, nursing services for residential and nursing home care had been paid for by social services. Nursing services for people in their own homes were provided, however, by the health services, and legislation had prohibited social services from paying for this. Thus 'there [had been] disincentive for the health authorities to see people placed in the community' (1993, Vol. 2:

7), and inevitably, stricter rationing procedures were used by community health personnel. The NHSCC Act failed to make mention of uncertain areas of responsibility and of avoiding delay in services caused by a dispute between different types of agency.

The issue of eligibility for continuing (long-term) NHS care (which arose as a problem following the 1990 Act) was not addressed until 1996 when the wide discretion of health authorities was confirmed by allowing them to determine their own criteria of eligibility of need.

Financing the reforms

The 1989 White Paper made clear that finance for local authorities' new community care responsibilities would be channelled through the revenue support grant and distributed between authorities in the normal way on the basis of their standard spending assessment (SSA). However, the government concluded that there was a case for modifying these principles in the early years of the policy and decided to introduce a ring-fenced special transitional grant (STG). The original grant was announced on 2 October 1992; it was later announced that a further amount would be included to recognize new burdens on local authorities as a result of changes to the Independent Living Fund (ILF). Table 2.1 summarizes these amounts.

The majority of funding consisted of moneys transferred from the social security budget already supporting those using residential services; relatively small amounts were to support changes in social services' infrastructure or for developing new projects. Key features of the STG were that the grant would be for a four-year transitional period, that it would be ring-fenced for use on community care services and directly related activities, be outside capping calculations and have a special transitional distribution formula. In the first year, the grant would include moneys transferred from the Department of Social Security (DSS) to local authorities in respect of their new responsibilities (£399 million). The second and third years would include the increase in the social security transfer and the whole of the ILF amount, phasing out in the fourth year. In each case, the previous year's grant would be added to the social services SSA

Table 2.1   Community care special transitional grant

Year	Amount (£ million)	Comment
1993–4	£565	DSS transfer plus £140 million additional funding plus £26.8 million ILF money
1994–5	£716	Increase in transfer plus £64.1 million ILF
1995–6	£618	Increase in transfer plus £99.9 million ILF
1996–7	Phase out	

Note: Apart from the ILF element, each year's grant goes into the subsequent year's SSA baseline.
Source: Department of Health and Social Security (1993)

baseline, meaning that over time an increasing proportion of funding for community care would be through the normal SSA.

The DSS transfer element of the STG was to be distributed among local authorities, half according to the existing pattern of DSS spending on income support in independent residential and nursing home provision, and half according to revised SSA calculations which were capitation-based and intended to reflect need in the whole population for which the local authority was responsible. The £140 million portion of the STG was to be distributed according to this SSA formula. Therefore, 37 per cent of the total STG in 1993–4 would be distributed according to current DSS spending and 63 per cent according to SSA.

Joint working

A precondition of receiving payment was for local authorities to provide evidence of joint agreements with health authorities by 31 December 1992 on: (1) strategies governing health and local authorities' respons-ibilities for placing people in nursing homes, and the numbers likely to be involved during 1993–4; and (2) how hospital discharge arrange-ments would be integrated with assessment arrangements. All 108 local authorities in England met this deadline, as the parliamentary under secretary phrased it 'for delivering proof of their partnership agreements with health authorities' (Department of Health 1993a).

The government originally proposed an additional condition that at least 75 per cent of each local authority's total grant was to be spent in the independent sector. Seventy-five per cent of the STG in fact amounted to £404 million, which was slightly more than the £399 million that constituted the DSS transfer element of the grant. In effect this meant that, according to the Local Authority Associations' (LAAs) own calcula-tions, some local authorities' share of the DSS transfer would amount to less than 75 per cent of their total grant, meaning that a proportion of their share of the £140 million would be required to meet this shortfall. After discussions with the LAAs and others, the requirement was changed to 85 per cent of the DSS transfer element. This worked out as 64 per cent of the total grant, somewhat less than the original 75 per cent. Local authorities had to demonstrate that they would spend 85 per cent over and above their baseline personal social services (PSS) expenditure on the **'independent sector'**, which was defined for these purposes as 'meaning not under local authority ownership, management or control' (House of Commons Health Committee 1993a: 54).

Funding was required for community health services to be commis-sioned by each local authority. Among the uses of an additional £800 million announced by the Department of Health for 1993–4 was that of providing extra support to cover costs of the health components of community-based care packages, such as district nursing, community psychiatric nursing, health visiting, physiotherapy and chiropody. From April 1993 general practice fundholders would be able to purchase com-munity health services and would therefore have a significant part to play in the planning and commissioning of appropriate community care services.

The government claimed that the criteria used for the funding settlement were transparent, adequate and fair and some attempt was made by the House of Commons Health Committee (1993b) to seek validation for this assertion. From the evidence it seemed that the argument was not upheld, despite continued efforts by government to justify its position – for example, allocated amounts for start-up costs, covering assessment procedures, development of financial systems and respite care were observed to have been chosen at random. On the question of adequacy, there were significant differences forecast between LAAs and the Department of Health as to overall funding requirements.

The issue of 'top up'

Most of the written evidence received during the Health Committee's inquiry referred to the shortfall between income support and homes' fees (House of Commons Health Committee 1993b: para. 66). The problems identified included concerns about the future for residents and their relatives who could no longer afford to 'top up' and the future of **charities** facing financial hardships. Local authorities made some use of their power to 'top up' for residents under pension age, although it was illegal for them to do the same for older residents. Some district health authorities also 'topped up' people with learning difficulties in independent sector homes who had been discharged from long-stay hospitals. A survey by the *Guardian* newspaper in 1993 showed that the number of NHS beds for elderly people with long-term illnesses had been cut by nearly 40 per cent since 1988, forcing people into means-tested private nursing homes (in total more than 10,000 beds had been closed). The means-testing regulations for private nursing home fees meant that people with assets of more than £8000, including their homes, received no financial help. As a result, nursing care became financed by house sales.

The funding gap

Evidence showed that in 1993–4 the gap between the Department of Health's and the LAAs' calculations of total funding requirements was £289 million, comprising £90 million for the DSS transfer, £145 million for the difference between income support and homes' charges and £54 million for support and other service costs. These figures were later revised to take account of inflation forecasts, benefit level uprating (1993–4) and the announcement that £26 million would be grantable to local authorities to replace the ILF. This showed a reduced overall gap of £138 million: £62 million arising from the DSS transfer, £66 million for the shortfall between benefits and charges and £10 million for support and other costs.

On unmet need, the Committee recommended that:

clear guidance be issued urgently to local authorities . . . and, if necessary, legislation introduced to make sure that there are no inhibitions on the ability of social services' departments and health authorities to make a full assessment of unmet needs. It will be difficult to judge in the future whether resources are adequate unless we have a clear indication of the level of need, both met and unmet.

(House of Commons Health Committee 1993b: para. 64)

The government response was equivocal, claiming that it was up to authorities to set out clearly their priorities and eligibility criteria for services and to collect the evidence they needed for planning purposes (House of Commons Health Committee 1993b: para. 7).

Implementing the reforms: A success story?

During the 1990s a number of studies emerged considering the effects of the reforms, including their impact on service users, and questioning whether there had been any clear benefits. One theme has tended to dominate, namely the failure of genuine needs-led assessment. A review of evidence of the early implementation of the reforms contrasts judgements about their successful introduction, based on administrative and political criteria (e.g. Wistow 1995) with reports that users and carers generally appeared to have experienced few improvements to services (Bewley and Glendinning 1994; Age Concern 1994; Hoyes *et al.* 1994; Warner 1994). Criticism (of lack of progress) has been grounded upon a failure to resolve contradictions and tensions inherent in the policies themselves; and upon a failure to define some of the terminology in use (Davies and Connolly 1995; Nolan and Caldock 1996; Malin 1997; Olsen *et al.* 1997).

A needs-led service?

A major source of difficulty in the implementation of care-management systems has been the tension between needs and resources. The new community care policy urged social services departments to make services needs-led. If assessment is separated from provision, it is argued, then the client's needs can be 'objectively' assessed and followed by the construction of a care package drawing on the wider range of services that will be available as a result of increased competition. Lewis *et al.*'s 1997 study of how the reforms bedded-down in five local authorities showed this to be unrealistic as it did not prove easy to separate assessment from service provision or from the knowledge of what resources are/are not available:

there are a number of tensions facing care managers in their work as assessors of need, and in deciding whether and how to provide service. The tension between the infinity of need and finite resources is hardly new, but it is highlighted within the new system, where purchasing is separated from provision and hence need from service, and where the caremanager must nevertheless decide what can actually be provided even if s/he does not do the providing.

(Lewis *et al.* 1997: 17)

A basic problem was resolving what an 'assessment of need' actually means (see, for instance, Nolan and Caldock 1996). The lack of clarity as to how to operationalize the **assessment** process lay at the heart of many difficulties that surfaced. Further dilemmas could be exposed by pointing to contradictions in policy pronouncements (the so-called gap between rhetoric and policy). Community care was all about client choice (Strong 1996) – indeed, the promotion of 'choice and independence' were fundamental values underlying the White Paper's proposals – as it was also about improving access to home-based care. Yet containing public expenditure was a central goal too and there was evidence later to demonstrate how home-based care was fragmented, uncoordinated and variable in terms of quality and level of payment expected by the local authority and private sectors. Successful implementation was also dependent on managing the changing boundary between health and social care. The reforms were being introduced at a time when the NHS was continuing to withdraw from providing long-term care and was moving instead into the acute sector heartland of high technology medicine and ever-reduced lengths of stay (Department of Health 1995a).

The following examples are given to highlight tensions arising from conflicting, oppositional ideas underpinning policy implementation.

Consumerism versus empowerment

According to research (for example, Nocon 1994; Parry-Jones *et al.* 1998) assessment and care management had failed to achieve greater autonomy, individuality and choice for service users, with residential care sometimes the only main option, rather than packages of care tailored to individual needs as the reforms proposed. Empowerment as portrayed in the practice guidance referred to users having choice about the process – that is, in deciding what type of care they would receive. This has been confused with empowerment used in another sense, where, for example, choice as exercised in the functioning of residential services – granting residents freedom of activity within limits – implies that a prime purpose of a service is to make individuals more independent, with the power to choose how they live their lives.

Traditionally service users have played a very small role in the organization and delivery of health and welfare services. Community care policy sought to develop and enhance this role: 'promoting choice and independence underlies all the government's proposals' (Department of Health 1989: 4). Subsequent practitioner guidance stressed that 'the rationale for this reorganisation is the empowerment of users and carers' (Department of Health and Social Services Inspectorate 1991: 7). In terms of practical application this involves service users taking or being given more power over decisions affecting their welfare and hence probably also involves taking at least some power away from health and social services providers.

This form of policy paradox provides one example of where practitioners are expected to empower service users (for example by granting more autonomy) but at the same time are also expected to minimalize risk. There is an argument that the ability of professionals to empower others stems from their possessing power in the first instance, implying that the service is, *de facto*, more powerful (and will remain so) than the service user/client. Jack (1995) describes this as paradoxical (power cannot be given but only taken) and states that recent legislation involves 'enablement, in the sense of promoting participation and involvement, not empowerment' (p. 18). He argues that the role of professionals is therefore peripheral to empowerment, that it is 'enablement' and that the two concepts are quite different. There are two competing models present in thinking about how community care is delivered: the charter approach, in which users are treated as consumers, and the aim is to maximize consumer satisfaction, and the empowerment model, in which the delivery of services is seen as a vehicle for providing users with power and development. In practice the reconciliation of views of, for example, users and professionals, creates problems not least due to the unequal power distribution.

A core stated objective of the community care legislation, as embodied in *Caring for People*, was that service users and informal carers should be given 'a greater individual say in how they live their lives and the services they need to help them to do so' (Department of Health 1989: 4, para. 1.8). This 'involvement' is along two dimensions: at the macro level it refers to the participation of service users and carers in the planning and delivery of aspects of service; at the micro level of individual assessments it relates to the users' and carers' role in identifying their needs and choosing means for meeting those needs. Baldock and Ungerson's (1994) study of 32 older people returning to the community after surviving a stroke showed users having a vague perception that they were in a 'care managed' process, and concluded that genuine participation by users in arranging their own care 'required large adaptations in established habits of behaviour and fundamental shifts in values' (Baldock and Ungerson 1994: 18).

Some of the difficulties have been caused not by systems or structural problems but by fundamental differences in service philosophies. For example, twin concepts of consumerism and empowerment have tended to be allied with 'management talk' and 'professional talk' respectively, suggesting that client needs are perceived differently. Davies and Connolly's (1995) study on the changed role of hospital social work and discharge planning illustrated this point describing the social workers' role as counsellors and advocates of patients' rights conflicting with that of managers anxious to see them concentrating on more functional duties, such as the 'need' to clear hospital beds.

The central issue is that the term 'choice' has come to have different and potentially conflicting meanings, and that since the reforms the evidence suggests that real choice for the service user may scarcely exist. The problem with using the term 'empowerment' is that the strategy embodies mixed assumptions: the charter and empowerment approaches described above compare to the 'exit' and 'voice' strategies (Hirschman 1970) described in Means and Smith (1994). The latter reinforce our understanding of the distinction: exit, or market approaches, are based on the assumption that the consumer can, in effect, take their custom elsewhere if dissatisfied with the service; voice, or democratic strategies, are based on the assumption that users and carers are able to change the system from within.

The problem with this aspect of the reforms is that the policy is unclear; expectations had been raised but the confusion arose on interpretation. A study by Myers and MacDonald (1996) demonstrated that involving users in needs assessment was hampered by a number of constraints: structural, procedural, cultural, practical and substantive (see Box 2.5).

Box 2.5   Constraints on involving users in needs assessments

- Structural: e.g. agencies separately defined their criteria of eligibility for a service; redistribution of knowledge from practitioners to 'consumer' may only be partial.
- Procedural: e.g. variability between practitioners in the degree to which they let users see, sign or retain copies of assessment documentation.
- Cultural: e.g. perceived reluctance by users to take up the mantle of power.
- Practical: e.g. communication difficulties – differences in language, means of expression or sensory impairment.
- Substantive: e.g. practitioners deemed some clients unable to make informed choices.

Another study on providing care for people identified as suffering from dementia showed a low level of service from agencies, particularly social work and specialist services, and in relation to multidisciplinary assessment (Burholt *et al.* 1997).

Managerialism versus professionalism

One effect of community care policy reforms has been deprofessionalization of the workforce: a reduction of professionally-trained staff in hands-on care and in areas outside management and need assessment (see, for example, Hatfield and Mohamad 1996 on community mental health support teams). Sheppard (1995: 75) refers to the 'marginalisation of a core of tasks centred around sentimental work such as interprofessional skills and reflective responses brought about by a different style of culture dominating health and social care'. As the Griffiths Report envisaged:

> the change in role of social service authorities might also allow them to make more productive use of the management abilities and experience of all their staff, including those who are not qualified social workers . . . the professional skills of community nurses and health visitors need to be effectively harnessed and their contribution in working with other professional groups fully recognised.
>
> (Griffiths 1988: paras. 8.1, 8.3)

Separating management from professional work dealing with clients, with the former dominating professional culture, has been accompanied by a belief that such management expertise is the sole legitimate criterion for decision making in public organizations.

Griffiths (1988) recommended: 'the creation of a new occupation of "community carers" to undertake the frontline personal and social support of dependent people . . . such job descriptions [should] enable individual workers to provide the assistance required without demarcation problems arising' (para. 8.4). There has since been some work supporting the claim that unqualified workers demonstrate greater flair and innovation in undertaking hands-on work (Cole and Perides 1995) and that **'quality'** is more associated with workplace ethos than with training and qualifications of staff (Wilding 1994). The division between managerial and professional/quasi-professional tasks has had a knock-on effect of deconstructing traditional professional competence (or professionals' right of ownership) and substituting routinization, rule-following and form filling. Many professionals, for example clinicians, have traditionally enjoyed high levels of autonomy reflecting both primacy of expertise over political control and the complexity of delivering services. The impact of **managerialism** and the growth in power of accountancy over health professionals have demonstrated how this autonomy and hegemony is now challenged and there is evidence of de-skilling, task fragmentation and centralization of work planning in both health and social care.

A further jolt to the 'cognitive superiority' argument used to recognize the essence of the professional claim (see Hughes 1971: 375) has been the impact of consumerism, where professionals are 'now being asked to share their knowledge with unqualified users and to join with these users in reaching care decisions' (Wilson 1995: 8). This has been interpreted as a form of devaluing professional training. The fact that consumers should be given considerably greater say in defining their own needs 'firmly places [professionals]' area of work, at least in part, in the arena of matters of everyday concern and competence. The need for any particular expertise is concomitantly reduced' (Sheppard 1995: 77).

Consequences for training

Training policy in residential, domiciliary and day care became directed during the 1990s towards a competence-based approach, a method of behaviour and performance assessment using core performance descriptors. An example is given in Box 2.6.

It was intended that evidence be collected through observation and oral questioning to gather 'proof' of a carer's skill acquisition. Together with other factors this signalled a pendulum shift away from 'indetermination' towards 'technicality' (see Jamous and Peloille 1970 for an explanation of indetermination-technicality ratio, where for example if there is insufficient indeterminacy, the occupation is likely to be perceived as a practical vocation). Despite the original antipathy of the nursing profession towards contributing to the development of competence-based training (Brown 1994), 'competence' became the currency in which training programmes were expressed. The emergence of employer-led training, which challenged the historical predominance of profession-determined education was promulgated by central government (for example, by involving employers at a regional level in training and enterprise councils (TECs), and in training health care and social workers). A question might arise as to whether a

> **Box 2.6 An example of a competence-based approach**
>
> *Methods of Client Assessment*: **A1**
>
> **Element A1.1 Gather and collate information from sources other than client.**
>
> *Performance Criteria*
> 1 His/her role is established with the appropriate persons.
> 2 The purpose and methods of the assessment are established with the appropriate persons.
> 3 Available factual information and views relevant to the assessment are obtained from appropriate sources.
> 4 Information is checked for accuracy where necessary.
> 5 Information is noted accurately, collated and stored in an appropriate form.
>
> **Element A1.2 Observe and discuss with the client.**
>
> *Performance Criteria*
> 1 The client's behaviour is continuously observed and recorded and valid conclusions drawn from the evidence.
> 2 The client's views relevant to the purpose are obtained.
> 3 Relevant factual information is obtained from the client.
> 4 All information is summarized and agreed with the client, collated and stored in an appropriate form.
>
> (*Source*: Care Sector Consortium 1990).

coherent staff training policy for community care existed. Implementing the reforms gave purchasers and providers the opportunity to reflect on staff training policies and the workforce infrastructure, which involved redeploying care staff and considering how staff might acquire new knowledge and skills. Some local authorities undertook a training need analysis of their workforce (e.g. Bradford and North Yorkshire Social Services Departments).

One reason for the move towards deprofessionalization was that the **contractual environment** meant that traditional patterns of service provision and training programmes were no longer sacrosanct. The discernible trend was for local managers to develop their own specific training courses rather than patronize courses offering regional, if not national, expertise, granting a feeling of local ownership. This raises the issue of comparability in standards between courses in different localities. Professional training bodies e.g. English National Board for Nursing, Midwifery and Health Visiting (ENB), Central Council for Education and Training in Social Work (CCETSW), were expected to take a back seat, as new National Vocational Qualifications (NVQs) were devised (following the government White Paper *Working Together: Education and Training* Department of Health 1986). In community care the emphasis was to be on 'pre-qualifying' (Levels 1 to 4) in the context of nurse and social work training (see Box 2.7).

Box 2.7 Levels of competence in nurse and social work training

Level 1 Occupational competence in performing a range of tasks under supervision.

Level 2 Occupational competence in performing a wider range of more demanding tasks with limited supervision.

Level 3 Occupational competence required for satisfactory, responsible performance in a defined occupation or range of jobs.

Level 4 Competence to design and specify defined tasks, products or processes and to accept responsibility for the work of others.

(*Source*: Brown (1992: 362)).

New NVQs were devised to meet the demands of needs-led assessment and care planning, involving wide-ranging consultation with users and carers. There have been studies illustrating how 'unqualified' (non-professional) staff 'appear to be working in appropriate ways' (Hatfield and Mohamad 1996: 217) and how they contribute significantly to the support of people with chronic psychotic illness living in the community; personal qualities being seen as more important than training. As stated earlier this has contributed to a perception in some quarters that anyone can perform a care task which has been disempowering to staff trying to promote the professional training argument (see Key 1995).

Need or risk

Traditionally, the demand for health and welfare services has been defined in terms of need. This concept is problematic and is open to different interpretations: i.e. it is absolute; it is relative; it has an inflationary tendency; it is easy to identify additional needs or higher levels of needs; it has been identified as part of the welfare culture. An alternative approach has emerged around the concept of risk: certain hazards can be identified (e.g. disease, ignorance) which can be most effectively dealt with collectively, and certain groups in society can be seen as vulnerable or at risk (e.g. children, adults with learning difficulties). The risk approach can be seen in the rethink of the mental health legislation (e.g. Department of Health 1995b). An advantage of the risk approach is that it focuses resources on specific issues and groups.

Policies setting out the community care reforms (i.e. Griffiths 1988; Department of Health 1989) did not articulate this alternative approach.

Instead, the language was that of 'needology'; the needs of each patient both for continuing health care and social care are (to be) assessed pre-discharge, so that effective arrangements are made as to how in principle those needs are to be met (Department of Health 1989: para. 7.7). Assessment guidance defined need as the 'capacity to benefit' from care, posing dilemmas for measuring outcome especially where preventative services (e.g. health visiting) were involved (see National Health Service Management Executive 1991; Department of Health 1993b). Contrasts occurred between health and social care guidance where need was assessed in the former by disease with pre-eminence to the expert view and in the latter by client group acknowledging the user perspective.

By April 1996 all health authorities were required to implement criteria determining their responsibilities for continuing health care, i.e. setting out which clients were in need of their services: 'not just hospital, nursing home or residential care but also community-based care and combinations of these different patterns' (see Southern Derbyshire Health 1995: 4). The ambiguity of community care policy aims showed up markedly, for example, in Lewis and Glennerster's (1996) study, with hierarchies of need emerging, whereby some clients were getting sophisticated packages of domiciliary care, and those classed as being not at high risk more likely not to have their needs met at all. In many instances eligibility criteria (for continuing health care) became defined by whether clients needed specialist professional services (e.g. regular contact of a consultant psychiatrist or specialist medical or nursing supervisor) adding further ambiguity to the equation. Perusal of several authorities' policies indicated a tendency towards defining categories of clients who were seen to be at risk, either physically or emotionally, and in need of treatment due to their severe behavioural difficulties.

The notion of risk has become a guiding principle in judging priority, entitlement or need (whether or not this was an intention of the reforms), and is particularly relevant in mental health services. This may have appeared to be an inevitability, given the variability in the allocation of resources which has unfolded. The care programme approach used by authorities to define the severity of mental health incapacity at individual level and hence entitlement to a community-based service has deployed a set of risk factors. An example is as follows: (where the individual has received) more than two admissions within the past year, continuous stay in hospital of more than six months in the last three years, four admissions to hospital within the last five years accumulating to one year, or attendance at a statutory mental health day resource for more than one year.

Risk has become an important concept in the management of welfare systems during the 1990s (Beck 1992; Giddens 1994). It has become incorporated within statutory training of health and social workers. It has helped to encourage a culture where practitioners focus more upon the consequences of actions and the probability that these consequences will occur. Inquiry reports (into child death, carer abuse) have reinforced a tradition of blame in social services; whereas inquiries into homicides, suicides among psychiatric patients (Boyd 1996) and studies of whistleblowing in the NHS (Hunt 1995; Public Concern at Work 1997) have focused upon the risks involved in practice self-regulation. In contrast, social workers have not been permitted to regulate their own practice – there is currently no social care council (for debate see Guy 1994; Department of Health 1996), making practitioners feel more vulnerable when measuring risks to their clients living in the community. Alaszewksi (1998), in discussing child protection, claims that there has been a shift away from preventative work, based on assessment of need, towards rapid response to risk, which is defined in terms of possible or actual harm (see, for example, Parton 1996). Nevertheless, social workers are now being criticized for responding to only one type of harm: parental abuse (Brandon et al. 1996: 19).

Providing care within the community creates more risk. For those with learning difficulties the move away from care within institutions has been motivated by a desire to grant individuals more autonomy (as overprotection and control were seen as harmful and unnecessary). Autonomy itself means greater risk which challenges most health and social services. For those with a history of severe mental illness or psychotic behaviour, community care is still being queried as a risk worth taking. Such 'autonomy' has, in instances where individuals are insufficiently protected, had grave consequences, particularly in terms of harm and danger to family members and members of the public.

Conclusions

This chapter has described how the ideology of the mixed economy has altered expectations in community care and shifted the role of the state from being a central provider to being an enabler, purchaser and planner. A conventional view in the 1990s has been to point to the more than partial failure of the reforms through chronic underfunding by central government, coupled with evidence of minimum success in extending user choice. The independent (private) sector has risen to the challenge of being a main provider, with variety and fragmentation seemingly characterizing patterns of services almost everywhere. Commentators (e.g. Means and Smith 1994) have suggested that the emphasis of the reforms upon user involvement and empowerment legitimized the voice of the user, carer and disability movements in a way that was not the case previously, although the market philosophy approach has aroused hostility among such groups. There have been many documented examples of good practice – for example local authorities consulting and involving users and carers – but an overwhelming impression, certainly in the first half of the 1990s, has been of agencies coming to terms with new responsibilities and introducing systems of monitoring, assessment, care management and care planning. There has been visible recognition of a need to transform the skills base of professionals delivering community care, but notwithstanding costing of provision being the main concern, the reality is that improving the skills of the 'caring' workforce has figured as a lesser policy priority than in previous decades.

Summary

- The move to reform community care policies was led by a drive to improve overall management and accountability and to cut growing social security costs of residential and nursing homes.

- The Griffiths Report (Griffiths 1988) and the White Paper *Caring for People* (Department of Health 1989) proposed an internal care market with emphasis on development of domiciliary, day and respite services and on maximizing choice among service users.

- Needs assessment and care management became the basis for resource allocation but implementation has been thwarted by confused terminology – for example, over the meaning of empowerment, and by group/professional interests and boundary issues ('grey' areas of responsibility).

- Government claims that funding of the reforms were intended to be transparent, adequate and fair, were not wholly justified and serious deficiencies in the funding formulae gradually emerged.

- The tension between needs and resources surfaced in a number of ways: in limiting the range of choices offered to clients; in deprofessionalizing parts of the workforce; and in extending assessment technology such as service eligibility criteria (e.g. legitimizing not meeting lower-level needs).

- Most evidence on the reforms suggests more effort is now being made to consult users and carers on the type of services they require but there is a clear distinction between a service which is needs-led as opposed to user-led – a potential conflict of interest which has not been resolved by policies introduced during the 1990s.

Further reading

Barnes, M. (1997) *Care, Communities and Citizens*. Harlow: Longman.

Bornat, J., Pereira, C., Pilgrim, D. and Williams, F. (eds) (1993) *Community Care: A Reader*. Basingstoke: Macmillan.

Jack, R. (ed.) (1995) *Empowerment in Community Care*. London: Chapman & Hall.

Lewis, J. and Glennerster, H. (1986) *Implementing the New Community Care*. Buckingham: Open University Press.

Malin, N. (ed.) (1994) *Implementing Community Care*. Buckingham: Open University Press.

Means, R. and Smith, R. (1994) *Community Care: Policy and Practice*. Basingstoke: Macmillan.

Wistow, G., Knapp, M., Hardy, B. and Allen, C. (1994) *Social Care in a Mixed Economy*. Buckingham: Open University Press.

References

Age Concern (1994) *The Next Steps: Lessons for the Future of Community Care*. London: National Council on Ageing.

Alaszewski, A. (1988) *The Dangers of Risk: Professional Practice and Organisational Policies*. London: PSI.

Audit Commission (1986) *Making a Reality of Community Care*. London: HMSO.

Baldock, J. and Ungerson, C. (1994) *User Perceptions of a 'Mixed Economy' of Care*. York: JRMT.

Beck, U. (1992) *Risk Society: Towards a New Modernity*. London: Sage.

Bewley, C. and Glendinning, C. (1994) *Involving Disabled People in Community Care Planning*. York: JRMT.

Boyd, W. (1996) *Report of the Confidential Inquiry into Homicides and Suicides by Mentally Ill People*. London: Royal College of Psychiatrists.

Brandon, M., Lewis, A. and Thoburn, J. (1996) The Children Act definition of 'significant harm': interpretation in practice. *Health and Social Care in the Community*, 4: 11–20.

Brown, J. (1992) Professional boundaries in mental handicap: a policy analysis of joint training, in T. Thompson and P. Mathias (eds) *Standards in Mental Handicap: Keys to Competence*. London: Balliere and Tindall.

Brown, J. (1994) The caring professions, in N. Malin (ed.) *Implementing Community Care*. Buckingham: Open University Press.

Burholt, V., Wenger, C. and Scott, A. (1997) Dementia, disability and contact with formal services: a comparison of dementia sufferers and non-sufferers in rural and urban settings. *Health and Social Care in the Community*, 5 (6): 384–97.

Care Sector Consortium (1990) *Residential, Domiciliary and Day Care: Project National Standards*. London: HMSO.

Cole, R. and Perides, M. (1995) Managing values and organisational climate in a multiprofessional setting, in K. Soothill, L. Mackay and C. Webb (eds) *Interprofessional Relations in Health Care*. London: Edward Arnold.

Davies, M. and Connolly, J. (1995) Hospital social work and discharge planning: an exploratory study in East Anglia. *Health and Social Care in the Community*, 3 (6): 363–71.

Department of Health (1986) *Working Together: Education and Training*, Cmnd. 9823. London: HMSO.

Department of Health (1988) *Working for Patients*, Cm. 555. London: HMSO.

Department of Health (1989) *Caring for People: Community Care in the Next Decade and Beyond*, Cm. 849. London: HMSO.

Department of Health (1993a) *Community Care*. Press release EL (93) 119/CI (93)35, 23 December.

Department of Health (1993b) *Implementing Community Care. Population Needs Assessment: Good Practice Guidance*. London: HMSO.

Department of Health (1995a) *Building Bridges: A Guide to Arrangements for Inter-agency Working for the Care and Protection of Severely Mentally Ill People*. London: HMSO.

Department of Health (1995b) *NHS Responsibilities for Meeting Continuing Health Care Needs*. London: HMSO.

Department of Health (1996) *The Obligations of Care*. London: HMSO.

Department of Health (1993) *Government Response to the Third Report from the Health Committee Session (1992–1993), Community Care: Funding from April 1993*, Cm. 2188. London: HMSO.

Department of Health and Social Service Inspectorate (1991) *Assessment Systems and Community Care*. London: HMSO.

Fox, N. (1993) *Postmodernism, Sociology and Health*. Buckingham: Open University Press.

Giddens, A. (1994) Agenda change. *New Society and Statesman*, 7 October: 23–5.

Griffiths, R. (1988) *Community Care: An Agenda for Action*. London: HMSO.

Guy, P. (1994) A general social work council: a critical look at the issues. *British Journal of Social Work*, 24: 261–71.

Harrison, S., Hunter, D. and Pollitt, C. (1990) *The Dynamics of British Health Policy*. London: Unwin Hyman.

Hatfield, B. and Mohamad, H. (1996) Case management in mental health services: the role of community mental health support teams. *Health and Social Care in the Community*, 4 (4): 215–25.

Hirschman, A. (1970) *Exit, Voice and Loyalty: Responses to Decline in Firms, Organisations and States*. Boston, MA: Harvard University Press.

House of Commons (1985) *2nd Report from the Social Services Committee Session (1984–85) Community Care: With Special Reference to Adult Mentally Ill and Mentally Handicapped People*, vol. I–II. London: HMSO.

House of Commons Health Committee (1993a) *3rd Report, Community Care: Funding from April 1993* (2 Vols). London: HMSO.

House of Commons Health Committee (1993b) 6th Report, Community Care: The Way Forward (2 Vols). London: HMSO.

House of Commons Social Security Committee (1991) *The Financing of Private Residential and Nursing Home Fees, 4th Report, Session 1990–91*, HC421. London: HMSO.

Hoyes, L., Lart, R., Means, R. and Taylor, M. (1994) *Community Care in Transition*. York: JR Foundation.

Hughes, E. (1971) *The Sociological Eye: Selected Papers*, Chicago: Aldine Atherton.

Hunt, G. (1995) (ed.) *Whistle Blowing in the Health Service*. London: Edward Arnold.

Hunter, D. and Judge, K. (1988) *Griffiths and Community Care: Meeting the Challenge*, briefing paper no. 5. London: King's Fund Institute.

Hunter, D., Judge, K. and Price, S. (1988) *Community Care: Reacting to Griffiths*, briefing paper no. 1. London: King's Fund Institute.

Jack, R. (1995) Empowerment in community care, in R. Jack (ed.) *Empowerment in Community Care*, London: Chapman & Hall.

Jamous, H. and Peloille, B. (1970) Professions or self-perpetuating systems? Changes in the French University hospital system, in J. Jackson (ed.) *Professions and Socialisation*. Cambridge: Cambridge University Press.

Key, B. (1995) Assessing your assets. *Community Care*, 5–11 October: 28–9.

Lewis, J. and Glennerster, H. (1996) *Implementing the New Community Care*. Buckingham: Open University Press.

Lewis, J., Bostock, P., Bovell, V. and Wookey, F. (1997) Implementing caremanagement: issues in relation to the new community care. *British Journal of Social Work*, 27: 5–24.

Malin, N. (1997) Policy to practice: a discussion of tension, dilemma and paradox in community care. *Journal of Learning Disabilities for Nursing, Health and Social Care*, 1 (3): 131–40.

Mandelstam, M. and Schwehr, B. (1995) *Community Care Practice and the Law*. London: Jessica Kingsley.

Massie, B. (1992) Empty wrappings inside: involving service users. *Community Care*, 26 March: i–ii.

Means, R. and Smith, R. (1994) *Community Care: Policy and Practice*. Basingstoke: Macmillan.

Myers, F. and MacDonald, C. (1996) Power to the people? Involving users and carers in needs assessment and care planning: views from the practitioner. *Health and Social Care in the Community*, 4 (2): 86–95.

National Audit Office (1987) *Community Care Developments: Report by the Comptroller and Auditor General*, HC 108. London: HMSO.

National Health Service Management Executive (1991) *Assessing Health Care Needs: A District Health Authority Project Disscussion Paper*. London: HMSO.

Nocon, A. (1994) *Collaboration in Community Care in the 1990s*. Newcastle: Business Education Publishers.

Nolan, M. and Caldock, K. (1996) Assessment: identifying the barriers to good practice. *Health and Social Care in the Community*, 4 (2): 77–85.

Olsen, R., Parker, G. and Drewett, A. (1997) Carers and the missing link: changing professional attitudes, *Health and Social Care in the Community*, 5 (2): 116–23.

Parry-Jones, B., Grant, G., McGrath, M., Caldock, K., Ramcharan, P. and Robinson, C. (1998) Stress and job satisfaction among social workers, community nurses and community psychiatric nurses: Implications for the caremanagement model. *Health and Social Care in the Community*, 6 (4): 271–85.

Parton, N. (1996) Social work, risk and 'the blaming system', in N. Parton (ed.) *Social Theory, Social Change and Social Work*. London: Routledge.

Public Concern at Work (1997) *Abuse in Care: A Necessary Reform*. London: Public Concern at Work.

Sheppard, M. (1995) *Care Management and the New Social Work: A Critical Analysis*. London: Whiting & Birch.

SSI/SWSG (Social Services Inspectorate/Social Work Services Group) (1991) *Caremanagement and Assessment: Practitioners Guide*. London: HMSO.

Southern Derbyshire Health (1995) *NHS Responsibilities for Meeting Continuing Health Care Needs: Principles, Policies and Eligibility Criteria. A Consultation Document*. Derby: Southern Derbyshire Health.

Strong, S. (1996) Care choices. *Community Care*, 11–17 January: 14–15.

Warner, N. (1994) *Community Care: Just a Fairytale?* London: Carers National Association.

Wilding, P. (1994) Maintaining quality in human services. *Social Policy and Administration*, 28 (1): 57–72.

Wilson, G. (1995) Introduction, in G. Wilson (ed.) *Community Care: Asking the Users*. London: Chapman & Hall.

Wistow, G. (1990) *Community Care Planning: A Review of Past Experience and Future Imperatives, Caring for People Implementation Document CC13*. London: DHSS.

Wistow, G. (1995) Aspirations and realities: community care at the crossroads. *Health and Social Care in the Community*, 3 (4): 227–40.

Wistow, G., Knapp, M., Hardy, B. and Allen, C. (1994) *Social Care in a Mixed Economy*. Buckingham: Open University Press.

TOWARDS A CONCEPTUAL FRAMEWORK

VALUES, ASSUMPTIONS AND IDEOLOGIES

Introduction

> The illusion is that we have created the most sophisticated society in the history of man. The reality is that the division of knowledge into feudal fiefdoms of expertise has made general understanding and coordinated action not simply impossible but despised and distrusted.
>
> (Saul 1992: 8)

As an opening exercise for undergraduates on the BA (Hons) Professional Studies: Learning Difficulties course at Stockport College, students are asked to write about aspects of their personal development which have led them to a degree strongly related to the world of community care services. Inevitably, as a first encounter between a group of people teaching and assessing students over a three-year period and those individuals themselves, a good deal is left unsaid that might represent students' true feelings, and a certain amount is written that is thought to be the 'expected' or 'right' thing to say. Given our undergraduate population is a roughly equal mixture of new school leavers and older people who have worked, or are working, in services there is also quite a difference in their respective answers. Those in services, as well as giving idiosyncratic personal details, most commonly talk about enjoying working with people with learning disabilities but wanting to progress in the service world. The school leavers, though all, as an entry requirement, have had a substantial period of time working with people with learning disabilities, are much more mixed in their views, particularly when it comes to their future. More see the degree as an end in itself, which while it may lead to a career in services, will be of value to them in their personal development. What very few of either group do, however, is to frame even part of their answers in what might be called 'values terms' – to say, for example, 'I think it is right to help other people' or 'I think people with learning disabilities get a bad deal in life, and I think that is wrong'.

This may be, as alluded to earlier, a reluctance to admit to **values** or **beliefs** before checking out what are 'approved' values or beliefs. It may also be the thought that 'personal opinions' don't really count when set against the wealth of knowledge that will descend from the lips of the omniscient lecturers over the next three years. What does seem to be true, however, and this is supported in ensuing, more relaxed conversations as the course proceeds, is that there is no questioning the existence of the need for community care services, or that it is 'right' for services to exist in an organized form that provides paid employment for those doing the serving and (usually more highly paid) employment for those managing those doing the serving. Further, it is extremely hard to get students to make the connection between their generalized values and beliefs, once those are made explicit (e.g. on the ethics of prenatal screening and selective abortion) and their understanding of **assumptions** behind the organization and functioning of services. This is scarcely their fault, or even really ours as teachers, given the paucity of material that itself makes these connections. Given that most of our graduates go on fairly rapidly to positions in the service world where they are able to exercise some influence over what happens in the lives of those who use services, the situation is also worrying, not only because our students are not making the connections, but because they apparently do not need to do so in order to progress.

As well as being worrying, however, it is hardly surprising, as this and the next chapter will attempt to elaborate. The argument put forward proposes that, for reasons which flow from society's highest order belief systems, through conscious and, more often, unconscious values and assumptions, via academic and professional **theories**, to the very use of language and what passes for knowledge about our fellow human beings, community care services are in chaos. This chaos is not brought about by incompetence or malevolence, but by the incompatibility of values both about and between what is thought to be 'right' and what is thought to be 'reasonable' or 'realistic'; indeed by the incompatibility of beliefs that one should even *consider* what is 'right' as opposed to what is 'reasonable' or 'realistic'. As an attempt to clarify, at least in readers' minds, that chaos, both sides of the assumed dichotomy will be examined and the range of influences on each considered, together with an attempt to clarify the differences between values, assumptions, theories and ideologies. This chapter will look at the broad picture, using a **model** which attempts to describe the dynamics of influences which result in particular service forms being played out in practice, both at the macro and micro level. Two different but complementary models have particularly informed this way of conceptualizing the situation. One, drawing on the work of Wolfensberger (1996a) and others (e.g. Armstrong and Malet 1978; Schoedinger 1992) uses the construct of **universals** and its application to human services in general. The other, coming from the field of learning disabilities (Dowson 1991) uses the analogy of an iceberg to describe services, with only the results, in terms of the manifest operation and effect of services being above the surface, while many of the dynamics, including the most powerful ones, operate beneath the surface. The model used here is not as broad as the concept of universals, nor, as we shall see, does it have quite the same notion of a hierarchy of phenomena. It does however, unlike Dowson's model, look at the impact of the various forces on the full range of community care services, though this does not imply a criticism of Dowson's model.

Having looked at the broad picture in this chapter, our model is then used in the next to describe the particular case of learning disability services and the influences on them.

The big picture: Influences and connections

It is probably no coincidence that the last ten years have seen the growth of discussion, dispute, and even whole livelihoods dependent on issues that could be described as 'questions of value', while at the same time the complexity of humans' arrangements for ordering themselves – communities, political allegiances, organizations and administrative processes among others – has increased massively, in some people's views to the point of unmanageability (Wolfensberger 1996a). What some have seen as the end, or at least the failure, of the rational and scientific domination of societal arrangements, leading to an era of **post-modernism** (Taylor-Gooby 1994), others have seen as an era where almost total control has been taken over our lives and how they are ordered, by an elite group of amoral technocrats, the natural heirs (or 'bastards' to use Saul's 1992 term) of the **Enlightenment** and the subsequent rise of **rationalism**. What appears certain is that within what have been called 'Western' societies a deep sense of unease, very often unarticulated and sometimes focused around a very specific issue, has arisen between what people feel 'ought' to be happening and what *is* happening in a given social situation. This is compounded by a further sense, as with some of our students mentioned in the introduction, that what one feels 'ought' to be happening is only one's 'ignorant' opinion and that only by reference to the 'experts' can that feeling be validated. These 'experts' are appearing not only in the more traditional areas of specialism, such as pure science or engineering, nor even in the more recently established, in historical terms, social sciences such as psychology or economics, but in aspects of our everyday lives such as child rearing, grieving and personal relationships (McKnight 1984). This is yet one more aspect of the increasing complexity of coping with modern life and one more symptom of the discomfort people feel when they address their own values and beliefs.

Values and working in community care services

When it comes to a particular issue that affects many people's lives, there-fore, such as the quantity, pattern and quality of services that have been subsumed under the umbrella title of 'community care' there is a tendency for those working in such services to do one of a number of things. They may, at one extreme, accept the rationalist approach, although probably calling it something like a need for 'education' or 'training' to increase their 'professionalism'. In doing this, they are implicitly accepting that there is a body of knowledge involved in their area of work, enough of which will be imparted to them to do the job at their current level in the system, and more of which will be given to them as they rise in that system, so that they will become, in time, 'experts' in their small corner of the service empire (Collins and Collins 1992). At the other end of the scale, though much less numerous, are those who hold it to be wrong for anyone but the people in receipt of services to define, plan or organize those services according to their own definition of their needs (Sutcliffe and Simons 1993). All that is required of service workers, in this view, is 'empowerment' of service users (Jack 1995). At both extremes, people working in services who hold these views can get along reasonably well with what is going on in their world – the former in the certainty of the professional and the latter in the certainty of permanent opposition, for whom no service defined provision will ever be satisfactory but who are rarely prepared to undertake the sacrifice and commitment required for alternatives – and can therefore remain in the service system but without any personal loyalty to it.

As noted above, these are extremes, though the former is more common than the latter. For most people in services, however, and for a number of writers (Tyne 1994; O'Brien and O'Brien 1997a, b) the dilemmas posed by those two extremes remain a constant source of tension. Put more simply, what is the average care worker to think about working in something called a 'home' when what is being provided bears no relation, either physically or, more importantly, socially to what they would come up with if asked what they valued and believed in most strongly about the idea of 'home' (Kinsella 1993)? What is the average care worker to think, if their most fundamental beliefs abhor violence and oppression, and yet they witness, and are part of, violent and oppressive things done to people, often in the guise of 'treatment' (Levy and Kahn 1991)? What is the average care worker to think, if they value and believe in the idea of service to needy people on the basis of the severity of those needs, when they observe, or are part of, a service system that rations services on the basis of the ability of people to pay for them (Lewis and Glennerster 1996)?

In an attempt to at least clarify that tension, we will now look at a model which tries to isolate and bring to consciousness the elements that influence what happens in services, and to examine the relevance and potency of those elements.

A model of influences on services

The following schemata (see Fig. 3.1) is intended to illustrate the dynamic interaction of forces in producing and maintaining at any one time a set of services for people defined as being in need of them. Unlike the idea of universals there is no indication in Fig. 3.1 of any relative weight in the interactions, though it would be true to say that it is compatible with that model in the sense that the more universal the individual elements are in any given society, the more powerful will be the effect of those elements on the other parts of the model and hence on the resultant service system. So, for example, if it is demonstrated that a particular set of values is dominant in a given society, then the results of those values on service delivery will be strong, even if a particular service has a set of values, or a **culture**, that may oppose the near universal ones.

In this chapter we shall look particularly at the two 'surrounding' influences of external economic, social and value forces, and the societal values of UK society, together with the inputs of 'shapers of values' and 'experts',

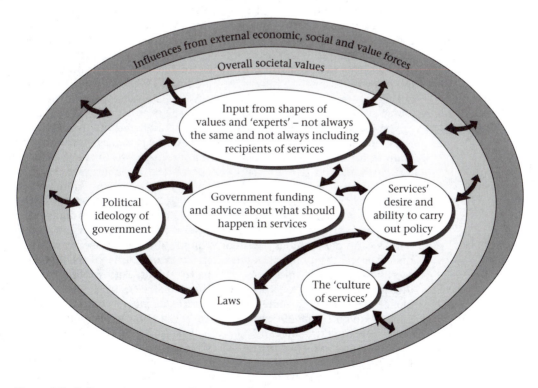

Figure 3.1 Influences on community care services.

leaving definitions of those groups to the proceeding discussion. The influence of the political ideology of the government will be briefly addressed, and all the discussion will be held with reference to the effects of these forces and their interaction with community care services in the UK.

External economic, social and value forces

Though described here as external, global forces of course have an input from, as well as an effect on, UK society. Nevertheless, developments outside the UK, in particular the end of the **cold war** and the development of a **global economy**, have a potentially major effect on the way we think about meeting the needs of our citizens. The apparent failure of communism has been greeted in many powerful quarters as a rejection not only of a centralized economy, but also of the responsibility of the state to make provision for its people by the creation and financing of public services. The 'freedom' for ex-communist countries triumphantly announced by commentators has in some cases included, for the poor, the aged and the infirm, a freedom from state care. Some would argue that the state care, particularly such institutions as orphanages for children and adults with disabilities, was also something from which people required liberating (Kaser 1976; McKee 1991) but many other examples of state provision, such as pensions, have also gone by the board or been made worthless by inflation of the national currency. The collapse of communism has also provided many opportunities for what could be called 'service imperialism,' where Western models are uncritically accepted into ex-communist countries only concerned with their technologies, rather than whether the underpinning values and assumptions of those Western models will fit into the host culture (Kalman 1996). All of this serves to bolster the self-belief of the established professional services in the West, which of course includes the UK.

Nor has the UK been isolated from global changes in the pattern of work, in particular the movement in most industrialized societies from manufacturing to **service based economies**. Many writers have observed this phenomenon (e.g. Dicken 1992; Foray and Freeman 1993), but few have indicated so clearly the effects on human services as Wolfensberger (1996a). Observing the economies of the West he points to the fact that such economies have little need for workers in the 'primary production' of food and basic necessities and so he names them 'post-primary-production' (PPP) economies. Among the many implications for societies noted in his paper the key point of interest here concerns his assertion that a PPP economy needs to, and does 'create dependent classes, who are then interpreted to "need" organised, paid human services of all kinds – but to make sure that these same human services do not accomplish any real good' (Wolfensberger 1996a: 141). There is not space to elaborate his argument here, but regardless of opinions regarding PPP economies, there is overwhelming evidence of the UK economy being of the PPP kind, and therefore generating among other things an expanding human service system. Further, the particular nature of the British class system, with its scorn for 'trade' among the aristocracy, the deference, and challenges to it, paid on the basis of subtle power relations of birth, location and education, and its need for a vast array of personal servants up until relatively recent times, has had its effect on both the economy and human services (Hutton 1996). The interaction of this service system with the ideology of a market-oriented and privatizing government in the 18 years up to 1997 has also meant that the system has increasingly been of a free market nature, reinforced of course by events that undermined the credibility of state services elsewhere, as mentioned above (Wistow et al. 1996).

What of global values issues? Here again opinion is divided, ranging from those who believe that a set of global values, based on ideals of democracy and human rights, is gradually taking over (Kanter 1995), to those who argue that this trend is a cover for global homogenization into an amoral technocracy dominated and determined by American power over both economies and media (Dicken 1992). Others point to the inadequacy of the idea of national values, given the information revolution and the power of multinational corporations, again over both economies and media (Foray and Freeman 1993). Still others claim that values can only be held by individuals, and the only values collectively held are those which shape individual identity through membership of a particular group. The common attribute of the group may be that it holds certain values in common, or experiences some other common feature, such as oppression (Haber 1994). This common feature then disregards national boundaries. In terms of community care services in the UK, the point of interest from all these differing views is how the global forces have interacted with UK society and what effect, if any, this has had on the dominant societal values and beliefs in this country.

Dominant societal values in the UK

At this point in our discussion some attempt should be made to define the different terms we have used rather casually up to now, particularly because it is part of the case being made that one of the key causes of the chaos in which services find themselves is lack of clarity about the difference between values, beliefs and technologies. Of course philosophers may object that modern **existentialist** philosophy has demonstrated that the very concept of a value system, or a sense of morality, is a totally invalid one, going beyond the bounds of 'knowledge and will' that they claim to be the only elements determining our actions (Hampshire 1982). Fortunately there are other philosophers who find this view of humanity 'alien and implausible' (Murdoch 1991: 9), and there is not space to rehearse their entire debate here. Instead, the definitions used for our discussion will attempt to be ones to which non-philosophers can relate, coming from reasonably everyday discourse.

First, the difference between values and beliefs. Put simply, values can be thought of as general statements of what a person or group of people hold to be 'right', not in the sense of 'correct,' but in the sense of 'morally right'. Beliefs, on the other hand, could be described as what an individual or group hold to be 'true', not in the sense of being 'proven', but in the sense that their 'truth' is what that individual believes in without proof. One can therefore say that one's beliefs lead to one's values. Let us try to illustrate the difference. A person can 'believe' in the existence of a **metaphysical** supreme being called 'God'. A corollary of that belief is that the person would look to guide their actions by reference to what that metaphysical being might want them to do. All the various faith systems have attempted to do this and yet anyone trying to get a sense of what is 'right' from these various faith systems (i.e., their values) would not come up with a consistent response. They would, however, find more in common between the faith systems, based as they are on a common belief in a 'God', than between a set of values based on a belief, say, in **materialism** – i.e. that there is nothing beyond the material and material processes. The value systems that might flow from materialism, such as rationalism and **utilitarianism** (i.e. what is right is what provides a logical solution to a problem with the greatest ratio of material benefits to material costs) are less often thought of as 'values', but if we say that what is thought to be right becomes a means of guiding and determining action and we observe that rationalism is a major influence on the processes of modern societies, then we can call rationalism a 'value system'. When beliefs and their resultant values are sufficiently held in common, then they could be called a 'religion', though that term tends to cause confusion between a set of beliefs and values and the institutions and organizational bodies that have arisen to promote and preserve those beliefs and values. However it may be instructive for a moment to use that term, as Wolfensberger (1994) does, to look at what beliefs and values are dominant in UK society at the end of the second millennium since the founding of one particular religion.

A new religion?

Surveys may still point to a majority of UK citizens who 'believe in God' and who will probably be baptized, married and buried in a church. Church membership in the traditional denominations of the UK, on the other hand, including the numbers coming forward to serve as priests, is declining rapidly (e.g. Diocese of Derby 1997). The influence of the churches in public affairs is still significant, at least in terms of the attention which is paid to utterances by church leaders, but if we look at the service system in this country, we see that it has probably come as far from its historical roots in the values of Judaeo-Christianity as any in the Western world, with the possible exception of some Scandinavian countries (Tawney 1938). This is due to a number of factors, not least among them the domination in UK society of a different set of beliefs from those historical roots. By 'domination' is meant a deduction of what the dominant beliefs in a society are from the way it behaves, and from the weight given to alternative courses of action, which reveal a society's values, rather than public utterances by politicians or others about what values 'the people' hold.

Space, and the terms of reference of this book, preclude an exhaustive analysis of all possible values held by all possible individual groups in society, and also any attempt to conclude what are the 'right' values for a society to hold. It is also important to acknowledge the overall impact on UK society, like most Western societies and many others, of institutionalized racism and sexism, but to withdraw from writing the book that incorporation of their relative influence would entail. This is on the grounds that, first, many other books have been written on this topic and second, and more importantly, that the analysis that follows is an attempt to examine the dominant values of UK society at a higher level of abstraction. In this context we would use the concept of universals to claim that overwhelming evidence exists for the universality of social stratification and oppression (e.g. Katz 1990), and that racism and sexism, in their broadest sense of prejudice with power, are a subset of that universal phenomenon.

The analysis that follows, therefore, is an attempt to examine values that, consciously or unconsciously, lead to behaviours in UK society, including its institutionalized racism and sexism (and, as we shall see later, many other 'isms' that have received less attention, such as disablism and ageism). For this analysis we draw still further on the work of Wolfensberger for our framework, though many other authors (Martin 1972; Mishra 1990; McKnight 1995, for example) support the overall contention.

The 'new value system'

Wolfensberger, in various publications e.g. 1994, 1996a, describes what he calls the 'new value system' being adopted by modern societies. It is summarized under four headings (Wolfensberger 1994 – all quotations in the list that follows are from p. 20).

1 **Materialism** – defined as having three 'potentially distinct expressions'. The first, and the most common understanding of the term materialism is 'a lust for possessions, wealth, goods and/or their consumption'. Less commonly understood, but what Wolfensberger claims as 'even more important' is 'an intense preoccupation with the material universe and human control over it, and especially with technological processes'. The third manifestation, regarded by Wolfensberger as 'the most important of all', namely 'a turning away from spiritualized belief systems and their derivative moralities, or in many people, at least a separation of morality from higher order spiritualized belief systems' is of course precisely the dilemma that is at the heart of this chapter.
2 **Individualism** – this followed historically from the 'materialization of worldview' which 'elevated collective humanity into the place of the divinity' but in its modern manifestation is 'an extreme form of individualism' which expresses itself as 'a different form of idolatry of the human, namely, no longer of humanity in the collective abstract, but of the human individual'.
3 **Sensualism** – again following from the other two elements, Wolfensberger claims that the casting off of 'any external moral constraints' combined with 'an exhaltation of individualism' leads inevitably to 'sensualism; a preoccupation with comforts, convenience, whatever feels good'.

4 **Externalism** – the fourth component again finds echoes in our introduction to this chapter, and is defined as people 'growing up empty,
shallow, superficial, without strength in spiritual values, morality, character, and often even personality. Accordingly, in their functioning, they
rely on, or even become dependent on external inputs and supports of
an ongoing nature'. One result of this is that people are 'very susceptible
to peer opinion and guru figures and are easily seduced into fads, crazes
and cults'.

Let us then see whether this framework, claimed by Wolfensberger to
apply to 'the modern world' has validity when applied to UK society.

Materialism

We have already discussed the apparent contradiction between what is
professed and what is practised in terms of the traditional organized reli-
gions of UK society and this can be extended to consider the place that
any metaphysical set of beliefs is given in the decision making arenas of
our society. Politicians may hold such beliefs, and even publicly proclaim
the fact, as is the case with the current prime minister, Tony Blair, but the
appeal to the public is overwhelmingly made in material terms. Education
is heralded as a 'value' but in the economic use of that term rather than
education being 'right' in itself. It is thus seen as simply a means to equip
our children to compete in the material market-place. Even allowing that
this takes account of the pressure of global influences outside national
control, we are not being asked to support education because it is right, in
a moral sense, but because it is a solution to a material problem, to be
solved by throwing out the technically, or professionally, inefficient and
replacing them with those who will make the educational machine work.
No debate is allowed on the values behind education, what it should be
for, or even who it should be for. Even a recent **Green Paper** on inclusion
(DfEE 1997) takes for granted that being in the school system is automatically a good thing, regardless of the wide range of beliefs and values that
the school system encompasses, some of which are basically incompatible
– e.g. examination success versus inclusiveness as a measure of the worth
of a school.

In medicine, despite some bows in the direction of alternative or **holistic**
approaches, the greatest areas of expansion are in the material worlds of
genetics and replacement therapy. Human machine design and maintenance,
like car design and maintenance, keeps the power in the hands of the de-
signer and mechanic with ever more complexity facing the average person.
The funding of health awareness campaigns for the non-professional
is dwarfed by the resources demanded by the human mechanics of the
medical profession. Like car maintenance, too, the economic benefits of
built-in obsolescence need the maintenance of ignorance in the population about how to keep themselves well, so that the latest model of drug
or therapy can be successfully marketed.

In community care services, too, the approach to people is characterized
in terms of a 'problem' of a material nature. Either something is 'wrong'
with the person that can be defined in a technical professional way, very

often as a 'disease' or a 'syndrome' (for an instructive and amusing list of the range of normative human conditions so defined, see Wolfensberger 1996a), or a whole class or group of people are categorized as being 'in need' of a technical service, rather than possessing more fundamental needs that they have in common with most other human beings (McKnight 1989). The vast bulk of literature on human services – and community care services in particular, at least for those in direct management or caring roles – consists of 'instruction manuals'. These range from books about ways to run particular services, borrowing heavily from the industrial management literature without too much regard for the differences between making cars and determining the shape of people's lives (e.g. Kalman 1996), to direct practice techniques for dealing with an increasingly differentiated set of users of services. So we don't just have books about – still less by – 'people with learning disabilities', we have them on issues ranging from 'techniques for dealing with challenging behaviour' (Emerson 1995), 'sexuality and learning disabilities' (Craft 1994) to a whole myriad of ways to deal with the material body with a label of learning disability that is presented to the service system (Stratford and Gunn 1996). The same applies to services for elderly people and people with mental health problems. Note that we are talking about the majority here. There are of course others who write about people who use services from a non-material point of view (e.g. Vanier 1979; McKnight 1987; Snow 1994). Ironically, because these writers talk about values, they are often criticized for attempting to 'indoctrinate' the reader, as if reading a whole series of technical manuals does not indoctrinate the reader into the materialistic, technical belief system. Similarly the growing, though still comparatively small, number of published accounts by people in receipt of services are regarded as idiosyncratic, non-generalizable and, anyway, about the past, from which 'we have moved on'.

Individualism

As for individualism, not only does it have a longer and deeper root in UK philosophy than its opposite value of collectivism, it also goes far deeper into the British social consciousness than many writers would have us believe, and therefore the UK could be said to be the most fertile ground for the growth of the 'radical individualism' of Wolfensberger's framework. The formation of the post-war welfare state, and the so-called 'consensus' in social policy that followed, is used by many social commentators (e.g. Sullivan 1992) to make the years of Thatcherism seem like an aberration in UK values, with individualism coming to the fore for a brief time while the money was good, but then firmly rejected by the re-election of a Labour government. This analysis ignores the appeal to individualism implicit in New Labour policies and the question of whether there really was 'consensus' prior to Thatcher (Hall 1992; Sullivan 1992).

The lack of collective memory described by Wolfensberger (1996a) and others (e.g. Saul 1992) is only rarely addressed by personal recollections of individuals, but what comes through from them is not that the welfare state was welcomed with open arms but with deep suspicion, especially from the professions most directly affected by it (Castle 1976; Foot 1983).

In addition, what Thatcher tapped into was not a new value strain in the UK population but a reaction to what many saw as a move away from individual responsibility by the provision of professionalized state services for people. The thought that 'unfit' individuals might be getting 'something for nothing' was always at the back of the mind of middle England, if not the rest of the UK. If to this is added the new part that Thatcherism, aided and abetted by global developments described earlier, *did* add to the values pot – namely the attachment to US rather than European notions of **rights** – then the picture of a UK still powerfully in the grip of radical individualism is clear.

The fact that, in a state without a written constitution UK citizens have few legal rights has not stopped the growth, again described in more detail in Wolfensberger (1996a) of a culture of felt individual 'entitlement' or 'rights'. This, again, becomes a question of values and beliefs. If we value our individual 'rights' so highly, and feel 'entitled' to certain things in life, where has that feeling come from? Not from traditional religion, since that teaches the denial of self as a major tenet, and in any case, as we have seen, traditional religious values are not those guiding UK society. The most convincing explanation comes in the embrace of individualism, where the individual human is seen as the centre of all things, and any external influence as being an interference with the individual's free choice.

In community care terms, this has resulted in the exaltation of *choice* within certain sections of the service world to something very akin to Holy Writ, though this usually means the choice between a number of undesirable alternatives for many service users, or trivial choices, such as meals, but in a place where the user has to spend the vast majority of their time, though they have not chosen to be there.

Individualism has also, when it has been allied with the ideology of the market, focused services on the individual as a consumer, able to choose between the array of options in the supermarket of services. Like the market in the wider world, however, as critics of so-called economic 'libertarianism' have pointed out (Haworth 1994), the ability to choose is not solely the result of being a 'rational consumer' but also dependent upon the ability to deal in the very material transaction of paying. The individual, without the bulk purchasing power of the collective, or the service agency, is much more like a consumer in a market survey in terms of affecting the product – i.e. one voice in a large group, where the majority opinion, or what is 'sellable' to the greatest number will determine the shape of the product. Nevertheless, individualism, particularly in the form of consumerism and consumer's rights, is a value dominant in UK society, and hence is a powerful influence on at least the rhetoric of services.

Sensualism

The next value, sensualism, is again one which has resulted from many global forces as well as factors peculiar to the UK, in particular the growth of global media and information sources which not only inform, but persuade people of the desirability of an almost infinite supply of 'experiences'. Not only that, these experiences are increasingly being materialized, even when they are not intrinsically of a material kind. Relationships can be bought, or at least defined in material terms in such things as 'pre-nuptial agreements.' A football match no longer becomes a matter of admiring the skill of two teams, or even of passionate local loyalties, but a family entertainment package, the result of which is almost secondary to the amount of money that can be made from subsidiary activities to the game itself.

The availability of credit in the UK, dramatically increased in the Thatcher years, allows another dimension of Wolfensberger's 'modernism' to flourish, what he has called 'here-and-nowism' (Wolfensberger 1996a). This is also reflected, as mentioned earlier, in the growing lack of a collective memory, as more and more inputs to the senses crowd out the time and space for reflection on, and lessons from, the past. Even academic writing, however brilliant, is not counted in research validation exercises unless it has taken place in the recent past. Reputation is now all about current image: you are only as good as your last performance, or article, or report, or presentation. What this has meant for services in the UK is a never-ending demand for 'newness', in particular in service technologies. In fact the newer a technique is, and the more 'high tech', the more likely are services to take it up. The emperor has never worn such new clothes. Unfortunately, like the guillotine, the latest technological method for doing something of questionable moral value does not make that thing any the less questionable.

Externalism

Finally, perhaps the most important value to be adopted in UK society, as far as the lives of certain recipients of services are concerned, is that of externalism. In particular, when the reliance on external supports, even the desirability or necessity of those external supports, becomes defined by others. If that definition of what someone needs is then informed by reference to utilitarianism, which is increasingly the case, then people's very lives can be threatened (Maclean 1993).

Like individualism, utilitarianism has a long-established place in UK philosophical history, and is very much to the forefront in ethical debates about abortion and euthanasia. There is too, as with individualism, considerable debate among philosophers about the interpretations of utilitarianism in the hands of non-philosophers (Maclean 1993). Nevertheless, if we follow the framework through and look at UK society we can see how much reliance is placed on other people's definitions of need being the powerful ones. If our society were made up of internally self-reliant people, using their collective power to support one another, then the power of those in services to define people's lives would be much diminished. It is the search for this sense of 'community' that has led many into false hopes of 'community care': 'the turbulent forces that fragment our times replace community with cleverly marketed counterfeits, like 'Community Care', which masks impersonal rationing by joining two words with high appeal, emptying them of content, and filling the hollowed out space with bureaucratic professional activity' (O'Brien and O'Brien 1997b: 87).

Those who have realized the power of the values forces pushing against this view still search for, and sometimes find 'community' in the lives of various devalued groups (Schwartz 1992; O'Brien and O'Brien 1997b), but a look at the majority of service literature, and the majority of services, suggests that professionalism has been successful in using and developing externalism in society to the point that people are even defining the quality of their lives by the availability of services. Interpretation of the 'quality of life' of individuals by external people in positions of authority in services has resulted in many decisions of a life and death nature being made on the basis of one set of values and beliefs, explicitly to the contrary of another, older set, or indeed of any other set.

Not that the utilitarians who make these decisions are claiming to be establishing, or opting for, an alternative set of beliefs and values. Instead they say that they are 'merely' looking at individual cases or providing general guidelines (Maclean 1993). These can then of course change with time, and the collective memory then forgets that a decision two years ago was hailed as definitive. So unborn children with disabilities can now be aborted right up to term, when only a few years earlier they were in a group for whom it was 'right' to abort only up until the 36th week. What the utilitarians are actually subscribing to is what Saul (1992) calls the 'theology of power' – that is, the dominance and blind faith in technological solutions to moral problems, worked out with 'pure reason' via a calculus that reduces more and more of people's lives to points on scales (Goode 1994). For those in the caring professions this is one of the key elements of the tensions mentioned earlier, between their own beliefs and values and what is going on in services.

What we have outlined here, therefore, is presented as evidence of a dominant set of beliefs and values in UK society, at least as observed by the behaviour of societal institutions, norms of general social behaviour and the prevailing pronouncements of the media. It is not, of course, being claimed that absolutely everyone subscribes to these beliefs and values, and one could present a long list of specific groups who would claim to oppose them. For our purposes, however, it is the dominance of that system of values and beliefs that is important and we now need to move on to a consideration of whether that dominance has come from the impact of those individuals and groups who attempt to shape values and beliefs, though they may not all claim to be doing so. We thus move to the next layer in the model shown in Fig. 3.1 as a link into the next chapter.

Theories, ideologies and assumptions: The impact of shapers of values

As a dynamic model, it should be clear that the elements in Fig. 3.1 have a powerful effect on one another. This is particularly true of the interaction between the values and beliefs that dominate a society and the attention society pays to those who shape those values and beliefs. We have used the term 'shaping' deliberately to try and convey the idea that such people are rarely, if ever, the *creators* of values and beliefs, but that they may have a powerful influence on the final form that the values and beliefs take in practice. This may happen by their clarifying the impact of a particular set of values and beliefs on the 'real world', by reinforcing commonly held values and beliefs through giving them the seal of approval of 'science', or by using the older magic of story-telling and personalization of beliefs to reinforce a particular view of human beings and the world. Given the focus of our discussion, i.e. the influences on community care services, what have the shapers of values had to say, and what effects have emerged from what they have said?

There is, once again, a temptation here to be caught in the modernistic tendency to disregard history and present to the reader a range of contemporary theorists as if that was all they needed to know. That, after all, would increase their 'professional knowledge' and enable them to hold erudite sounding conversations at interviews and elsewhere. It is the thesis of this chapter, however, that services are rarely shaped by theorists alone, and that 'experts' are not just those who claim to be such. Unfortunately, the limitations of space prevent major elaboration of the contribution of historical experiences and the collective unconscious retention of those experiences towards the shaping of beliefs and values that are still a major part of contemporary community care. What will have to suffice is a brief overview, leaving the reader to explore its relevance in more detail.

Historical shaping of values

Beliefs and values of primary historical relevance to contemporary services concern the tension between the effects of our Judaeo-Christian heritage and an increasing sense of what Wolfensberger (1996b) has called 'menacization' of those seeking assistance. If to this tension is added the rise of science and reason to the level, in some people's view, of a religion (Saul 1992), then the ingredients of the contemporary soup of values and beliefs is complete.

Judaeo-Christian values, though of course not always their practice, have been around in the UK, as they have in most Western European nations, for at least sixteen hundred years, since the Romans declared Christianity as the imperial religion. The expression of these values in service to the poor and weak in society had its earliest expression in individual service in one's own community – including in one's own home – and then in service in various forms of community-based institutions (Davies 1909). These could be part of the facilities of various religious orders, or simply an individual community's way of looking after its own. What matters here is not the precise form that such facilities took though Wolfensberger (1996b) provides a fascinating account of the origins of some of our contemporary service forms, including the still high proportion of residential facilities that have 'beds' in multiples of 12, a reference to the 12 apostles, but the beliefs of those doing the serving, and the values that sprung from those beliefs. Essentially, the beliefs were in the Christian God, and the value position that service to those in need was service to God. Those being served are pictured, in the Middle Ages and beyond, as being thanked by the servers for giving them the chance to fulfil their Christian mission more readily.

As an *ideal*, this value position lasted for many centuries (Kilvert 1860; Dow 1922), though of course there were many variants on how people put these values into practice, and many, much more destructive, things done in the name of the same religion. During the Middle Ages, a contrasting pressure on values, however, came from a combination of wars in Europe (leaving large numbers of wandering ex-soldiers that stretched notions of hospitality to strangers to their limits), the growth of Protestantism (with its notions of sinfulness and affliction as the reward of sin) and the various serious plagues that swept Europe (Tawney 1938). The notion of needy people as either sick, and therefore contagious, or sinful, and therefore dangerous, led to a rather different set of values towards the poor and needy (note again that they still stemmed from the same basic belief in God). A differential system of obligation, based on notions of deserving and undeserving began to arise. Historians of welfare tend to cite the Elizabethan Poor Laws as a key embodiment of these values, though they were to receive the full force of value endorsement in the Victorian era (Dalley 1992).

Again, the point for our discussion is the dominant value position. In the centuries up to the period known as the Enlightenment (*circa* 1750–1800) provision of services was still largely local, though for large cities this would mean large institutions (such as the Hopitale Generale in Paris). In addition, payment for service and the running of institutions on military, rather than religious lines, was an increasing trend. The underlying values of service to others, or at least service to *deserving* others, being service to God were still, however, dominant.

The Enlightenment, and the rise of science, has been documented at great length, though more in terms of its effects on ideas than its effects on services. We have already mentioned the effects of this on the values of society, at least in some writers' views. Looking at services as they developed in the eighteenth and nineteenth centuries we can begin to see their effects slowly enter the thinking of those in positions of influence. It should also be remembered here that, by today's terms, such people were few in number. Most parishes still carried out their systems of 'poor relief' in their own way, with Poor Law guardians being made up largely of local people of substance.

The effects of rationalism and utilitarianism were beginning to be felt however, sometimes with what might be seen as 'good' outcomes, as in the various nineteenth-century attempts to educate 'ineducable idiots' (Race 1995), sometimes with less favourable outcomes, such as the 'less eligibility' principle of the Victorian workhouse. In the former, rather than serve the 'idiot' as he or she was, rationalist thinking thought to use educational technology – i.e. the asylum – to keep the person away from the diversions of the world so that they could be taught to read and write and perform tasks and thus be 'improved.' In the latter the rational pauper was to be so put off the workhouse that they would take even the meanest work to escape, and thus 'improve their soul' at the same time as easing the financial burden on the parish and so providing an interesting way to serve both God and Mammon (Coll 1969).

For most of the eighteenth and nineteenth centuries, however, the values behind the provision of services were still dominated by the belief in Christianity and the various values that stemmed from this. As the twentieth century dawned, the doubts sown by the Enlightenment, and the burgeoning of science, particularly the development of 'human science' in the form of, first, **Darwinism** and **eugenics** and second, psychology and the social sciences, began to push the Christian God out of the picture, to be replaced, at least in terms of values and beliefs, by the God of reason.

Though we have presented it as such to some extent, this change was not sudden, nor is it complete, but in relation to services it is typified by the growth in what might be called the 'human professions'. Beginning with medicine, then nursing, with teaching providing a curious mixture of the moral and the technical, these human professions have come to dominate the twentieth-century world of services. Offshoots of the original professions – what Etzioni (1969) memorably called the 'semi-professions' – have also blossomed. There is debate as to whether they have all produced fruit, but the presence of psychologists, social workers, therapists of various varieties, and the most recent hybrid, the counsellor (*consultores ubicumques*) is a significant feature of the service garden. Again, our point is not to debate whether their presence is appropriate, but to assert that their presence, and their claims to 'professionalism' are the triumph not only of the new values system we described earlier, but of a multigenerational breeding programme of rational, technical shapers of values, whose key influence has, paradoxically, been largely to deny the need for a consistent set of values to determine how services ought to be carried out. Instead the professions have evolved into bodies solving problems of their own defining, and thus influencing services to become the laboratory where they can test out their technological theories (Saul 1992; McKnight 1995). When this is taken alongside the growth in PPP economies, including the UK, with its demand for more and more people being defined as in need of services, and the political ideology of a government which saw services as another commercial 'good', to be subject to the same exposure to market forces as other previously sacrosanct public obligations, the success of the rational technocrats in shaping the services to their own ends is, if not guaranteed, given a very strong hand.

One has only to look through the vast range of textbooks on any aspect of community care (Williams 1989; Thompson and Mathias 1992 are only examples, and are not singled out here as being the epitome of this approach) to see the absence, at least in overt terms, of any indication of the values behind the instructions being given. Except, of course, the ideology of self-determination, choice and individual rights, which in these sorts of books are repeated as a sort of mantra at the beginning and then ignored as the range of technical professional options is presented. This is inevitable, of course, given that the predominant value system would deny that it is possible to have a communal set of values that determine the nature of service delivery. It also enables the apotheosis of the rational technocrat, the manager, to divide and rule in the service organization between the various professions and to hold to the view that managing and ensuring 'quality' in a service organization is no different to managing any other, since a change of organization does not mean a change of values, but merely a different set of professionals to organize. (Much more discussion on this issue from a policy perspective has already taken place in Chapters 1 and 2).

What, though, of other shapers of values, or 'experts'? We will conclude this chapter by looking at the influence of two groups, both of whom could be claimed to be 'experts', but who have both had relatively limited success in shaping values as they are applied to services, with some notable exceptions. The first group are academics, and the second are people who use community care services.

Academics and service users: Shapers of values or experts?

In attempting an 'academic' analysis of the effects of academics one could be said to be the pot calling the kettle black. Nevertheless in looking at community care services it is possible to divide, somewhat crudely, the effects of academia into groups along the same lines as the previous analysis.

The first group would be those who go along with the prevailing values of society and the dominance of the rational professional view of services. In terms of affecting the technology of service delivery, this group is likely to have the greatest effect, if our argument on the dominant value position is granted. Certainly, as noted above, the service literature, and many of the research journals, are full of reviews of existing technologies, announcements of new 'breakthroughs' in the treatment of this or that client group (the word 'client' fits most nearly to the professional notion of people who use services, as it has since the oldest profession) and training manuals for all of them.

Within their own terms, many new innovations have had a significant effect on services, in that such technologies have not only been applied, but also could be said to have benefited those to whom they are applied. As Illich *et al.* (1977) and others in this tradition (e.g. McKnight 1989) have pointed out, however, this is rarely the majority of clients, and usually at the expense of either *not* doing something more basic, in terms of well tried and tested technologies, or trusting in historical community solutions to certain problems (Schwartz 1997). In the main, this first group of academics would want to reinforce the values of materialism, via technological solutions: sensualism, by promising ever-changing, new experiences via new technologies; individualism, by the technologies being available to a tightly-defined category, or those who can pay for them, or those who are judged to 'deserve' them; and externalism, by the reliance on ever-changing fashions in the criteria for rationing those technologies according to some artificially constructed utilitarian measure of 'quality' or 'benefit'.

The second group of academics, at least as far as community care services are concerned, are those who have sought to construct a theory around what is happening to people. Some of these are general theorists of social policy, who have tended to reflect on social arrangements from a particular political perspective (e.g. Katz 1990; Mishra 1990). Some are academics producing theories about particular groups and how they are dealt with by society (e.g. Oliver 1990; Haber 1994). Finally, there is a small, but growing, group who disavow the possibility of theory, some of whom see the construction of reality for those who use services as unique to them (Wilson 1995). Though fairly large in number (or perhaps output), a look at the development of community care policy, as described in Chapters 1 and 2, should make it clear that these theorists have been heavily outnumbered – in terms of effect – by the technocratic academics, and that other influences in our model have had a more direct influence on the development of services than either group. This point will be taken up in more detail in the next chapter, as we also consider the influence of the other group of 'experts' – the people who use services.

As has been noted above, the value of choice is very much part of the individualistic value system, and it would therefore be expected that users of community care services of all kinds would have a powerful voice in their development. In reality, though current community care services are often described as consumer led, or more commonly, 'needs led', by far the greatest area where the voices of service users have been heard is their accounts of the effects of services on them, rather than their being a significant influence on service development. Far too often these accounts are used for breast beating by others about how bad things used to be (i.e. when different technologies were being applied) rather than examining the beliefs and values behind those older technologies and seeing how many are still, consciously or unconsciously, being applied. It has, however, been argued (Oliver 1990) that the one area where both theorists and the users of services themselves have had a significant influence on service development has been in the field of disability. To examine this further we need to use the other elements of our model. This we will do in the next chapter by looking specifically at influences on services for people with learning disabilities.

Conclusion

In examining the effects of the different forces on community care services by use of the model shown in Fig. 3.1 we have attempted to demonstrate that issues well beyond the particular specialized disciplines that make up community care services have a major impact on those services. In particular issues of global concern and issues to do with the values that are dominant in UK society lay the ground for a major tension between what individual service workers hold as values and the realities they observe in the services in which they work. This tension, particularly if it is concluded that the dominant values of Western societies are those identified by Wolfensberger as materialism, individualism, sensualism and externalism, requires service workers to deal with a world dominated by professional enclaves, each with their own technologies and each vying for power, which contrasts with the historical roots of services in the Judaeo-Christian values of service to fellow human beings. This professional division, one might even say chaos, in the service world is reinforced by the 'shapers of values', particularly a majority of academics who produce textbooks and guides to action very much in line with a materialist technological view of human beings and human problems. Though some writers oppose this view, as we have reviewed, their influence does not appear to be great, as with the views of those who use services, when it comes to affecting the overall shape of the service world, and hence the world of community care services.

Summary

- A tension exists, for many service workers, between the values they hold and the assumptions and influences on the services in which they work.

- A schematic model is used (Fig. 3.1) which attempts to map out the various influences on services and their interaction one on another.

- External societal forces are described, particularly the influence of globalization and the PPP (i.e. service based) economies of the West.

- Dominant values of UK society, the next element of the model, are found to be concordant with Wolfensberger's (1994) notion of a new 'religion', defined by the dominance of materialism, individualism, sensualism and externalism.

- The impact of shapers of values is looked at historically, and is seen to have moved on from an ideal (though not always the practice) of service based on Judaeo-Christian values to a materialist technology of service based on professional technical expertise and the separation of service according to that technical expertise.

- Academics are mostly seen as being allied with the professional/technical dominance of services, though those proposing an alternative view are noted as a small but growing group.

- The view is also expressed that service users, despite rhetoric to the contrary, have yet to become a powerful influence on the majority of community care services. This, and the rest of the model will be examined in the next chapter with specific reference to services for people with learning disabilities.

Further reading

Adams, R. (ed.) (1996) *Crisis in the Human Services: National and International Issues*. Conference held at the University of Cambridge, September 1996. Lincoln: University of Lincolnshire and Humberside.

Lewis, J. and Glennerster, H. (1996) *Implementing the New Community Care*. Buckingham: Open University Press.

McKnight, J. (1995) *The Careless Society: Community and its Counterfeits*. New York: Basic Books.

Saul, J.R. (1992) *Voltaire's Bastards: The Dictatorship of Reason in the West*. London: Sinclair Stevenson.

References

Armstrong, D.M. and Malet, D. (1978) *Universals and Scientific Realism*. Cambridge: Cambridge University Press.

Castle, B. (1976) *The Castle Diaries*. London: Jonathan Cape.

Coll, B.D. (1969) *Perspectives in Public Welfare: A History*. Washington DC: US Government Printing Office.

Collins, J. and Collins, M. (1992) *Social Skills Training and the Professional Helper*. Chichester: John Wiley.

Craft, A. (ed.) (1994) *Practice Issues in Sexuality and Learning Disabilities*. London: Routledge.

Dalley, G. (1992) Social welfare ideologies and normalisation, in H. Brown and H. Smith (eds) *Normalisation: A Reader for the Nineties*. London: Tavistock/Routledge.

Davies, M. (1909) *Life in an English Village*. London: T. Fisher Unwin.

DfEE (Department for Education and Employment) (1997) *Excellence for all Children: Meeting Special Educational Needs*. London: HMSO.

Dicken, P. (1992) *Global Shift: The Internationalization of Economic Activity*. London: Paul Chapman Publishing.

Diocese of Derby (1997) *A Better Way: A Strategy for Ministry in Derby Diocese*. Derby: Council for Ministry in Derby Diocese.

Dow, G.S. (1922) *Society and its Problems: An Introduction to the Principles of Sociology*, 2nd edn. New York: Thomas Y. Crowell.

Dowson, S. (1991) *Moving to the Dance: Service Culture and Community Care*. London: Values into Action.

Emerson, E. (1995) *Challenging Behaviour: Analysis and Intervention in People with Learning Difficulties*. Cambridge: Cambridge University Press.

Etzioni, A. (1969) *The Semi-professions and their Organisation: Teachers, Nurses, Social Workers*. New York: The Free Press.

Foot, M. (1983) *Aneurin Bevan 1945–1960*. London: Paladin.

Foray, D. and Freeman, C. (1993) *Technology and the Wealth of Nations: The Dynamics of Constructed Advantage*. London: Pinter Publishers.

Goode, D. (ed.) (1994) *Quality of Life for Persons with Disabilities: International Perspectives and Issues*. Boston, MA: Brookline Books.

Haber, R. (1994) *Beyond Postmodern Politics: Lyotard, Rorty, Foucault*. New York: Routledge.

Hall, S. (1992) No new vision, no new votes. *New Statesman and Society*, 17 April.

Hampshire, S. (1982) *Thought and Action*. London: Chatto & Windus.

Haworth, A. (1994) *Anti-Libertarianism: Markets, Philosophy and Myth*. London: Routledge.

Hutton, W. (1996) *The State We're In*. London: Vintage.

Illich, I.K., Zola, J., McKnight, J., Caplan, J. and Sharten, H. (eds) (1977) *Disabling Professions*. London: Marion Boyars.

Jack, R. (ed.) (1995) *Empowerment in Community Care*. London: Chapman & Hall.

Kalman, A. (1996) Strategies of adult education and methods in change management: the training of administrative staff in the light of an educational system, in R. Adams (ed.) *Crisis in the Human Services: National and International Issues* (conference held at the University of Cambridge, September 1996). Lincoln: University of Lincolnshire and Humberside.

Kanter, R.M. (1995) *World Class: Thriving Locally in the Global Economy*. New York: Simon & Schuster.

Kaser, M. (1976) *Health Care in the Soviet Union and Eastern Europe*. Oxford: Oxford University Press.

Katz, M. (1990) *The Undeserving Poor*. New York: Pantheon Books.

Kilvert, F. (1860) *Memoirs of the Life and Writings of Richard Hurd, Bishop of Worcester, with a Selection from his Correspondence and Other Unpublished Papers*. London: Richard Bentley.

Kinsella, P. (1993) *Supported Living: A New Paradigm*. Manchester: National Development Team.

Levy, A. and Kahn, B. (1991) *The Pindown Experience and the Protection of Children – The Report of the Staffordshire Child Care Enquiry 1980*. Stafford: Staffordshire County Council.

Lewis, J. and Glennerster, H. (1996) *Implementing the New Community Care*. Buckingham: Open University Press.

Maclean, A. (1993) *The Elimination of Morality: Reflections on Utilitarianism and Bio Ethics*. London: Routledge.

McKee, M. (1991) Health Services in central and eastern Europe: past problems and future prospects. *Journal of Epidemiology and Community Health*. Vol. 45.

McKnight, J. (1984) *John Deere and the Bereavement Counsellor*, Fourth Annual E.F. Schumacher Lecture, Massachusetts. Great Barrington, MA: E.F. Schumacher Society.

McKnight, J. (1987) Regenerating society. *Social Policy*, Winter: 54–88.

McKnight, J. (1989) Why servanthood is bad. *The Other Side*, Jan/Feb: 38–9.

McKnight, J. (1995) *The Careless Society: Community and its Counterfeits*. New York: Basic Books.

Martin, E.W. (1972) *Comparative Development in Social Welfare*. London: G. Allen & Unwin.

Mishra, R. (1990) *The Welfare State in Capitalist Society*. Hemel Hempstead: Harvester Wheatsheaf.

Murdoch, I. (1991) *The Sovereignty of Good*. London: Routledge.

O'Brien, J. and O'Brien, C.L. (1997a) A tune beyond us, yet ourselves: power sharing between people with substantial disabilities and their assistants, in P. O'Brien and R. Murray (eds) *Human Services, Towards Partnership & Support*. Palmerston, NZ: The Dunmore Press.

O'Brien, J. and O'Brien, C.L. (1997b) *Members of Each Other: Building Community in Company with People with Developmental Disabilities*. Toronto: Inclusion Press.

Oliver, M. (1990) *The Politics of Disablement*. London: Macmillan.

Race, D.G. (1995) History of service provision, in N. Malin (ed.) *Services for People with Learning Disabilities*. London: Routledge.

Saul, J.R. (1992) *Voltaire's Bastards: The Dictatorship of Reason in the West*. London: Sinclair Stevenson.

Schoedinger, A.B. (ed.) (1992) *The Problem of Universals*. Atlantic Highlands, NJ: Humanities Press.

Schwartz, D.B. (1992) *Crossing the River: Creating a Conceptual Revolution in Community and Disability*. Cambridge, MA. Brookline Books.

Schwartz, D.B. (1997) *Who Cares? Rediscovering Community*. Oxford, PA: Westview Press.

Snow, J. (1994) *What's Really Worth Doing*. Toronto: Inclusion Press.

Stratford, B. and Gunn, P. (eds) (1996) *New Approaches to Down's Syndrome*. London: Cassell.

Sullivan, M. (1992) *The Politics of Social Policy*. Hemel Hempstead: Harvester Wheatsheaf.

Sutcliffe, J. and Simons, K. (1993) *Self Advocacy and Adults with Learning Difficulties: Contexts and Debates*. Leicester: National Institute on Continuing Education.

Tawney, R. (1938) *Religion and the Rise of Capitalism: A Historical Study with a Prefatory Note by Charles Gore*. Harmondsworth: Penguin.

Taylor-Gooby, P. (1994) Postmodernism and social policy: A great leap backwards? *Journal of Social Policy*, 23(3): 385–404.

Thompson, T. and Mathias, P. (1992) *Standards & Mental Handicap: Keys to Competence*. London: Bailliere Tindall.

Tyne, A. (1994) Taking responsibility and giving power. *Disability & Society*, 9(2): 249–54.

Vanier, J. (1979) *Community and Growth: Our Pilgrimage Together.* Toronto: Griffin House.

Williams, E. (1989) *Caring for Elderly People in the Community.* London: Chapman & Hall.

Wilson, G. (ed.) (1995) *Community Care: Asking the Users.* London: Chapman & Hall.

Wistow, G., Knapp, M., Hardy, B., Forder, J., Manning, R. and Kendall, J. (1996) *Social Care Markets: Progress and Prospects.* Buckingham: Open University Press.

Wolfensberger, W. (1994) A personal interpretation of the mental retardation scene in light of the 'signs of the times'. *Mental Retardation*, 32(1): 19–33.

Wolfensberger, W. (1996a) Major obstacles to rationality and quality of human services in contemporary society, keynote address, in R. Adams (ed.) *Crisis in the Human Services: National and International Issues* (conference held at the University of Cambridge, September 1996). Lincoln: University of Lincolnshire and Humberside.

Wolfensberger, W. (1996b) A history of human services. Presentation given at the University of Cambridge, September 1996.

VALUES, THEORIES AND REALITIES: THE CASE OF LEARNING DISABILITY SERVICES

Introduction

> It is natural to think that an innovation in social care which has benefited a few people should be turned into standard national policy, so that the benefits can be extended to all. In reality, however, the outcome may be to standardize mediocrity and destroy those pockets of excellent innovation which inspired the policy. It is beginning to look as if the UK's policy on community care for people with learning difficulties (and other user groups) may prove to be a case in point.
>
> (Dowson 1997a: 11)

Among the people with learning disabilities known to the author are two individuals whose ages differ by 35 years. When the older of the two was born, in 1950, her parents experienced an uncommon reaction from medical staff attending the birth of a child with Down's syndrome. Instead of telling them to 'leave her with us' or to 'go home and try for another', which was the usual advice at the time, they were told 'take her home and bring her up like your other daughter'. The younger person, born in 1985, also with Down's syndrome, met with a different response, but here too the place of his birth had a major effect on his life. Just as pressure on the woman's parents would have been different had she been born in another place, indeed in the majority of other places, the young man would, in all probability, still be with his natural parents had he been born ten miles further north in the next town. The fact that, again in all probability, had his parents lived in a town ten miles further south he would not have been born at all indicates what changes there have been in services to people with learning disabilities in the time between the two people's births.

In the town to the north of where the young man was born, a scheme for reconciliation of parents rejecting disabled children was in operation, and had a very high success rate. In the south, the next town had a famous teaching hospital, which was one of a number pioneering the use of screening by amniocentesis beyond the original target group of older mothers. Those who participated were put under some pressure to have children identified by this process aborted. As it was, the young man, by being born in a town in-between the two mentioned, was put up for adoption a short time after his birth, following rejection by his parents, whose only knowledge of people with Down's syndrome was a particularly impaired and very disruptive child of a family in their town.

In the 35 years between the birth of these two people, and in the 12 years since then, the pattern of services for people with learning disabilities in the UK has changed considerably. The woman and her parents faced a service world consisting almost entirely of one model of care: the large 'mental deficiency asylum' or 'hospital' as they were just beginning to be called. The young man was born in the middle of what has been described as a 'revolution' in care, with those same hospitals closing, with schooling available (some of it even in mainstream schools), with people leaving home to live with a few other people, and with some people holding down jobs. Other influences, however, were also at work, and as the two peoples' story moves into the present day these influences have had their effect in determining the current pattern of services that they are being offered.

As the chapter proceeds, and we use the model of Fig. 3.1 from the previous chapter to look at these influences, it will be up to the reader to decide whether they have resulted in a set of services that offer more to the young man as he grows up than was offered to the woman, and if so, whether more necessarily means better.

External economic, social and value forces on learning disability services

It should be apparent from the previous chapter that the major external influences affecting learning disability services do so as part of their influence on the whole range of human services. The pressures from the global economy and the PPP nature of Western economic structures applies equally to people with learning disabilities as to other users of services. Further, there is nothing particularly unique about the UK policy of 'community care'. Deinstitutionalization has occurred to a greater or lesser extent in most of the industrialized countries (see Mansell and Ericsson 1996; Cocks 1997) and as it was applied specifically to people with learning disabilities UK services looked beyond these shores for examples of 'models' to import. World views on 'freedom' and 'democracy', and especially US-dominated interpretations of 'rights' have also been significant influences on the UK learning disability scene.

The renaming of the International League of Societies for Persons with a Mental Handicap as Inclusion International is symbolic of a growing global pressure for the 'right' to inclusion for people with learning disabilities. That this international body should adopt the American notion that values can be imposed as 'rights' and that therefore calling something that you want to happen a 'human right', even when it is unenforceable by law in countries that do not have a written constitution, is indicative of the power of global influences on the discourse of services. Whether or not these particular global forces have had an influence on the values of societies – and thus their enactment of those values in the form of services – is more debatable, particularly when that other global force, technologization, is taken into account. When there is talk of the need for the UK to be a 'learning society' this is, as the previous chapter noted, in response to the perceived need to compete in the global, technologized, economy. Since people with learning disabilities, almost by definition, have some problems dealing with technological processes and the intellectual and conceptual jumps from one form of technology to another, this results in global pressures being yet another means by which such people will be marked out as of lesser value and dependent on services to enable them to cope with the 'modern world'. The 'clientage' spoken of by Wolfensberger (1996) as a need of the PPP economies will thus be reinforced.

Overall societal values and learning disability services

As with the external influences described above, the effect of overall societal values on learning disability services, assuming the case made in the previous chapter for their fit with Wolfensberger's (1994) framework is granted, will be as part of the effect of those values on human services as a whole. As a subset of those services, 'community care' receives its share of the influence from those values, as does the subset of community care services for people with learning disabilities. This last subset also has its own particular spin in relation to what those values say about people with learning disabilities and their place in the world, including whether, in fact, they should be denied that place.

The influence of materialism

As we have noted, the influence of materialism on services in general has enhanced the notion that they are about 'fixing' people. That the 'fixing' now sometimes takes place, at least in 'community care' services, in locales where other people, not just users of services, live or work does not negate the belief that specialist 'fixers' are required. Indeed, even the notion that people should live in or near their own homes or neighbourhoods is secondary to the desire for 'efficiency' in people fixing. Therefore 'affordability' is dependent on the cost of the material resources of service technologies and the people to run them, rather than the intangible, and thus non-material and non-measurable, costs of, say, having a friend.

The **medical model** of care for various client groups has been identified and criticized in some quarters, and this will be covered in more detail later (Oliver 1990; Swain *et al.* 1996). However, the model still remains dominant, with its materialist assumptions about the 'problem' resting in a sick, impaired or merely wearing-out body or mind.

Services in the UK for people with learning disabilities, other than education, are still controlled in large part by the Department of Health, either directly or through its 'advisory and inspectorial' role *vis-à-vis* social services departments. **Evidence based practice**, by which is meant evidence collected on the assumptions of a materialistic empirical research methodology (DoH 1995) is currently the watchword at the Department of Health and is already being spread to the wider service world.

Within learning disability services, the evidence of the effect of materialist values is revealed most clearly by the increasing power going to clinical psychology, and in particular behavioural psychologists. This is partly as a result of increased pressure to deal with people with so-called 'challenging behaviours', and partly as a result of a gradual take-over of the majority of the literature in learning disability by academic psychologists. Not that there was much to take over, as the field has always represented something of a backwater for academics, but the point is exemplified by noting what was included and excluded from a 'review of research' into residential care for people with learning disabilities commissioned by the Department of Health (Emerson and Hatton 1996). The dominance, in this review, of empirical studies carried out by psychologists would be partly justifiable in terms of their greater numbers in the field (though this reinforces the influence of materialism) but it cannot fully explain the virtual absence of work using assessments of services based on other values or ideologies (Williams 1995) or assessments made by people who use services (Sinson 1995). This is despite, as we shall see, many recent services having been set up precisely as a result of those values and ideologies, some with the expressed aim of providing power to service users.

The effect of individualism

Individualism, too, has had a major effect on services at two levels. First, in direct practice, the rhetoric of individual choice is manifest in many a brochure or mission statement, but its use in practice very often has a double negative effect on service users. On the one hand it can be used very easily by care staff to abdicate responsibility for the people with whom they are working by doing nothing that the person has not specifically chosen. This abandonment to choice hits particularly hard those who have experienced a lifetime of deprivation of experience of the world, and hence of the options for choice, by being shut away in the institutions which the new services are designed to replace. It is made more ironic when the notion of choice is heavily promoted to disguise the fact, often quite unconsciously, that the major areas of a person's life (where to live and with whom; where to earn money or how much money they will receive) are all determined by the service system, often for reasons that are far removed from the expressed or even assumed choices of the individual service users.

The second level is that of societal attitudes. It is at this level that individualism affects services for people with learning disabilities most. The notion of individual 'rights' to freedom from inconvenience or suffering promoted by radical individualism, as noted in the previous chapter (Wolfensberger 1996) has come to mean that people with disabilities, and particularly learning disabilities, have been seen as both a 'personal tragedy' (Oliver 1990) and as an intolerable burden for parents. This has led to the changes in the way services deal with the prospect of (or the actual) birth of a disabled child demonstrated by the examples of two people mentioned at the beginning of this chapter. While it was common for the service system, in the case of the woman, to say to parents 'you can't cope, leave the problem to us', it is now much more common for the attitude to be 'you shouldn't have to cope even with the fact of giving birth to a disabled child, let alone be responsible for demanding services from us'. Since the young man was born, the practices pioneered in the town south of his birthplace have become commonplace, and it is now possible to abort a child diagnosed as disabled at any point up to delivery, and even for treatment to be withheld for minor defects after birth (Norburg et al. 1994; Rachels 1986).

Of course it could be argued that the same deep-rooted fears of disabled people as menaces, as sick, or as a curse for some evildoing on the part of parents were behind both the old institutions and the 'new eugenics' (Ryan and Thomas 1987), but the key point here is that the current state of affairs offers a way out of the perceived 'problem' with the moral sanction that a person is asserting their individual 'rights', which is a direct result of the worship of the individual identified as a major value position in UK society.

The influence of sensualism and externalism

Sensualism and externalism also have their part to play in the effect of current values on services for people with learning disabilities, and again at both the levels identified previously. At the direct service level there has been, at one end of the spectrum, an insistence, almost to the point of force, that the sensual experiences that *care workers* find the most important, especially sexual activity, the diversions of the media and recreational drugs such as alcohol, should be provided for people with learning disabilities. This view rarely takes account of service users' life experiences, often associated with abuse (Sinason 1994) nor makes any judgment as to the degree of vulnerability of individuals. At the other extreme, ironically, there are those who hold that people with learning disabilities are incapable of dealing with such 'risky' experiences as sex or alcohol, including those who label a desire for such things as evidence of 'challenging behaviour' (Mitchell 1987), and thus go to great lengths to prevent people with learning disabilities from adopting a responsible attitude to such matters. Externalism then adds to the dilemma, with services being unable to trust their, or their staff's, own judgement in such matters and thus having to draw up elaborate codes of conduct (which can never cover all eventualities) to 'guide' staff. Then, whenever something goes wrong, staff are defended as long as they have kept to the externally-set rules, rather than being guided by their personal sense of right and wrong – i.e. their values (Fruin 1994).

At the societal level, the negative views of people with learning disabilities are also reinforced by the elements of sensualism and externalism. Sensualism has been used by many writers (sometimes in the guise of getting an individual's views of their own situation and sometimes with just the writer's own views) to derive scales of **quality of life** (Crisp 1991). Included in many of these scales are judgements on the sensual experience, be it pain or pleasure, that an individual is perceived as receiving. Behind this is an assumption that no meaning can be found in suffering, particularly sensual suffering, and therefore no life is better than a life of suffering. This is compounded by ever shifting views, guided by external fashion and gurus, of what constitutes the 'good life'. What seems clear from the experiences of people with learning disabilities, and the overall public attitude to them, is that they are not regarded as being likely to have a good 'quality of life' however it is measured.

Shapers of values and their effects

The effects of the modernistic value system have been compounded, as the previous chapter noted, by the dominant position of certain shapers of values in the service world. In particular we noted the predominance of an approach to both management and professional practice in services which, while not presented as a set of values (in fact often loudly proclaiming its 'value free' nature), nevertheless draws heavily on the post-Enlightenment religion of science and rationality (Saul 1992).

In the area of disability, including learning disability, this has been described as the 'medical model'. As we also noted above, this approach has gone well beyond disability in its effect on service delivery and professional practice, but it is from the disability field that the two most articulated theories critical of the medical model have emerged. In learning disability the ideas around what was originally defined as the 'principle' of **normalization** (Nirje 1969; Wolfensberger 1972), and then as the 'theory' of **social role valorization** (SRV) (Wolfensberger 1992) have been said to have had a major effect on services in the UK and elsewhere. In the wider disability world a combination of growing communication between disabled people themselves and an articulated **social theory of disability** has also been said to have had a major effect on services, though some would argue that this has been realized more for people with physical disabilities than those with learning disabilities (Chappell 1997).

Two other concepts, **advocacy** and **inclusion**, which have sprung from the same roots, have also occupied much space in the literature of learning disability. Within the former, the notion of 'self-advocacy' as a distinct, and some have argued superior, advocacy form has been realized, at least on paper, in many services (Walmsley and Downer 1997).

We will examine all of these in turn, not to try and form a judgement of which is the 'best' set of ideas, though readers are invited to match the ideas with their own experience, but to see which, if any, has had an influence on services for people with learning disabilities.

Clarification of terms

Before that, however, an attempt will be made to clarify some further usage of words, in particular the distinction between what we have called **ideas** and **theories**, and their distinction from our earlier definitions of values and beliefs. As before, we have to acknowledge that there is no consensus on what these terms mean, or even that they can exist, but again will try and at least explain in reasonably ordinary language what they are taken to mean in this chapter.

In this case we have at least the additional support that the authors of SRV and the social theory of disability actually call what they have produced a theory, and those involved with advocacy and inclusion talk about them as ideas. For our purposes, therefore, a theory consists of a set of explanations of a particular phenomenon, be it a physical phenomenon or, as in our discussion, a human phenomenon such as the treatment of people with disabilities. These explanations are put forward as a proposition, or hypothesis, which is then subject to examination as to how much of the evidence gained from observing the phenomenon fits the proposition. If sufficient evidence exists, at least in terms of the weight of probabilities, then the theory can be said to be valid.

Ironically, in view of the use of this approach by SRV and the social theory of disability to criticize the dominant model in services, it is of course precisely the same one that is employed in the great majority of academic and service discussion about what is 'best' or 'evidence based' practice. As we have noted, there is a growing body of writing which claims this approach to be fundamentally flawed, particularly its reliance on objective and therefore value-free 'evidence' (Sarantakos 1994).

'Ideas' on the other hand do not claim to be value free, certainly not those of inclusion or advocacy which feature in this chapter, and therefore would not receive the same objection from the critics of theory. We take the notion of 'ideas' to be a formulation of actions or guides to action based on certain assumptions. Those assumptions could be called 'working beliefs' or 'working values' in the sense that they represent the starting point from which the ideas flow. So, for example, if certain people did not believe that it was 'wrong' for individuals to be excluded from certain functions of society (a values position) then they would not have developed a set of ideas to combat this wrong, which fall under the heading of 'inclusion'.

Despite these differences in definition, however, both the theories we are considering in this chapter (i.e. SRV and the social theory of disability), and the ideas (i.e. inclusion and advocacy) can be said, at least in good part, to be a reaction at a values level to the results of the dominant (medical) model influencing services for people with learning disabilities, and thus a reaction at that same level to the dominant values of society.

Impact on services of alternative theories

Unfortunately, because of the very nature of the dominant values, in particular individualism and externalism, people who adhere to the medical model do not think of it in terms of an over-arching theory which explains the behaviour of much of today's community care and other services. There does not appear to be, except as produced by opponents of it, a generalized theory that corresponds to and justifies the medical model. Instead, as well as claiming to be 'value free', its adherents only use 'theory' to refer to very specific, empirically testable propositions about particular groups of service users. Most actions by services are then presented as specific 'solutions' to individual service user's 'problems'. Hence the increased search for ever-changing technologies to solve ever-changing 'problems'. The overall belief, as discussed in the previous chapter, is in the power of human reason to overcome all problems, and therefore if only the 'problem' of people with disabilities can be defined and classified, then solutions can be found.

The result, as those proposing theories in reaction to this belief have variously articulated, is to see people's identity as being bound up in this diagnosis, and in their 'need' to adjust this identity to deal with their impairment. Those who cannot do so, or are perceived as being incapable of adjusting sufficiently to meet society's standards of what is acceptable in terms of behaviour or appearance, have been, and still are in many services for people with learning disabilities, segregated from society to a greater or lesser extent, congregated with others with a similar diagnosis who are assumed to have the same 'needs' and to whom similar service technologies can thus be applied more efficiently.

SRV and the social theory of disability

The notion of people with learning disabilities as passive, incompetent recipients of service was, and is, thus nurtured. Oliver (1990), one of the main contributors to the social theory of disability, describes this version of events as the 'personal tragedy theory' of disability and there are direct comparisons with the fundamental basis of SRV, and of its predecessor, normalization – namely the 'wounds' imposed by society on an individual as its reaction to a functional or social impairment (Wolfensberger 1972). Both theories, therefore, SRV and the social theory of disability, though their various adherents have disagreed among themselves, are based firmly on an analysis of the situation of people with disabilities being created and perpetuated by how they are viewed and the reaction of society to that view. It is also ironic that the power of this analysis, while it has been important in generating an influential social movement with a number of developing ideas, not least those of inclusion and advocacy (Tyne 1994), has been somewhat dispersed in factional disputes about what it is thought the theories 'say' should be *done* about the situation that the analysis reveals. The irony comes in that those involved in the disputes are arguing about what they perceive to be the *solutions* offered by the theories, rather than the validity of the theories themselves, and are thus falling into the modernistic rationalistic trap of judging things on outcomes, rather than looking at the truth or otherwise of their basic premises.

The impact of the disability movement

With the social theory of disability has certainly come an increasingly powerful disability lobby, many of whom claim the theory as their inspiration and driving force. By 'uniting against the common oppressor' organizations such as those which make up the British Council of Organizations of Disabled People (Davis 1996) have achieved a much wider recognition of disability issues in UK society, and the beginnings of effective legislation from the then reluctant Conservative government. They have also been active in opposition to the 'new eugenics' described earlier, though not with any notable success in amending legislation that allows abortion of disabled people up to term.

There have been some difficulties, however, in the reaction of the disabled persons' movement to people with learning disabilities and the implications of the social theory when set against the personal experiences of some disabled people, notably women. A number of the adherents of the social theory have claimed that the 'disabled identity' is entirely a matter for positive assertion (as in the case of 'black pride', feminism and 'gay pride') against the socioeconomic and ideological oppression accorded to people with that identity. Others, especially disabled women writers, claim this is denying the concomitant need to focus on 'what it feels like to be unable to walk, to be in pain, to be incontinent, to have fits, to be unable to converse, to be blind or deaf, to have an intellectual ability which is much below the average' (Morris 1991: 70).

In other words the personal experience of the impairment, though socially created in many of its aspects, nevertheless has real 'wounds' unique to each person. Actions based solely on changing society's view of disabled people, therefore, particularly if they are channelled through 'legislative persuasion' – i.e. anti-discriminatory laws – are in this view important, but should not be the only actions to address the oppression identified by the social theory of disability. Like all theories as we have defined them, in fact, the truth or otherwise of their premises, while they might suggest action to address the situation, do not have a unique control over actions, or even over the need to take action at all. It is perfectly possible for readers of the social theory of disability to say 'the evidence to support this theory is convincing' but then to say 'so what, that's tough on people with disabilities' or 'if this is the natural reaction of society, then the majority must be right'. Even if one accepts that the social theory describes a societal reaction that one feels, at the level of values, to be 'wrong' what one then does about it is not prescribed by that theory but, again, by one's values.

Normalization and SRV theory

This argument is precisely the one used by Wolfensberger (1995) in his attempt to address the many years of dispute about what normalization and then SRV theory 'said people should do' in reaction to the analysis of devaluation, via the 'wounds', that the theory provided. In developing his 'principle' of normalization – which contained a number of statements about working with individuals that some writers concluded amounted to authoritarianism (Dalley 1992) – into the theory of SRV which addresses the issue of *devaluation* by 'The application of what science has to teach us about the defense or upgrading of the socially perceived value of people's roles' Wolfensberger (1998) was doing more than just changing the name. He was firmly putting the theory, like the social theory of disability, into the realm of social science – playing the medical model at its own empirical game, it might be said.

What a reader then *does*, assuming the theory is demonstrated to their satisfaction, will again depend on their values. Reaction to Wolfensberger's theory from the disabled people's movement has been rather mixed, partly as a result of somewhat ambivalent attitudes to people with learning disabilities from people with physical disabilities (Chappell 1997), with SRV being seen as having come from services for the former group, and partly due to a tendency for writers attached to the social theory to be as involved in modernistic values, particularly individualism, as many others in UK society.

As before, it is more what readers impute as demanded by the theory, rather than its invalidity, which has caused the trouble. This has, in the case of SRV in the UK, been compounded by a number of misunderstandings of what the theory actually says, and by a number of misuses of its predecessor, normalization. In particular, though both normalization and SRV have always, at least as taught by their author, maintained that devaluation of impaired people took place, and therefore should be addressed, at all levels of society, from individuals through intermediate groups to whole social systems, attempts within the service world to address devaluation have primarily come at the individual level. Though some impact was initially made at the level of service systems, in particular the pressure to move people out of hospitals and smaller institutions such as hostels, the focus of training in normalization, and particularly SRV, has become direct care staff and their immediate managers.

So, along with many positive results, not least the change of dwelling for many people from institutions to ordinary houses and the raising of consciousness of staff, the decline of interest at senior levels in the service system has led to the thought that simply by moving some people into such houses normalization had been 'done'. This focus on the individual level, without continued support and involvement from above, then resulted in many restrictive if not outright abusive things being done in the name of normalization. In addition, the development by Wolfensberger of SRV as a social science theory became increasingly unexamined, with front line staff assuming, and often being told, that normalization and SRV were 'the same thing'.

UK academics, who had been initially rather sniffy about normalization as 'lacking empiricism' but then had to acknowledge its power in affecting services for people with learning disabilities, found the development of SRV equally hard to deal with. Most developed attacks, not on SRV, but on normalization, and this included some of the academics supporting the social theory of disability (Chappell 1992; Walmsley 1994). In particular they sought to ally normalization with the medical model's power over the individual, and with its notion that the professional system knows what is right for people. In doing this, they were drawing on a limited version of the written material on SRV, usually referring back to written material on normalization, but also to the genuinely poor experiences that some parts of the service system had imposed on people because of their interpretation of normalization (Race, in preparation).

If all the parallels with the social theory of disability are drawn, and the effects of the wider forces of our model are allowed, it is at the societal and intermediate social systems level where oppression and devaluation are at their most powerful. This being the case, a concentration on the individual level is at best likely to bear small fruit (though of course very important for the individuals concerned) and at worst likely to divert potential allies with accusations of paternalism and collusion with an oppressive society (Brown and Smith 1989).

This is, unfortunately, what happened in a good many services for people with learning disabilities in the 1980s and early 1990s, to the extent that when the full impact of government legislation and policy on community care services was felt as the 1990s progressed (as we shall discuss shortly) there was a rather threadbare resistance from the service system. There were a number of changes brought about in the 1980s as a result of normalization and more (as we shall see) from offshoots of the same analysis of devaluation and exclusion, but, perhaps because of the influence of the other forces of our model, people seemed unable to separate out the issues of values from the theoretical analysis of people's position contained in SRV theory.

Thus, rather than use the analysis as their spur to action, with values determining the precise nature of that action, SRV was interpreted as a procedure manual. Action as a result of the theoretical analysis was what needed to be tempered by values, but instead SRV was seen as yet another technology, and all the efforts of its proponents have not prevented the maintenance (and some would argue the increase) in the medical model of care services for people with learning disabilities. We have perhaps, as Linda Ward feared in her foreword to one of the more widely quoted critiques of normalization, succumbed to the 'real risk that the baby would be thrown out with the bathwater' (Ward 1992: xi).

Impact on services of two ideas

Advocacy

Both advocacy and inclusion, as we argued earlier, could be said to be responses to the observed devaluation of people with disabilities, and both have their roots in the value position that it is wrong for this devaluation to occur.

The first, again originating from Wolfensberger (1969), at the same time as the earliest versions of normalization, takes as its starting point that vulnerable people are devalued by society, and that as part of society, and subject to the same value influences, the human service system cannot meet all the needs of those vulnerable people. Indeed, the analysis of 'wounds' in normalization and SRV takes the argument further to posit that the human service system contributes to and sometimes enhances that devaluation.

In attempting to get fellow citizens alongside vulnerable people, a response to that devaluation being unacceptable, advocacy in its original form was trying to develop a means by which their interests could be defended by someone without conflict of interest. Since its origins as citizen advocacy, this idea has formed what Tyne (1994) identified as one of three 'movements' in the UK, along with normalization and the disabled persons' movement, which struggled with the status quo of services for people with disabilities. Unfortunately, as Tyne and others go on to note, a combination of internal wrangling among the advocacy movement, disputes between the three movements, particularly as normalization was developed into SRV, and annexation by the service system of the idea of advocacy (Dowson 1997b) reduced its impact considerably. Again, this is not to deny the advances made in some parts of the advocacy movement, particularly the development of a number of groups trying to use their collective voice in what has become called 'self-advocacy'.

What writers such as those contributing to Ramcharan et al. (1997) are celebrating, however, remains small and still riven by internal disputes. In particular, those emphasizing the superiority of self-advocacy are again concentrating on the application of a general idea to individual circumstances, and do not seem prepared to accept the notion that O'Brien and O'Brien (1994) identify as 'interdependence'. To those former writers, who do seem to be very hooked on the modernistic value of individualism, all advocacy can, and should, do is enable the voice – and, importantly to them – the choice of the individual, to be heard. There is then an assumption that this is, in itself, 'empowering'. Any assumption of responsibility by an advocate for the interests of people with learning disabilities is thus reduced to being a mouthpiece. If the advocate goes further than this, in the view of these writers, then they are 'taking over' the person's life, 'imposing their values' and generally doing the sorts of things that critics of professionalized services say is their greatest fault. What they do not seem prepared to accept, as Tyne (1994) goes on to point out, is that one of the key reasons why people with learning disabilities are devalued is that they are excluded from the sense of commonality with other people, and that simply by standing with a devalued person, as someone who is not able to be categorized into their identity as 'other', an advocate is denying that exclusion.

Evidence from writings on advocacy (e.g. Simons 1995) suggests, however, that though there are many people who would be prepared to stand by devalued people, their numbers, and therefore their potential influence has been affected by, on one side, those thought to be in the vanguard who tell them that self-advocacy is the only 'true' advocacy and, on the other side, the massed battalions of the professional service system who tell them that all that is required is more resources to deal with the 'problem' of learning disability.

Inclusion

If factionalism, assimilation and the prevailing values of society, shaped by academics and others, have minimized the effect of advocacy (though not, let it be repeated, for certain individuals for whom it has been, sometimes literally, a lifesaver) the idea of inclusion, though spoken and written about more frequently, has also struggled to affect the overall pattern and quality of services. As an idea, it has far broader historical roots, coming from a whole series of historical exclusions of people from society, and a values-led reaction to that exclusion. In positing that there could exist a fully inclusive society, where people are welcomed with the gifts that they have, regardless of how these might be valued, and difference is celebrated, its advocates are of course presenting an 'ideal state'. This is, however, no different in form to the 'ideal state' held by the Judaeo-Christian belief system, and therefore in presenting this as a direction to travel its adherents are reflecting, as we have done in the previous chapter, how far present reality differs from that ideal state, and how far the dominant beliefs and values are from those behind inclusion. Tied up with this is the underlying belief that human service systems cannot reproduce, with all their technologies and systems, the 'membership of each other' (O'Brien and O'Brien 1997) which is the essence of community.

Many of the writers in this area (e.g. McKnight 1995; Schwartz 1997) are not from the UK, and there is some sense, in that part of its history which leads to its particular interpretation of modernistic values, of a special UK twist to the notion of community. This stems in no small measure from the still prevailing sense of class, discussed earlier, with its particular subtleties of behaviour and social relations. That it is still present can be judged, at a perhaps trivial level, by the continued success of television comedy series that rely for their underlying humour on the class positions of their characters, and by the even more overwhelming popularity of dramatizations of novels dealing with periods when class was the most powerful determinant of a person's identity.

With that caveat, there have been some notable successes for the inclusion movement in the field of learning disabilities, particularly in the field of education. The young man mentioned earlier attends a mainstream secondary school, though he is the only child with Down's syndrome in a town of 20,000 people to do so, and it has in the main been individual successes, rather than a change of the overall pattern of services that has occurred. Even here, the incompatibility between the values behind a competitive school system – largely those of individualism – and inclusion – those of mutuality and sharing – has meant that those being newly-included face many further trials after passing through the school gates. Further, though inclusion in schools is a challenge to formerly held ideas, it is not in itself a challenge to the established school system, or its professional authority.

Inclusion in community, however, does represent a challenge, not only to received ideas, but also to the professionalized service system. Advocates for inclusion range from those such as McKnight (1995) who see community as being able to provide for all its members, to others such as O'Brien and O'Brien (1997) who make the distinction between certain supports that professional service workers can provide, and other elements that need to be in a person's life if they are to be fully included members of society. As with advocacy, though perhaps less vitriolically, people in this range have disagreed with one another, and, also as with advocacy, the service system has annexed some of the ideas and called them its own. The impact, therefore, of inclusion as a shaper of values in the service world when set against the prevailing societal values and their own shapers in the form of the medical model of care for people with learning disabilities still remains small, though it could be said to be growing. One of its attempts at influence has been to try, and some would say succeed, to change the situation by the use of the law, and another has been the hope that by a change of government, and a different political ideology, services might change.

In the final part of this chapter we shall look at the remaining elements of our model. The view is put forward that, despite changing political ideologies and legislation, and advice from governments, the underlying values of society, as embodied in the desire and ability of services to put policies into operation and the developing 'culture' of services, still maintains and reinforces the power of a system that says many things about its values but does many things that keep people with learning disabilities in a devalued state.

Politics, legislation and the service system

In the previous chapter we noted that, though drawing on the notion of universals, our model did not imply the hierarchy of phenomena implicit in that concept. We also noted, however, that the elements of our model were not of equal weight – i.e. some have more influence than others on the overall pattern of services, and some have more influence *on the other elements*. For this reason we will be spending less time on the remaining elements of our model than the previous ones.

This may go against what readers may have expected, or at least against their experience of what occupies the energy of people who work in services, and others who seek to influence them. It is certainly true that many planning meetings are held in the service world that make no reference to values, or influences from the wider world (except perhaps a bid from someone to be put on the Internet). Nor, very often, are the views of shapers of values an everyday subject of the service world (except, as we have noted, the acceptance of professionalized values through more and more technologies). What is much more frequently discussed, and acted on, is legislation and advice from central government on what should happen in services. It would therefore be thought that these elements have a much greater influence on the pattern of services than the other previously mentioned ones.

In the field of learning disabilities, the past decade has seen an abundance of legislation and advice, mainly about community care in general, but also with some specific parts of its own. It is not the purpose of this chapter to go into the detail of this legislation and advice, a lot of which has, in any case been covered by the first two chapters of this book. The key point to be made is that, while it has had considerable effects on the *organization and financing* of services for people with learning disabilities, all the legislation and advice of Thatcher's Conservative government made little difference to the changes that were going on in the *sort* of services being provided. Those latter changes, influenced as we have seen by the dominant values of UK society and some opposition to them, have been far less great than the legislation and advice might suggest.

The range of services available to the woman and the young man mentioned at the beginning of this chapter are said to have changed dramatically in their lifetime, and certainly from the birth of the woman at the beginning of the 1950s this could not be denied. The advice in the White Paper *Better Services for the Mentally Handicapped* (DHSS 1971) and some of the recommendations of the Jay Committee (1979) on Mental Handicap Nursing and Care, are, however, far closer to what has emerged as the sort of services currently being provided than anything to be found in the Griffiths Report (DHSS 1988), the White Paper *Caring for People* (DoH 1989), or the NHS and Community Care Act (1990). The earlier documents were produced at a time when professional domination of the service system was no less than it is today, but when governments were prepared to listen more to the academic shapers of values, and when the full impact of the dominant value system on services had yet to be realized.

So, while services are today delivered by a much wider range of providers than just the two public agencies of health and social services, and a new breed of technocrat has been produced in the purchaser or commissioner, exactly *what* is provided in the way of services has a lot in common with what was provided ten years ago. As we noted, services have developed with some influence from shapers of values opposing the dominant value position, through theories like SRV, the social theory of disability and ideas like inclusion and advocacy, as have some ways of addressing devaluation outside the service system. They are still only a small part of what is provided for people, however, and even where use of the law has been tried, as in the 1981 Education Act or the 1986 Disabled Persons (Services, Consultation and Representation) Act, the service system has contrived either to thwart the legislation by delay and lack of professional resources (in the former case) or to get a not unwilling government to delay implementation in the latter.

This should not surprise us, given all that has gone before. The resources of the service system, its training and education, and ultimately the culture that it develops, are highly bound up with the overall values of society, as influenced by and influencing external pressures and the shapers of values. The service system is strongly subject to the political ideology of the government and to legislation in terms of what it *must* do, in particular how much, or how little, of taxpayers' money it can ration out in the form of services, and to whom that money should be paid to provide services. This has greatly affected the financing and organization of services, but governments – regardless of political ideology – have in recent years left decisions of a 'professional' nature to the service world, though in the case of community care services and services for people with learning disabilities in particular that has covered a pretty broad range of people.

Knowledge regarding people with learning disabilities held by those making decisions about whether or not someone gets a service, and what sort of service they receive, has changed as the culture of services has changed, from the all-encompassing professional providers to the purchaser/provider split (Lewis and Glennerster 1996). However, though purchasers, typically without much knowledge of learning disability, have the nominal power in that they control the budget, the specifications they put out for the sort of services to be purchased bear all the hallmarks of a view of services dominated by providers. This therefore continues to reflect the 'professional' view which, though it has changed in its physical appearance from large institutions to smaller ones, and from people doing nothing in the name of work training to people doing nothing as their 'choice' of daytime leisure activity, retains its intrinsic faith in 'value free' technologies.

Conclusion

So we are back to where we started in Chapter 3, with a tension between people's personal values and beliefs and what is happening in services, and the suction into professional service technologies of attempts to address the devaluation of vulnerable people. What seems to be the most influential of all our elements is the dominance of a set of beliefs and values that, when combined with the dominance of a technocratic élite, have maintained the power of the service system in defining the lives of a large number of people with learning disabilities.

As we said at the end of the last chapter, services for people with learning disabilities are supposed to be the one area where alternatives, based on a different set of values, have had the most effect. Readers from other branches in the community care system are invited to consider whether that proposition is true and, if it is, what the relatively small effects that those alternatives have had on what is available for people with learning disabilities means in terms of their own field. For the woman and the young man, being born where (rather than when) they were seems to have made the most difference, along with who was alongside them. Perhaps Voltaire, ironically one of the leading thinkers in the Enlightenment which has led inexorably to our present-day values, was being more prophetic than he knew when he advised people to 'cultivate their own gardens', if that can be a metaphor for cultivating our own families and communities before the combine harvester of the service system comes along. The more sobering thought is that, if values trends continue, people like the man and woman we have talked about will be weeded out before any cultivation can start.

Summary

- The impact of external economic, social and value forces on services for people with learning disabilities is largely the same as it is for other people who use services, as discussed in the previous chapter. Increased technologization, however, is particularly likely to reinforce the devaluation of people with learning disabilities.

- Overall societal values also have a similar effect to those with learning disabilities as on other groups, in that the materialist medical model still dominates services and academic research. Individualism has also had an impact, with the changing expressions of 'choice' and 'rights' resulting in a mixture of outcomes for people. Sensualism and externalism – in particular the latter – have had a major impact on what has been defined as the 'quality' of people's lives, and on who makes a judgement as to whether that 'quality' is so low that people would be better off dead.

- Theories and ideas are defined, and two theories, SRV and the social theory of disability are examined in terms of their impact. Though they have had some successes, particularly for individuals, overall change in the service system has been slow, with the medical model still dominant.

- The same results are apparent for the ideas of advocacy and inclusion, which again have made some important gains for individuals, but have not really affected the overall pattern of services.

- Finally, changes in legislation and the party in government are not seen to have had a major impact on the sort of services being provided to people with learning disabilities, nor on the dominance of a professional technologized service. So, while changes, some extremely important, have occurred for individuals, the overall dominance of a service culture by a modernistic value system prevails, which does not bode well for people with learning disabilities as a group. If this is the group where challenges to the prevailing system have been the greatest, possibilities for other community care users look bleaker still.

Further reading

Barton, L. and Oliver, M. (eds) (1997) *Disability Studies: Past, Present and Future*. Leeds: The Disability Press.

O'Brien, J. and O'Brien, C.L. (1997) *Members of Each Other: Building Community with People with Developmental Disabilities*. Toronto: Inclusion Press.

Wolfensberger, W. (1972) *The Principle of Normalization in Human Services*. Toronto: NIMR.

Wolfensberger, W. (1998) *Social Role Valorization*, 3rd ed. Syracuse, NY: Training Institute for Human Service Planning, Leadership and Change Agentry, Syracuse University.

References

Brown, H. and Smith, H. (1989) Whose ordinary life is it anyway? A feminist critique of the normalisation principle. *Disability, Handicap and Society*, 4 (2): 105–19.

Chappell, A.L. (1992) Towards a sociological critique of the normalisation principle. *Disability, Handicap and Society*, 7 (1): 25–51.

Chappell, A.L. (1997) From normalization to where? in L. Barton and M. Oliver (eds) *Disability Studies: Past, Present and Future*. Leeds: The Disability Press.

Cocks, E. (1997) Agency change: a case study, in P. O'Brien and R. Murray (eds) *Human Services: Towards Partnership and Support*. Palmerston North, New Zealand: The Dunmore Press.

Crisp, R. (1991) QALYs and the mentally handicapped. *Bulletin of Medical Ethics*, 67: 13–16.

Dalley, G. (1992) Social Welfare ideologies and normalisation, in H. Brown and H. Smith (eds) *Normalisation: A Reader for the Nineties*. London: Tavistock/Routledge.

Davis, K. (1996) Developments in the disabled persons' movement, in J. Swain, V. Finkelstein, S. French and M. Oliver (eds) *Disabling Barriers – Enabling Environments*. London: Sage.

DHSS (Department of Health and Social Security) (1971) *Better Services for the Mentally Handicapped*, Cmnd. 4683. London: HMSO.

DHSS (Department of Health and Social Security) (1988) *Community Care: An Agenda for Action*. London: HMSO.

DoH (Department of Health) (1989) *Caring for People: Community Care in the Next Decade and Beyond*, Cm. 849. London: HMSO.

DoH (Department of Health) (1995) *The Nursing and Therapy Professions' Contribution to Health Services Research and Development*. London: DoH.

Dowson, S. (1997a) UK policies destroying pockets of excellence. *B.C. Community Living News*, 15 (1): 11–12.

Dowson, S. (1997b) Empowerment within services: a comfortable delusion, in P. Ramcharan, G. Roberts, G. Grant and J. Borland (eds) *Empowerment in Everyday Life: Learning Disability*. London: Jessica Kingsley.

Emerson, E. and Hatton, C. (1996) *Residential Provision for People With Learning Disabilities: A Research Review*. Manchester: Hester Adrian Research Centre.

Fruin, D. (1994) Almost equal opportunities: developing personal relationships guidelines for social services department staff working with people with learning disabilities, in A. Craft (ed.) *Practice Issues in Sexuality and Learning Disabilities*. London: Routledge.

Jay Committee (1979) *Report of the Committee of Enquiry into Mental Handicap Nursing & Care*, Cmnd. 74611(1) & 7468(11). London: HMSO.

Lewis, J. and Glennerster, H. (1996) *Implementing the New Community Care*. Buckingham: Open University Press.

McKnight, J. (1995) *The Careless Society: Community and its Counterfeits*. New York: Basic Books.

Mansell, J. and Ericsson, K. (1996) *Deinstitutionalization and Community Living: Intellectual Disability Services in Britain, Scandinavia and the USA*. London: Chapman & Hall.

Mitchell, L. (1987) Interventions in the inappropriate sexual behaviour of individuals with mental handicap, in A. Craft (ed.) *Mental Handicap and Sexuality: Issues and Perspectives*. Tunbridge Wells: Costello.

Morris, J. (1991) *Pride Against Prejudice: Transforming Attitudes to Disability*. London: The Women's Press.

National Health Service (1990) *NHS AND COMMUNITY CARE ACT*. London: HMSO.

Nirje, B. (1969) The Normalization principle and its human management implications, in R.B. Kugel and W. Wolfensberger (eds.) *Changing Patterns in Residential Services for the Mentally Retarded*. Washington DC: President's Committee on Mental Retardation.

Norburg, A., Hirschfield, D.M. and Davidson, B. (1994) Ethical reasoning concerning the feeding of severely demented patients: an international perspective. *Nursing Ethics*, 1 (1): 3–13.

O'Brien, J. and O'Brien, C.L. (1994) *Assistance with Integrity: The Search for Accountability and the Lives of People with Developmental Disabilities*. Lithonia, GA: Responsive Systems Associates.

O'Brien, J. and O'Brien, C.L. (1997) *Members of Each Other: Building Community in Company with People with Developmental Disabilities*. Toronto: Inclusion Press.

Oliver, M. (1990) *The Politics of Disablement*. London: Macmillan.

Race, D.G. (in press) *Social Role Valorization, and the English Experience*.

Rachels, J. (1986) *The End of Life*. Oxford: Oxford University Press.

Ramcharan, P., Roberts, G., Grant, G. and Borland, J. (eds) (1997) *Empowerment in Everyday Life: Learning Disability*. London: Jessica Kingsley.

Ryan, J. and Thomas, F. (1987) *The Politics of Mental Handicap*, 2nd edn. Harmondsworth: Penguin.

Sarantakos, S. (1994) *Social Research*. Basingstoke: Macmillan.

Saul, J.R. (1992) *Voltaire's Bastards: The Dictatorship of Reason in the West*. London: Sinclair-Stevenson.

Schwartz, D. (1997) *Who Cares? Rediscovering Community*. Oxford, PA: Westview Press.

Simons, K. (1995) Advocacy, in N. Malin (ed.) *Services for People with Learning Disabilities*. London: Routledge.

Sinason, V. (1994) Working with sexually abused individuals who have a learning disability, in A. Craft (ed.) *Practice Issues in Sexuality and Learning Disabilities*, London: Routledge.

Sinson, J. (1995) *Care in the Community for Young People with Learning Disabilities: The Client's Voice*. London: Jessica Kingsley.

Swain, J., Finkelstein, V., French, S. and Oliver, M. (eds) (1996) *Disabling Barriers, Enabling Environments*. London: Sage.

Tyne, A. (1994) Taking responsibility and giving power. *Disability & Society*, 9 (2): 249–54.

Walmsley, J. (1994) Learning disability: overcoming the barriers, in S. French (ed.) *On Equal Terms: Working with Disabled People*. Oxford: Butterworth-Heinemann.

Walmsley, J. and Downer, J. (1997) Shouting the loudest: self-advocacy, power and diversity, in P. Ramcharan, G. Roberts, G. Grant and J. Borland (eds) *Empowerment in Everyday Life: Learning Disability*. London: Jessica Kingsley.

Ward, L. (1992) Foreword, in H. Brown and H. Smith (eds) *Normalisation: A Reader for the Nineties*. London: Tavistock/Routledge.

Williams, P. (1995) The PASS and PASSING evaluation instruments, in D. Pilling and G. Watson (eds) *Evaluating Quality in Services For Disabled And Older People*. London: Jessica Kingsley.

Wolfensberger, W. (1969) The origins of our institutional models, in R. Kugel and W. Wolfensberger (eds) *Changing Patterns in Residential Services for the Mentally Retarded*. Washington DC: Government Printing Office.

Wolfensberger, W. (1972) *The Principle of Normalization in Human Services*. Toronto: NIMR.

Wolfensberger, W. (1984) A reconceptualization of normalization as social role valorization. *Mental Retardation* (Canadian) 34: 22–5.

Wolfensberger, W. (1992) *A Brief Introduction to Social Role Valorization as a High Order Concept for Structuring Human Services*, 2nd (revised) edn. Syracuse, NY: Training Institute on Human Service Planning, Leadership and Change Agency, Syracuse University.

Wolfensberger, W. (1994) A personal interpretation of the mental retardation scene in light of the 'sign of the times', *Mental Retardation*, 32 (1): 19–33.

Wolfensberger, W. (1995) An 'if this then that' formulation of decisions related to social role valorization as a better way of interpreting it to people. *Mental Retardation*, 33 (3): 163–9.

Wolfensberger, W. (1996) Major obstacles to rationality and quality of human services in contemporary society – keynote address in R. Adams (ed.) *Crisis in Human Services: National and International Issues* (conference held at the University of Cambridge, September 1996). Lincoln: University of Lincolnshire and Humberside.

Wolfensberger, W. (1998) *Social Role Valorization,* 3rd edn. Syracuse, NY: Training Institute on Human Service Planning, Leadership and Change Agency, Syracuse University.

USERS' AND CARERS' PERSPECTIVES

USERS' PERSPECTIVES: DO SERVICES EMPOWER USERS?

Introduction

This chapter brings users of community care services to the centre stage of our discussions. It starts with an analysis of the concept of being a service user – an important identity but one which is subject to confusion and contradictions. As we shall see in Chapter 6, on carers, the construction of identities such as users and carers can clarify discussion of community care but it can also draw artificial distinctions. This chapter goes on to explore the engagement of users with services as a way of understanding users' experiences, and argues that users' perspectives may be related to the circumstances and timing of their relationships with services. Discussion of the concept of empowerment follows, empowerment being a word often identified as an objective by service providers and policy makers, but one which is difficult to put into operation. In contrast, the term exclusion – the subject of the next section – seems to be a more common experience. We end the chapter with a discussion of users' emergent roles in professional training.

Constructing the user of community care

The term user, or service user, is of relatively recent origin in respect of community care. For some individuals, working in addiction services, the word 'user' implies a person currently using or misusing illicit drugs or alcohol. But in community care the word user is now frequently encountered. What does this new category mean? Why has it achieved such rapid acceptance?

To answer these questions we can sift through the White Paper *Caring for People* (DoH 1989) to determine how government conceived of users of community care services at this important time. In its definition of community care the government chose to relate it to the provision of services and support to: 'people who are affected by problems of ageing, mental illness, mental handicap or physical or sensory disability [who] need to be able to live as independently as possible in their own homes, or in "homely" settings in the community' (DoH 1989: para. 1.1).

Throughout this document the term 'people' is used (or 'such people'), and occasionally the terms 'client', 'those who need care', 'individuals', 'vulnerable people', 'consumer' and 'user' (DoH 1989: para. 3.2.3). It is clear that either *Caring for People* was assembled by a variety of authors and/or that the interchangeable terms reflect a flexibility of categories.

Biggs (1997: 199–200) has argued that clear professional boundaries and distinctions between helpers and the helped belong to a world where service systems were unchanging and predictable, but that:

> under postmodern conditions one would expect positions to become more flexibile and, indeed, interchangeable. The identities of people who make up the system would change, chameleon-like, depending on the situation in which they found themselves. Service users become people in need in one context, experts in the consumption of services in another and decision-makers in yet another.

Constructing the term 'user'

The category of user, or service user, is therefore not a fixed entity or identity, and its popularity lies perhaps in a variety of other explanations. The word 'user' is efficient: as the extract from *Caring for People* illustrated, including all conditions and categories can be lengthy and cumbersome. Other words, however, such as 'client' or 'patient' carry with them specific historical associations with services (generally client within social work/ law and patient within medicine/nursing) and to some may indicate a supplicant or unequal relationship. As an umbrella term, user is also defined by what it is *not*, in more recent contexts – it is neither customer nor consumer despite the language of markets and economy so influential in the Thatcher years. People receiving community care services may share some of the characteristics of customers and may be well-served by attention to quality, but some are reluctant or even resistant to services. For example, an individual who has been compulsorily detained in hospital under the Mental Health Act 1983, who is released from detention but subject to supervised discharge procedures – ordering where he or she should live, where he or she should attend in the daytime and who should be admitted into the home, and in addition perhaps having his or her benefits controlled by another person – may feel that 'consumer' is a term that does not convey the nature of the relationships involved.

While such examples may be in the minority the label consumer is also related to having control over purchasing decisions. While this may be encouraged in the name of choice, most users of community care services will find that financial decisions are determined by others. For example, the amounts that will be paid by social services for help with personal care and the levels of eligibility determining the level of services, if any, are set by the local authority. The term 'quasi-consumer', relating to the quasi-market of community care, may thus be more accurate. However, it is hardly accessible.

The word user is employed generally but it is also allied with other words to delineate membership of a 'client group'. Users of mental health services and users of learning disability services are more frequently cited as examples of user groups, and at times user movements are associated with people with physical disabilities (often themselves referring to and terming themselves disabled people). Older people, however, appear to be less frequently categorized as users perhaps because the term 'older people' does not so markedly point to impairment or illness. The word user is further complicated by its association with specific services. People may be identified as users of a day centre but are rarely described as users of residential services.

Essentially we need to see the word user as a category or label, both applied by professionals in attempts to humanize and empower individuals, and seized by some individuals to mark aspects of their relationship with services. To 'use' a service is an innocuous phrase, denuded of market overtones and glossing over power relationships. In its context, of course, the word user may mask long-standing inequalities.

To be a user moreover implies a relationship with services or professionals in the area of community care. Individuals provided with care by family or friends may be termed users for convenience and in particular to avoid the pejorative term 'dependent' and the slightly unwieldy term 'care recipient'. To be a user provides the counterweight to the word carer, and as Poole (1993) noted the terms user and carer have been closely linked and at times merged together. Much greater distinction is now made in the late 1990s between the two by practitioners and policy makers as well as many of the individuals concerned (Manthorpe and Twigg 1995).

The conceptualization of the term user is thus relatively recent and many texts refer to specific client groups or disabled people while others discuss similar subjects using the term user (see Barnes 1997 as an example). The Griffiths Report (Griffiths 1988) argued for a focus on users and carers, emphasizing that this could be equated with 'the consumer's point of view' (para. 3.4). To other commentators the label user seemed to be the preferred term to imply involvement, participation and choice (Ramcharan *et al.* 1997). The following discussion investigates the perspectives of people so labelled through their own volition or others' decisions.

Research and self-advocacy publications have commented on the shaping of user voices, and by seeking to collect examples of users' experiences and feelings have brought new understandings of the human aspects of community care. For some individuals it seems that although professionals might see community care services as crucial, they can be marginal. Anya Souza (1997: 13) for example, writing as a person with Down's syndrome, observed in her account of her life:

> You will have noticed that I have not talked about the service sector and in my case that is because they have not really affected my life that much. My mum and I did have some respite care (from each other as much as anything) from time to time, both on a parent-to-parent scheme and in a hostel setting. I have also had social workers in my time. But they are not in a position to be my friends, to be there when I need them, to have a relationship which will last for a lifetime.

Not simply a service user

In researching the experiences of individuals who had acquired a physical disability, mostly in adulthood, Pilgrim *et al.* (1997: 11) found that many did not appreciate being defined as service users: 'Essentially, the respondents utilised two strategies in relation to services. Some opted for independence and non-contact – they would go it alone. A second group would be selective about their use of services, when "getting by alone" became untenable'.

In their discussions, respondents did not identify services as their main priority, although for many they were useful at times, albeit in a limited way. Pilgrim *et al.* (1997) contrasted users' aims (using the term user despite the ambivalence expressed by their respondents) with those of the commissioners of services, both from health and social services. Briefly summarized, these included the comments shown in Box 5.1.

Box 5.1   Users' aims

- 'Disabled people seek direct user power'.
- They 'emphasise the complexities of their experience and their identity'.
- They 'seek to achieve social rights'.
- They 'emphasise citizenship' and 'collective participation'.
- They 'demand more resources'.

Source: Pilgrim *et al.* (1997: 13).

Provided with opportunities to express their views through new service agendas which seek consumer comment, service users may be able to wield more influence, even if their concerns are much broader than those of welfare services.

The agenda created by service users is broader than community care but this book needs perforce to focus on such services. In doing so artificial categories are sometimes created and it is important to remember that an identity as a user of services is fluid in the amorphous mass called the community. Users can also be carers and can also be practitioners. French (1994), for example, has commented on the role of disabled professionals as having the potential to 'undermine traditional professional values and beliefs' (p. 209). Further research would be helpful in identifying the contributions and challenges of disabled individuals and service users who are elected to powerful policy making positions within local government, central government and the independent sector.

Finally, the categories of users and carers have been very much constructed in the context of adult services, particularly in respect of individuals with learning disabilities or mental health problems and disabled people who are below retirement age. In respect of children who receive community care services the user label is at times applied to the children but also to their parents. As Cigno and Burke (1997: 177) noted in a report of their study of 67 families where a child had learning disabilities:

> When does a carer become a user? In the case of parents with children 'in need' as defined in Section 17 of the Children Act 1989 and elaborated in subsequent guidelines (Department of Health, 1991) it could be argued that, in an important sense, parents are also service users, and need to be, in order to benefit their child.

Cigno and Burke (1997) argued that single mothers, in particular, should be classed as service users since the need for support to enable them to care for their child was inextricably linked to the family's relative lack of support systems. To some extent the Carers (Recognition and Services) Act 1995, which is applicable to parents of disabled children, may reflect a greater acknowledgement of parents' needs than children-focused legislation which emphasizes the paramount position of the child's interests. In relation to young disabled children however the term user is not frequently employed. Children, it would seem, are children first and their parents are proxy users. Much remains to be researched about children's views and experiences, to identify what disabled children value and how their views accord with those of their parents. In doing so community care debates will necessarily intertwine with the education sphere. The separation of education and care services means that user views are rarely collected, if at all, in parallel. Those working in community care arenas will have much to learn, for example, from studies such as Swain's (1994) research into student participation in decision making at a school for young disabled people (aged between 3 and 19 years). Here the challenge to existing power relationships was very clearly identified, perhaps made more stark by the adult-child boundaries. Being categorized as a user conveys a sense of adult status and this may be why the term has become associated with challenging established structures. A seemingly neutral word cannot remain neutral when applied to the contested area of community care.

Engaging with services

In this section we draw out some of the experiences of service users to paint a picture of their relationships with the service system. In contrast to institutional provision the picture of users' engagement with services is depicted as dynamic and multi-faceted. The environment of a large long-stay hospital for patients was itself probably a far more complicated and changing experience than is generally portrayed. The changes in community services, however, arguably are more rapid and the area more differentiated by local variations in providers, eligibility criteria and service content. In the move to direct payments made possible by the Community Care (Direct Payments) Act 1996 in England and Wales, services can be individualized to an extreme. The disabled person him- or herself is now permitted to construct a personalized package of services and to pay and to control the providers. New patterns of service engagement look set to emerge. As Campbell and Oliver (1996: 171) observed, this 'is solely attributable to the disability movement'. Although direct payments are currently restricted to people under pensionable age and local implementation looks set to vary considerably, engagement with services in a monolithic sense may well become highly individualized.

Patterns of engagement with services by individuals

The engagement of individuals with welfare services is determined by a number of factors. Some people approach services directly for assistance, others walk a pathway of referrals and reasons for contact. Morris (1993) conducted 50 interviews with disabled people aged between 19 and 55 and found that help from services was vital in preventing a damaging dependence on family members. One of the 'clearest messages' from those she interviewed was that services needed to be responsive and appropriate (p. 103). Pankash, for example, paid for a local authority care service to help him get to work in the mornings: 'Because I am working at a full-time job so I need it in the morning, early morning. I go out by 8.30 so they must make sure they get here at 7. They get me ready' (p. 104).

In contrast, many respondents found services restrictive, particularly in the changes from domestic care to personal assistance. While help with personal care is needed, domestic services can also be important to people's sense of dignity and comfort (see also Walker and Warren 1996).

Morris (1993) also identified a problem for users in the tendency for services to 'fit' clients to their own structures and priorities. Elizabeth, for example, observed that her needs had to fit in with the needs of other service users: 'I don't feel I have much control at all over the amount and kind of help I get. It's very difficult . . . I have to walk on eggshells' (p. 108).

The effect of the National Health Service and Community Care Act 1990

While these interviews were conducted prior to the implementation of the NHS and Community Care Act 1990 it is clear that the new climate of financial restrictions has also restricted services' abilities to be more responsive or more extensive. For some writers this relative lack of progress can be set at the door of poor professional practice in the past, and its legacy. Hughes (1995), for example, pointed to the absence of good assessment practice and models of social work with older people and the insistence of policy guidance at the time of implementation that users should be assessed comprehensively and should be active participants in the assessment process.

Indications from early research post-implementation indicated that these aims continued to be relevant, for practitioners' abilities to respond flexibly and imaginatively to the needs of older people were still constricted. For example, writing of community care overall, Lewis and Glennerster (1996: 203) observed that although some highly complex packages of care had been possible, most services remained on a 'set list': 'The spot purchase of a pub meal or a trip to the opera instead of day care that would constitute a truly individually tailored response to need has not happened'. They argued that the community care reforms indicated a potential for services to listen to users' views – a 'fundamental step' to changes in practice. One manager presented this cautiously optimistic view: 'I think you can say that it's changed our way of examining our responsibilities. It's allowed for a lot more voices to be heard'. (Lewis and Glennerster 1996: 204)

An explanation for apparent contradictions in the rhetoric of consumer empowerment and its slow but patchy progress may lie in the various layers of implementation operating concurrently. At one level, as Gostick *et al.* (1997) suggested, empowerment of users could command broad acceptance of the reforms for, as we have seen, criticisms abounded from users that services were inflexible and unresponsive. In practice, moreover, at agency level, both users and carers appear to have been involved in consultation to some extent. It is at individual level that progress appears to be slow and it is here that most knotty dilemmas remain. As Gostick *et al.* (1997: 169) observed: 'only by their [users and carers] involvement in the strategic commissioning process can some of the more difficult decisions about future service configurations effectively and confidentially be addressed'. Users are thus required to engage with services at two levels: over individual commissioning and over strategic decisions.

Users of mental health services

In the context of service users who may be reluctant, but not always, to engage with services, individuals with mental health problems have generally been identified as a group requiring particular constellations of services. In a balancing attempt to acknowledge the losses of self-determination and liberty under the Mental Health Act 1983 the state has given this group of service users rights to complain, rights to services and rights in respect of the coordination of agencies. Community-based services have sought to provide accessible, non-stigmatizing services in many areas.

Flexibility has also been identified by research into the needs of users of mental health services, who received much publicity in the 1990s. Generally the media has portrayed this group of service users as abandoning or rejecting of services. Crepaz-Keay (1996: 41) noted that the media often referred to users 'escaping' or 'slipping through' the service net, or being 'set free' from institutions to kill others or harm themselves (p. 42). However, the influential inquiries into homicide (for example Ritchie 1994; Woodley 1995) underlined the complexities of each situation for each inquiry and also proferred a chronology of the individual's contacts with services and his or her social environment (to some extent). Users' needs may be highly individual but it is no accident that inquiries frequently have reported a need for more specialist staff, for better resources and greater attention to matters such as employment, personal relationships and accommodation.

The *targeting* of services has generally meant that users may now only be deemed eligible for services when they have high levels of need or are at great risk. We are beginning to see growing numbers of people who are no longer assessed to be eligible for assistance. The group judged to be 'not in high enough need' and yet excluded from social contexts of employment and mainstream social life may well challenge services who in the past have been able to rely on social services to provide low-level support, preventive work and a safety net. From users' points of view such services were often described as restrictive and disempowering. Sinson (1995), for example, noted the loss of skills in ordinary living among young people who had left a well-resourced educational facility to live in a world of patchy community care services. Writing as a member of a self-advocacy group, Enzo also described what he felt to be a low level of service during his 19 years at a day centre: 'At first I thought [it] was OK. I mixed in with a load of friends but as the years went on I thought it was pretty boring . . . After about the first eight, nine years it became a waste of time. I knew what to expect every day' (Peterborough Voices 1997: 10).

It is evident that engagement with services is now centred on issues of targeting and availability and that for many service users, as well as professionals, the targeting of services on those with the highest levels of need will inevitably exclude those with needs at lower levels. Engagement with services is changing to a more intensive relationship. For users the price of achieving independence may be to put their services in jeopardy. In order to argue the perversity of this approach many users have advocated that narrow definitions of need are discriminatory: later in this chapter we will discuss the expression of this disquiet by focusing on empowerment.

Towards user-led services

In a wide-scale survey of users of mental health services, Shepherd *et al.* (1994: 63) noted that many expressed feelings of 'powerlessness and alienation'. Users often called for more information and greater involvement in treatment and care. As one person with schizophrenia commented:

'. . . knowing about the medication and its side-effects is important, otherwise you don't know whether you have new symptoms or if it is side effects. Makes something else to puzzle about' (p. 45).

In a later research project, Carpenter and Sbaraini (1997) also argued that users could be involved in care programmes and that a regular and reliable professional contact helped them to feel that services were appropriate and encouraging. Most people remembered the formal arrangements of care plans made with professionals, had signed their agreement to them and could recall the accompanying meetings. The researchers argued that the comments shown in Box 5.2 were typical, not just the most congratulatory.

Box 5.2   Users' views of 'user-led' services

- 'I feel I am treated with respect'.
- 'I'm working together with my CPN'.
- 'I'm very happy with my care manager'.

Source: Carpenter and Sbaraini (1997: 45).

User-led services have many different manifestations, the examples of care plans given above are, perhaps more correctly, services which involve users and integrate their perspectives into professional assumptive worlds.

Empowerment

The metaphors of a ladder and sometimes a spectrum of empowerment are used to convey a sense of the variations behind this word. It is generally agreed that empowerment constitutes a transfer or gain in power by service users or disabled people, but Ramcharan and Borland (1997) have argued that the broad debate about empowerment reflects the general ease of defining and illustrating the characteristics of disempowerment compared to empowerment. They continue: 'But simply removing the barriers to individual examples of disempowerment is not sufficient to produce an overall sense of empowerment in everyday life' (p. xii).

Empowerment can be observed to be a process of participation, democracy, consultation, choice, autonomy, independence and, as Ramcharan and Borland (1997: xi) recalled, its positive image and sense of warmth can be paralleled with those associated with community care itself. For Braye and Preston-Shoot (1995: 50) this mass of generalized attributes can be seen through two perspectives:

- a traditional value base describing a process which involves people in acquiring skills and confidence to improve services;
- a radical value base challenging existing power structures.

Braye and Preston-Shoot's analysis constructed a forcefield (1995: 111) to explore the pushes for empowerment and the pressures at work to

resist such demands. They argued that the forces working for empowerment included the elements shown in Box 5.3.

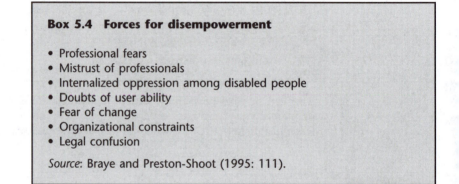

Box 5.3 Forces for empowerment

- User/self-advocacy mandates
- Professional/practitioner persuasions
- Legal and policy imperatives

Source: Braye and Preston-Shoot (1995: 111).

In contrast, lie the 'power of orthodoxy and convention', including the
elements shown in Box 5.4.

Box 5.4 Forces for disempowerment

- Professional fears
- Mistrust of professionals
- Internalized oppression among disabled people
- Doubts of user ability
- Fear of change
- Organizational constraints
- Legal confusion

Source: Braye and Preston-Shoot (1995: 111).

This latter list contains powerful forces and both lists are helpful in noting that groups and individuals can find themselves working for change
while simultaneously doubting that it can or should happen.

To further complicate the notion of empowerment, rather than seeing it
as a unified term in which one either works for or against change, it is
possible to see it across a spectrum. Means and Lart (1994) provided a
ladder of empowerment indicating the steps or rungs from low to high
versions of empowerment. At the low level 'information is given about
decisions made'; at the polar opposite 'users have the authority to take
decisions' (p. 34). Both forms of empowerment can be applied to different
ideological bases lying behind community care.

Means and Lart gave as extremes the market and democratic approaches.
In a *market approach* consumers are empowered through the exercise of
choice and the option of 'exit': 'In other words, if you don't like your day
centre, you move to another one' (1994: 35). In a *democratic approach*
users are empowered by their ability to change that with which they are
unhappy: 'In other words, if you don't like your day centre, you join the
user committee and change it to your liking' (1994: 35). Means and Lart
pointed out that these models generally combined in practice but took
different emphases. They also warned that different client groups and
different social groups might experience and interpret empowerment in
particular ways.

The traditional 'client group' categories of older people, physically disabled people, people with mental health problems, people with learning disabilities and children with disabilities are familiar to welfare practitioners: services are often organized around such categories and education of professionals has been built upon such divisions at times.

Empowerment and older people

While older people form the majority of users of community care services this numerical superiority has not been associated with user empowerment. This may be rooted in older people's reluctance to be critical or to appear ungrateful (Means and Lart 1994). Alternatively it might be associated with greater levels of illness, isolation and mental confusion among sizeable groups of older people. As Archibald (1996: 123) observed, the feelings of people with dementia have not generally been sought, but carers are consulted in their stead. In an innovatory project, Tozer and Thornton (1995) recruited older people as participants in a project to comment on community care and other services. Some were users of services and others were described as potential users (see Box 5.5).

Box 5.5   Summarized findings of user comments on services

- Older people were a very diverse group
- Service users could be perceived as different by other older people
- Living alone may militate against initial abilities to participate in discussion
- Being involved should be a purposeful and a positive experience

Source: Tozer and Thornton (1995: 41–2).

Barnes (1997) has questioned whether there is a 'user movement' of older people. She acknowledged that such are the differences among older people and their needs that it may be difficult for them to act together. In fact, as Ginn's (1996) research on 'grey power' has shown the most powerful organizations of older people are often market or class orientated and thus their seeking of empowerment may be linked to market or commercial decisions round consumer issues or pensions. If we take the ladder of empowerment model, groups such as older people appear too heterogeneous to neatly classify. For individual older people matters in addition to chronological age may be relevant to empowerment. None the less the impact of **ageism** may affect older people and the relationship between ageism and empowerment needs to be considered in practice and theoretically.

Empowerment and physically disabled people

The neglect of ageism in debates about empowerment stands in contrast to the links identified between disabled people and user empowerment.

Oliver (1990: xi) argued that capitalist society 'individualised and medic-alised' disability, and that the disability movement should be conceived of as a new social movement, linking the personal and the political. Oliver identified a dilemma for the movement – should it play a role in provision, or should it:

> remain separate from the state and concentrate on consciousness – raising activities leading to long-term changes in policy and practice and the empowerment of disabled people, with the attendant risks that the movement may be marginalised or isolated?
>
> (1990: 128)

The route of the disabled people's movement to empowerment has been associated with a negative social trait – institutional discrimination. While the movement was associated early on with campaigns around finance and benefits, attention has moved to focus on social rights and access to information and redress. In relation to health and social support services Barnes (1996: 100) has argued that: 'Independent living means disabled people have access to and control of a range of community-based services which empower them to identify and pursue their own lifestyle'.

For disabled people the linking of empowerment with independence is a strong motif, yet the word independence has also had to be recon-structed to convey *control* rather than individualized autonomy. As Morris (1998: 167) noted:

> Control over the assistance that is required to go about daily life is crucial, therefore, to the concept of independent living. It is this control which enables the expression of individuality and from this then flows the assertion of disabled people's human rights and their status as citizens.

Furthermore, disabled people's organizations have recognized that dif-ference between disabled individuals is important and that the identity of disabled people can be refracted by other social categories. Morris (1993) has been influential in drawing British feminists to the need to develop a relationship with disabled women and for the disabled people's movement to acknowledge the gendering of disability. She argued:

> Disabled and older people are treated as social policy issues and there has been very little challenging of the public attitudes which are held on impairment and old age, and a significant failure to explore the experiences in terms of the subjective reality of those who are old and/or disabled.
>
> (1993: 48–9)

In her research, Morris (1998) pointed to the ways in which disabled women tried to maintain their independence and social identity as home makers or mothers. Such identities were empowering but could be under-mined by gender-insensitive services. Morris provided the example of Valerie's comments to illustrate this:

> I think the community care philosophy doesn't understand what independent living is . . . They seem to think that community care is

about someone being cosy and comfortable, being kept clean. To me that's a step back into the situation of residential care – living in the contained environment of your own home.

(1998: 169)

Identity in relation to *race* and *ethnicity* has also emerged as an important aspect of the disability movement. Stuart (1996: 99), for example, has drawn attention to the common identity sought by the disabled people's movement and the position of black disabled people: 'in the context of community care policy, black disabled people have not been the main beneficiaries of services, such as those characteristic of the independent living movement, which are designed to empower them'. This may be associated with socioeconomic disadvantage and with racism, so Stuart has proposed that attention is given to the diversity of individuals overall. By so doing we may begin to listen carefully to black disabled people's views.

Empowerment and mental health service users

Empowerment for users of mental health services has its roots in critiques of the services and definitions of mental illness. Barnes (1997) has provided a history of the complex groupings that constitute the mental health movement in the UK, noting that the movement is made up of national and local groupings, some organized around particular issues, others around specific networks. Most groups appeared to work with 'sympathetic' professionals but few were engaged in direct service provision, outside more traditional voluntary sector groups. As Barnes observed this user group in particular faces problems in presenting its own cause since individuals are often considered to 'lack insight and . . . [be] incapable of defining either themselves or external reality' (p. 70).

One strategy for achieving empowerment when individuals are unwell or in great distress has been to develop systems of advocacy to counter the 'drift to disempowerment' identified by Cocks and Cockram (1997: 232). Vulnerable people, at certain times or in certain circumstances, may be able to access one of a range of advocacy types: individual advocacy, legal advocacy, systemic advocacy and citizen advocacy. In relation to users of mental health services, as with other individuals, access to advocacy varies according to whether there is a specific formal decision making process in train or local definition of a need for an advocacy service.

In an individual advocacy relationship a user may develop a relationship with another person who puts forward his or her case or acts to represent his or her known or anticipated views. In legal advocacy a user may be entitled to professional representation in respect, for example, of a mental health review tribunal. System-based advocacy may furnish a user with an advocate (independent or otherwise) to argue his or her case – for example, in complaints procedures. In many services a key worker, care manager or named nurse might well be expected to act as a person's advocate but with the general realization that conflicts of interest might arise. Finally, citizen advocacy may provide an individual to establish and represent the wishes of the user. They may not necessarily act in the user's best interests, but will equip decision makers with the nature and extent of the user's priorities and preferences. The non-statutory basis of representation for disabled people currently means that most service users will probably find advocacy services stretched.

Empowerment and people with learning disabilities

Some models of empowerment gloss over the problems of those whose abilities to make or communicate choices are limited or hard to identify. In relation to service users who have a learning disability there are a number of national organizations, such as People First, and local groupings, which effectively support individuals who wish to achieve more control over their lives. For some individuals with profound intellectual and multiple disabilities, self-advocacy may be insufficient and what is needed is enablement, or substitute decision making, in respect of some choices.

Fitton *et al.* (1995) illustrated some of the complexities in this area in their account of the support structures necessary to provide high quality support for young women in a home of their own. In the early stages of the project there was general agreement that the young women concerned – Kathy, Victoria and Lisa – would benefit from someone to represent their needs and wishes. Despite this positive welcome, the project found it would not find it easy to recruit and sustain advocates; being such an advocate requires training, commitment and imagination:

> such a project succeeds when it provides meaningful choices for people like Kathy, Victoria and Lisa. Ways of interpreting and translating those perceived wishes must be constantly sought, so that the young women are genuinely involved in developing their capacity to choose and initiate, in areas such as food, clothes and daily routines, as well as in more complex areas such as relationships.
>
> (Fitton *et al.* 1995: 98)

Empowerment and disabled children

To conclude this section we briefly discuss the empowerment of disabled children. Children themselves as users of services are not always consulted or listened to, though Aldgate *et al.* (1996) explored children's understanding and experience of respite accommodation. This study was unusual in including young children and reported that children generally were confident and articulate, giving opinions through play and descriptive accounts if relevant (p. 153). In a guide to practitioners, Dalrymple and Burke (1995) reported that involving young people in decision making should include providing information, offering opportunities for consultation and allowing young people 'to make choices and risk making mistakes' (p. 142). As they noted: 'A key message in the Children Act 1989 is that young people should be involved in the decisions that are made about their lives' (p. 140).

There are strong echoes here of policy in relation to adult users of community care services. It serves as a reminder that although one of the outcomes of the community care reforms has been to separate children's and adults' services in many agencies, there are important links, no more so than a need to recognize that adult service users may have their experiences shaped by children's services. Listening to the voices of children as active agents in their community care may well be an important development in the future.

That it is possible to collect and analyse children's views is evident. Mayall (1996), for example, has proposed that children need to be seen as much more than the objects of health and education services since they are active in the project of their own lives. In the same way that sociology has added gender as an element to be considered in social studies and then has had to radically revise its basic theories and understandings, Mayall has argued that the study of childhood will be similarly modifying and revolutionary to understanding the social world.

To empower children with disabilities will require further new mechanisms and practices. In their review of models of child participation Flekkoy and Kaufman (1997) provided examples of arenas where children practise taking responsibility and making decisions. Many of these models relates to a linear model of development and growth, with emphasis on learning through information and experience. Nevertheless, the empowerment of children with disabilities needs to be considered more imaginatively.

This section has focused on empowerment and the understandings given to this concept in general and more specifically. It should be remembered of course that empowerment is not confined to community care – it can be manifested or restricted within personal relationships, public attitudes and other aspects of social life. The association of disempowerment with facets of institutional life does not mean that the community is by nature empowering. In the next section we shall place discussion about users in the context of social exclusion and inclusion.

Exclusion and inclusion

While the rhetoric of empowerment and to some extent its reality have been a central feature of community care services in the 1990s, the broader social policy arena has focused on social exclusion and inclusion. Empowerment and inclusion are plainly related and indeed the experiences of many recipients of or applicants to community care services have been used to illustrate social exclusion. Disabled people in particular have argued that the experience of social exclusion sums up some of their feelings and analyses of a disabling environment and social prejudice against disabled people. Discrimination against disabled people in employment and aspects of public life, for example, has been challenged by disabled people, and the Disability Discrimination Act 1995 was in some measure a response to disabled people's campaigns against exclusion. This Act is instructive to those working in community care, for it is precisely welfare services that are left to one side by this legislation, almost as if the interests of disabled people lie in matters such as access, employment, education and contract law. While this does not remove the fact of heavy reliance on and support from community care services in some instances it signifies that services are generally not the totality of a person's life. One key characteristic of traditional institutions has been that they affect all aspects of people's lives – restricting life styles, individuality and access to ordinary living.

The language of exclusion and inclusion is relevant to two important matters: money and sexuality. These two illustrations, taken from areas in which values and emotions play a major role, can be used to draw out the experience of users currently.

Money

Power over one's money has long been recognized as an important indicator of adult status. People with learning disabilities however have at times been disempowered from exercising control over their own benefits. For some this is the result of legal intervention removing from people who lack 'capacity' the legal status to operate their own finances (for example, through receivership of the Court of Protection). For others the benefits agency receives an application to set up a system of appointeeship for a claimant who cannot manage money. To some extent such individuals are 'excluded' but overall the intention is that they and their best interests are protected. A lack of clarity and accountability in both such systems has led to calls for legal reform (Law Commission 1995).

Behind this organizational framework lie much broader issues relating to the exclusion of people with disabilities, illness, and older people from social participation. Bewley (1997), for example, pointed to the extent of poverty among people with learning disabilities and the lack of attention to matters of low income among such individuals. She observed:

> many thousands of pounds are paid out in benefits and service costs on behalf of people with learning difficulties and yet many people are extremely poor in terms of the actual money which they have access to and control of. Money is part of life; it is intimately tied to choice and empowerment.
>
> (1997: 109)

The disempowerment of people from their own income has been highlighted particularly in studies relating to people with learning disabilities. Bewley's (1997) research provided one such illustration representative of a number (see Box 5.6).

This exclusion within families and also within care settings takes place in a context of exclusion from the labour market: less than one-third of disabled people of working age are in employment, and those who are generally earn lower than average wages (Alcock 1996: 244). The resultant reliance on disability benefits may in itself promote social exclusion since benefit levels are generally low. This is furthered by many disabled people's higher costs of living (for example, for extra heating, travel costs and special equipment). Benefits targeted at people with disabilities may

> **Box 5.6 A representative case example**
>
> Dorothy's mother gives her £16 a week and puts £3 in a Christmas savings club. Dorothy has never been told how much more money is claimed in her name. There was an argument about the Christmas club money: Dorothy's family threatened to take the money away, but it is a lifeline for Dorothy because she chooses to use it to pay for two weeks' respite care every year, her only chance to get away from her family. Dorothy was 54 and lived with her family in a small village.
>
> *Source*: Bewley (1997: 10).

be inadequate, and there is now evidence that charges for community care services are taking up such benefits to pay for help in the home, personal care and day care services. While many practitioners may find implementing charges morally difficult if the result is to lower a person's income considerably (see Bradley and Manthorpe 1997), the market of community care has created a situation in which service users are expected to contribute benefits awarded in respect of disability's extra costs to pay for services which are helpful, yet partial. For some users and some practitioners a contradiction exists in promoting empowerment but reducing disabled people's ability to participate in activities of ordinary living as a result of charging.

It is necessary to remember that 'Disability does not necessarily create disadvantage' (Hirst and Baldwin 1994: 109) for evidence exists that not all disabled people are equally economically excluded. Moreover individuals' circumstances change over time. Hirst and Baldwin's survey of young disabled people and non-disabled peers, for example, pointed to the growing gap in terms of independence between the young people. The circumstances of these two groups 'drifted apart' (Hirst and Baldwin 1994: 111) as they moved from childhood to adult status and each group's level of independence was interrelated: so those with disabilities had less money of their own, went out less often and had less personal autonomy than their non-disabled equivalents. The researchers estimated that between 30 and 40 per cent of disabled young people would find great difficulty in attaining similar levels of independence to their non-disabled counterparts and proposed proactive help at crucial transition stages. While individuals might be helped by an advocate, it also appeared that extending civil rights (for example, over access to employment) would be of overall advantage to the young people with disabilities.

The advent of the Community Care (Direct Payments) Act 1996 promised much in relation to personal control over community care purchasing, and as described earlier, has been central to many disabled people's demands that real empowerment entailed access to funding. Under this Act local authorities have the power to make payments to users instead of arranging services themselves. As one respondent commented in a prospective study of the Act, direct payments have the potential to lead to: 'more independence, greater privacy, more friendships and going to places I want to go to' (Collins *et al.* 1997).

It would appear that individuals will be able to use the money independently or through a trust fund, independent living scheme or agency. The experience of users is eagerly awaited to determine the extent to which empowerment is advanced through such schemes. It should be noted though that not all community care users are eligible – for example, older people were initially prevented, by virtue of their age, from participating in the scheme. As with many debates around money, the advantages of empowerment will also have to be considered in the light of some people's heightened vulnerability to abuse and exploitation.

Sexuality

Empowering individuals in the area of personal expressions of sexuality has also been an influential aspect of community care. This stands in contrast to institutional living where sexual relationships were generally discouraged. Powerful myths exist none the less in relation to sexuality despite widespread community care services and illustrate the difficulty for practitioners in putting into practice theories of empowerment.

Many such myths relate to older people and the exclusion of sexuality from well-meaning but narrow assessment processes. Older people, for example, may find community care packages bring the institution into the home with its visiting, routines and medical equipment. Patterns of intimacy can be disturbed and partnerships change into carer and care-recipient. Such risks have been chronicled in relation to younger partnerships (see Morris 1993; Parker 1993) but may be appropriate to the experience of older people.

Lesbians and gay men

Community care services have also been accused of neglecting the needs of older lesbians and gay men. In one of the few research studies in this area from the UK (Hubbard and Rossington 1995), three-quarters (88 of 117) of respondents wanted specific community care services for lesbians and gay men. Reasons for this centred around wanting a service that was responsive and non-discriminatory. One service user commented: '"They [home carers] don't know I'm gay and if they did I know they wouldn't treat me the same, as they sometimes make comments that are overtly homophobic" – Jim (65), London' (Hubbard and Rossington 1995: 42).

Other reasons arose from feelings relating to community and its meanings in relation to overall community care. One respondent considered specific services would meet her needs more appropriately: '"[I] would feel more comfortable with gay attendance, around personal care, etc." – Leslie (82), Hampshire' (Hubbard and Rossington 1995: 42).

In the widespread absence of specific services, social care and health care practitioners will have to work with existing resources to ensure that such service users are not discriminated against and that their sexual orientation is respected. Moreover, as Bullock (1994) has argued, the experience of all lesbian or gay service users is unlikely to be similar. Bullock drew attention to the views of black lesbians who may feel rejected by a predominantly white movement and to the apparent invisibility of older women within the lesbian community (1994: 21). Her prediction was that many lesbians might choose to empower themselves in later life, should the need for care arise, with ideas for innovative service provision merging housing, friendship and care.

People with learning disabilities

Sexual empowerment in relation to people with learning disabilities has been less swept under the carpet. As part of philosophies of normalization and ordinary life, the right to sexual expression has been seen as one of the positive aspects of community care. Specifically, community care services have empowered individuals to join in social activities, to participate in programmes encouraging social skills and provided, through a care manager, a skilled helper who can identify opportunities for social integration. Community care in practice however has sometimes failed to live up to these expectations. It may restrict participation in ordinary activities by continuing to contract for segregated services in day care, for example. It may leave issues of social skills, friendship and community participation to one side in its concentration on personal and health needs in a narrow sense.

Furthermore, community care again has to take into account the vulnerability of many individuals receiving community care services. Recent evidence has revealed the extent of abuse and mistreatment among vulnerable adults and this needs to be brought into the context of debates about empowerment. When does empowerment become neglect and to what extent should principles of acting in a person's best interests replace acting in accordance with a person's expressed wishes?

Empowerment and advocacy

Debates about empowerment need to be more closely related to these dilemmas. To some extent empowerment as a concept sits comfortably and is acceptable ethically in respect of individuals, particularly adults, with mental competence. It needs to be flexibly interpreted when individuals have, for example, dementia or profound learning disabilities. It is such individuals whose need for empowerment is arguably the greatest. At times, only a practitioner is available – not an independent advocate. The same practitioner may perforce have to advocate for both user and carer, to the best of his or her ability. Bland's (1996) study of care managers' work with people with dementia, for example, found that care managers had to act as advocates for both carers and people with dementia. This advocacy role was combined with their roles as the family's confidantes and being the family's line of communication to the world of services. In some situations it may not be possible for a practitioner to find an advocate who is able to engage with the service user in such depth and it may not be possible for advocates to convince carers of their integrity.

To tackle such problems service systems and disabled people themselves have identified advocacy as an appropriate source of assistance. Having an advocate of course does not resolve problems or conflicts necessarily, but it may bring them into sharp relief. Professionals may find their interpretation of empowerment challenged by advocates and by self-advocacy in particular, as the following example from a study of service user involvement illustrates: '"... we want to run the services along with those who do now. They don't think we are capable. If only they came to our meetings they would understand and learn a lot from us" – member of a self-advocacy group' (Croft and Beresford 1990: 8).

In the face of such claims from service users community care services need to make fundamental changes. While it is government policy to involve users and carers in community care, it is clear that other pressures now come from users and carers themselves in a powerful and bottom-up movement.

One method of working together to make involvement meaningful is to involve service users in training and education.

Learning from users

The reforms of the NHS and Community Care Act 1990 were implemented amid an acknowledgement that training would be integral to their success. Gostick *et al.* (1997: 164) termed the process 're-visioning' and commented on the tendency of social workers to believe that they possessed already the necessary skills for care management while in practice they focused on assessment rather than overall care management skills. Involving users of services in professional training has been seen as one way in which the mechanics of community care provision might be better tuned to the needs of users.

Initiatives exist at a variety of levels. Many agencies and higher education institutions have developed user involvement in course design and delivery. This reflects a perspective that users are the experts with regard to their own needs and with regard to local community care provision – in reality. The view of one users' network reported in Harding and Oldman's (1996) guidelines on user and carer involvement conveyed this belief:

> The things that stand out about the workers we identify as empowering are such things as being treated as individuals and real people. They engage with us as equals rather than distancing themselves and seeing us as dependent clients. Part of this is recognising the expertise that we have gained from our lives by living with or being a user.
>
> (Harding and Oldman 1996: 3)

Models exist of involving users from a simple 'bringing on board' model where individual users are recruited to provide evidence of their own experiences, to representative models where groups of users are provided with opportunities to develop their own agenda for training within a specific session. Further along the spectrum lie courses and training programmes where users are involved in overall course design, delivery, assessment and evaluation.

Users, or 'survivors', of mental health services have been at the forefront of such developments, often stimulated by positive experiences from other areas. Crepaz-Keay *et al.* (1997) have drawn together guidelines and advice for managers and trainers, noting the importance, for example, of contracts, clarifying outcomes and setting targets. Despite the possible extra work involved they concluded: 'Whatever your role in mental health training and staff development, involving survivors effectively will help you to balance better the other competing demands and give you a larger repertoire of resources' (p. 31).

Conclusion

The emphasis on empowerment within community care forms a useful counterweight to a focus on disempowerment. It entails a reorientation of practitioner support, from whatever agency, to maximize community care service's abilities to enhance skills, independence and decision making from childhood through to old age. Even in the most difficult and perhaps distressing circumstances, service users can be empowered at a personal level. Croft (1992), for example, has written of the ability of practitioners to empower people who are dying through offering advocacy and enabling choices, being honest, providing information and recognizing and negotiating around possible conflicting interests. Beyond the personal level other service users may be able to empower themselves at interpersonal or organizational levels, with support from community care rather than in spite of its ministrations.

More work has been done in engaging with users to establish their needs in respect of community care, less on how to translate these needs into patterns of resources and priorities. In the coming years we may anticipate further refinement of concepts such as need. For policy makers rationing through eligibility criteria may be the favoured or only affordable option but for service users specific entitlements or rights may be a position which would sit comfortably with many user groups' growing sense of empowerment.

Summary

- The category or label of 'user' of community care services reflects changes in the way services are constructed and the ideas and values of professionals. Some service users welcome this label arguing that it is a positive move to partnership.

- Service users encounter community services at different times and have varied experiences. The targeting of services is a process of rationing. Service users in priority groups may benefit from flexible and imaginative care packages; others may find assistance is limited.

- Empowerment promotes choice and control. It is not an excuse for neglect. Professionals face dilemmas in managing the risks around protection and conflict.

- Involving users in service delivery can be positive practice. In training and education they may present powerful challenges to students' and course organizers' preconceived ideas.

Further reading

Ahmad, W. and Atkin, K. (eds) (1996) 'Race' and Community Care. Buckingham: Open University Press.

Allott, M. and Robb, M. (eds) (1998) Understanding Health and Social Care: An Introductory Reader. London: Sage.

Barnes, M. (1997) Care, Communities and Citizens. Harlow: Longman.

Campbell, J. and Oliver, M. (1996) Disability Politics. London: Routledge.

Ramcharan, P., Roberts, G., Grant, G. and Borland, J. (eds) (1997) Empowerment in Everyday Life. London: Jessica Kingsley.

References

Alcock, P. (1996) Social Policy in Britain. London: Macmillan.

Aldgate, J., Bradley, M. and Hawley, D. (1996) Respite accommodation: a case study of partnership under the Children Act 1989, in M. Hill and J. Aldgate (eds) Child Welfare Services. London: Jessica Kingsley.

Archibald, C. (1996) Home and away: people with dementia and their carers, in K. Stalker (ed.) Developments in Short-Term Care. London: Jessica Kingsley.

Barnes, C. (1997) Institutional discrimination against disabled people and the campaign for anti-discrimination legislation, in D. Taylor (ed.) Critical Social Policy: A Reader. London: Sage.

Bewley, C. (1997) Money Matters. London: Values into Action.

Biggs, S. (1997) User voice, interprofessionalism and postmodernity. Journal of Interprofessional Care, 11 (2): 195–204.

Bland, R. (1996) On the margins: care management and dementia, in J. Phillips and B. Penhale (eds) Reviewing Care Management for Older People. London: Jessica Kingsley.

Bradley, G. and Manthorpe, J. (1997) Financial Assessment: a Practitioner's Guide. Birmingham: Venture Press.

Braye, S. and Preston-Shoot, M. (1995) Empowering Practice in Social Care. Buckingham: Open University Press.

Bullock, F. (1994) Invisible Older Lesbians? Birmingham: Department of Social Policy and Social Work, University of Birmingham.

Campbell, J. and Oliver, M. (1996) Disability Politics. London: Routledge.

Carpenter, J. and Sbaraini, S. (1997) Choice, Information and Dignity. Bristol: Policy Press.

Cigno, K. and Burke, P. (1997) Single mothers of children with learning disabilities: an undervalued group. Journal of Interprofessional Care, 11 (2): 177–86.

Cocks, E. and Cockram, J. (1997) Empowerment and the limitations of formal human services and legislation, in P. Ramcharan, G. Roberts, G. Grant and J. Borland (eds) Empowerment in Everyday Life. London: Jessica Kingsley.

Collins, J., Holman, A., Aspis, S. and Amor, Y. (1997) *Funding Freedom*. London: Values into Action.

Crepaz-Keay, D. (1996) A sense of perspective: the media and the Boyd Inquiry, in G. Philo (ed.) *Media and Mental Distress*. Harlow: Longman.

Crepaz-Keay, D., Binns, C. and Wilson, E. (1997) *Dancing with Angels: Involving Survivors in Mental Health Training*. London: Central Council for Education and Training in Social Work.

Croft, S. (1992) Empowerment in action (inside supplement). *Community Care*, 26 March: ii–iii.

Croft, S. and Beresford, P. (1990) *User Involvement in the Social Services*. London: The Open Services Project.

Dalrymple, J. and Burke, B. (1995) *Anti-oppressive Practice and the Law*. Buckingham: Open University Press.

DoH (Department of Health) (1989) *Caring for People: Community Care in the Next Decade and Beyond*, Cm. 849. London: HMSO.

Fitton, P., O'Brien, C. and Willson, J. (1995) *Home at Last*. London: Jessica Kingsley.

Flekkoy, M. and Kaufman, N. (1997) *Rights and Responsibilities in Family and Society*. London: Jessica Kingsley.

French, S. (1994) Experiences of disabled health and caring professionals, in J. Swain, V. Finkelstein, S. French and M. Oliver (eds) *Disabling Barriers – Enabling Environments*. London: Sage/The Open University.

Ginn, J. (1996) Grey power: age-based organisations' response to structured in-equalities, in D. Taylor (ed.) *Critical Social Policy: A Reader*. London: Sage.

Gostick, C., Davies, B., Lawson, R. and Salter, C. (1997) *From Vision to Reality in Community Care*. Aldershot: PSSRU/Arena.

Griffiths, R. (1988) *Community Care: An Agenda for Action*. London: HMSO.

Harding, T. and Oldman, H. (1996) *Involving Service Users and Carers in Local Services*. London: National Institute for Social Work.

Hirst, M. and Baldwin, S. (1994) *Unequal Opportunities: Growing Up Disabled*. London: HMSO.

Hubbard, R. and Rossington, J. (1995) *As We Grow Older: A Study of the Housing and Support Needs of Older Lesbians and Gay Men*. London: Polari Housing Association.

Hughes, B. (1995) *Older People and Community Care*. Buckingham: Open University Press.

Law Commission (1995) *Mentally Incapacitated Adults and Decision-Making: An Overview*, Law Com 231. London: HMSO.

Lewis, J. and Glennerster, H. (1996) *Implementing the New Community Care*. Buckingham: Open University Press.

Manthorpe, J. and Twigg, J. (1995) Carers and care management. *Baseline*, October: 4–18.

Mayall, B. (1996) *Children, Health and the Social Order*. Buckingham: Open University Press.

Means, R. and Lart, R. (1994) User empowerment, older people and the reform of community care, in D. Challis and B. Davies (eds) *Health and Community Care: UK and International Perspectives*. Aldershot: Gower.

Morris, J. (1993) *Independent Lives: Community Care and Disabled People*. London: Macmillan.

Morris, J. (1998) Creating a space for absent voices: disabled women's experience of receiving assistance with daily living activities, in M. Allott and M. Robb (eds) *Understanding Health and Social Care*. London: Sage.

Oliver, M. (1990) *The Politics of Disablement*. London: Macmillan.

Parker, G. (1993) *With this Body: Caring and Disability in Marriage*. Buckingham: Open University Press.

Peterborough Voices (1997) *Extraordinary People, Extraordinary Lives*. Peterborough: Council for Voluntary Service.

Philo, G. (1996) Users of services, carers and families, in G. Philo (ed.) *Media and Mental Distress*. Harlow: Longman.

Pilgrim, D., Todhunter, C. and Pearson, M. (1997) Accounting for disability: customer feedback or citizen complaints? *Disability and Society*, 12(1): 3–15.

Poole, B. (1993) *Carers, Care Management and Assessment*. London: Central Council for Education and Training in Social Work/Contact a Family.

Ramcharan, P. and Borland, J. (1997) Preface, in P. Ramcharan, G. Roberts, G. Grant and J. Borland (eds) *Empowerment in Everyday Life*. London: Jessica Kingsley.

Ramcharan, P., Roberts, G., Grant, G. and Borland, J. (eds) (1997) *Empowerment in Everyday Life*. London: Jessica Kingsley.

Ritchie, J. (1994) *The Report of the Inquiry into the Care and Treatment of Christopher Clunis*. London: HMSO.

Shepherd, M., Murray, A. and Muijen, M. (1994) *Relative Values*. London: Sainsbury Centre for Mental Health.

Sinson, J. (1995) *Care in the Community for Young People with Learning Disabilities*. London: Jessica Kingsley.

Souza, A. (1997) Everything you ever wanted to know about Down's syndrome, in P. Ramcharan, G. Roberts, G. Grant and J. Borland (eds) *Empowerment in Everyday Life*. London: Jessica Kingsley.

Stuart, O. (1996) 'Yes, we mean black disabled people too': thoughts on community care and disabled people from black and minority ethnic communities, in W. Ahmad and K. Atkin (eds) *'Race' and Community Care*. Buckingham: Open University Press.

Swain, J. (1994) Taught helplessness? Or a say for disabled students in schools, in J. Swain, V. Finkelstein, S. French and M. Oliver (eds) *Disabling Barriers – Enabling Environments*. London: Sage/The Open University.

Tozer, R. and Thornton, P. (1995) *A Meeting of Minds: Older People as Research Advisers*. York: Social Policy Research Unit.

Walker, A. and Warren, L. (1996) *Changing Services for Older People*. Buckingham: Open University Press.

Woodley, L. (1995) *The Woodley Team Report*. London: East London and City Health Authority/Newham Council.

CARERS' PERSPECTIVES: DO SERVICES SUPPORT CARERS?

Introduction

This chapter moves the debate about community care to consider those individuals who are now frequently described as *carers*. Central to government policy, carers have many varied experiences of community care services. One of the aims of this chapter is to tease out some of the reasons behind carers' differing experiences of community care and to communicate the many perspectives adopted by carers. All social care and health care practitioners will encounter carers in their work: some will also simultaneously be carers themselves or will have taken on this role in the past, while for others it will be a future role, anticipated or otherwise. Within our own families there will be a whole range of caring experiences: such matters are important for practitioners to reflect on since they have potential to influence our own values and attitudes to others.

The structure of this chapter is as follows: we start by exploring various definitions and terms, outlining how the world of caring is perceived by policy makers and service delivery systems. We then move to consider carers' own perspectives and how their voices may be heard by practitioners and politicians. We explore coping strategies among carers and particular challenges from practical, emotional or relationship difficulties. Attention is then paid to the key differences emerging between carers and the impact of factors such as gender, sexuality, ethnicity, economic status and age. The chapter then focuses on policy and practice: examining the construction of carers' needs and the service response. We end with a brief note of the potential for carers to be involved in education and training and their consultative and critical roles in service development and innovation.

Defining caring, carers and care

Few people pause to define what they are doing when it is taken for granted or a mundane task. Much caring involves such work: its very domestic and sometimes commonplace facets may seem uncomplicated and unproblematic. Activities of daily life such as shopping, making a cup of tea or being on the end of a telephone can seem unworthy of the concern of policy makers or professionals. However it is such care that sustains the very notion of community care. It is carers who are the community and they who provide most care.

There are a number of qualifications to such an overview. For example, some caring provided by relatives or friends is highly expert and may involve skills generally considered within the remit of professionals. Caring is not randomly or evenly distributed between individuals or groups: as we shall see later it falls disproportionately on those who are female and on those who are poorer. Finally, caring does not always involve physical activity or quantifiable transactions: much of it is bound up with emotion and complex relationships between family members. Such feelings can affect the meaning of caring for the individual and make an objective view of a caring relationship rather one-dimensional.

In considering *care* we first need to recall that most care received by any of us, disabled or otherwise, is provided by ourselves. Self-care is often overlooked but it remains fundamental to community care, the emphasis of which is primarily on fostering and sustaining independence. Self-care however may be part of a spectrum ranging from self-sufficiency in many aspects of ordinary life to relative dependence. Technological developments may play an important part in reducing or changing the necessity for any of us to rely on the direct assistance of others. Certain individuals are protected from the demands of self-care such as very young children, or have their abilities for self-care restricted, such as hospital patients or prisoners. Not being able to care for oneself, unless given up by choice, has often been viewed negatively or with pity: for children it is regarded as a transitory period marked by their increasing abilities to take on responsibilities for their own care.

Caring then has to be seen within this context as something beyond ordinary support. Yet we know that there is a wide range of what passes for ordinary support between adults and in relation to their children or members of their extended families. Parker (1981) teased out some of the essentials behind caring and argued that it frequently involved:

- *duration* (it lasts or is predicted to last a period of time);
- *intensity* (it is perceived as an 'extra' activity or as work);
- *prognosis* (the condition is not temporary but long-term and may well deteriorate).

Parker, rather unsuccessfully, proposed that the word caring should be replaced by the word *tending* to distinguish it from the emotional back-cloth surrounding the word. To 'care about', he argued, is different from 'caring for', the former having the potential to appear rather general. However, tending has not entered our vocabulary and professionals, policy makers and the media within the UK are commonly using 'carer' and 'caring'. In the USA the terms care-giver and care-giving appear to be more frequently employed, with the term 'care-recipient' more neatly summing up the awkward British circumlocutions of 'person receiving care' or 'person being looked after'. Unwieldy as these phrases are they represent progress from the more pejorative term 'dependant'.

Concepts of care and carers only enter everyday language when there is general agreement that the role is distinctive from others. While professional material has moved to use 'caring' it still often employs the tag 'informal' when referring to carers to distinguish them from formal providers such as social care staff or nurses. Carers however argue that their role is not 'informal' but highly formal at times, involving skilled interventions or structured routines.

To label one individual as a carer and the other as a 'disabled person' or service user (referring to formal services) serves to simplify many relationships. In many families there is much interdependence and reciprocity. This can apply to older couples, for example, when one person's physical disabilities are managed in the context of the spouse's own problems. Equally, Walmsley (1997: 45) writing of Lynne, a woman with learning disabilities, illustrated how a person receiving care in some aspect of her life can also be a carer and be under pressure to fulfil this role:

> In terms of care, she was both carer and cared-for. The formal care she received was very much geared to sustaining her ability to carry out her job . . . The care work Lynne did for her father was actually quite substantial, but she got little credit for it and no rewards.

For other individuals to be seen as a carer can be a matter of status and a very positive role. Rose and Bruce (1995) have pointed to the impact of caring for a wife with Alzheimer's disease as sometimes bringing new interest and purpose to men in retirement. In their study some husbands had acquired new skills and were well regarded by others as effective carers, indicating that reciprocity in care is not confined to the two individuals involved but may be part of much more diffuse relationships.

Discovering carers

Research and professional discussions contributed to what may be viewed as the 'discovery' of carers in the 1980s. But the emergence of carers as a distinct subject for study or focus for service delivery should not be seen in isolation. It is questionable whether interest in carers would have been so pronounced without the context of community care or without the influence of feminism and pressure-group politics.

Early on in discussions about informal care the self-reported experiences of families were dominant. Such accounts featured in newspapers and other popular media and highlighted the extent to which caring for a disabled relative at home was both hard work and emotionally draining. Services were either irrelevant or too sparse on the ground.

It is possible to see caring as being constructed as a **social problem** in the 1980s. Blumer (1971) has proposed five distinct stages or phases for the development of social problems – the processes whereby some issues or features of social life become seen as problems about which something can and should be done. Employing such a framework permits us to see why caring might have emerged as a 'problem' and thus why it is so central to ideas about community care. Blumer's five stages are shown in Box 6.1. Blumer suggested that there might well be overlaps and linkages between them in practice.

Box 6.1   Blumer's five stages for the construction of social problems

1 The emergence of the problem
2 The legitimation of the problem
3 The mobilization
4 The formulation of an official action plan
5 The plan's implementation

Source: Blumer (1971)

In the confusing and complex area of welfare, Blumer's analysis has proved helpful in other respects, notably elder abuse (see Penhale and Kingston 1995; Manthorpe 1999). We now discuss how caring can be seen through the lens of social problem construction.

Caring: A social problem

Emergence

This first stage is illustrated by the personal experiences of carers, notably through the organization formally known as the Association of Carers which has since then become Carers National Association (see Briggs and Oliver 1985).

Other similar organizations were formed by groups of carers (in the case of MENCAP), by parents of children with learning disabilities (formally often known as mental handicap) and by the pioneering National Council for the Single Woman and her Dependants (again merging into the Carers National Association).

Legitimation

The next stage, legitimation, was partially achieved through the impact of research studies of the 1980s, notably the work commissioned by the Equal Opportunities Commission (1982a, 1982b). These studies formed a link between personal testimonies of experience and the professional and policy making communities, which issued publications based on official statistics, for example, using data from the General Household Survey (GHS) (Green 1988). The GHS overview of caring within domestic households has been influential on a number of levels and provided 'evidence' of the scale of individuals involved in providing care, their relationships with care recipients, the extent of care and its financial impact. In parallel with growing interest in social models of disability, the subject of informal care, as opposed to professional or paid assistance, was increasingly seen as the proper subject for policy.

Mobilization

Being the focus of policy makers attention however does not necessitate action: the third phase of social problem construction requires 'mobilization'. The early 1990s witnessed accelerating demands for support or 'care for the carers' with pressure from interest groups now joined by professional bodies who argued that community care would entail recognition of carers' needs in conjunction with the needs of disabled people. One strand of this involved arguments for discrete financial support for carers to replace income forgone; another strand involved provision of many forms of respite care, giving carers a 'break'. However, action in respect of carers has been step-by-step, or incremental, with carers' benefits being limited and at low level. There has been no legislation in the area of employment protection or rights to leave. There is no guarantee of services or a minimum level of support.

None the less, carers have featured in government policy when it is centrally concerned with community care, and more latterly with health provision. The White Paper *Caring for People* (DoH 1989) had six key object-ives and second in this list was 'To ensure that service providers make practical support for carers a high priority' (para. 1.11). The same docu-ment observed that: 'the reality is that care is provided by family, friends and neighbours ... Helping carers to maintain their valuable contribution to the spectrum of care is both right and a sound investment' (para. 2.3).

In relation to assessment, *Caring for People* advised:

> Assessments should take account of the wishes of the individual and his or her carer, and of carer's ability to continue to provide care, and where possible should include their active participation. Effort should be made to offer flexible services which enable individuals and carers to make choices.
>
> (DoH 1989: para. 3.2.6)

Caring for People is the apogee of policy attention in relation to carers and their centrality in keeping the ship of community care afloat. Carers are repeatedly referred to yet are distinguished from those receiving care. In this document the government openly revealed its (and society's) in-debtedness to carers and by default acknowledged that choice, flexibility, sensitivity and support had not always been available to carers from wel-fare services. Presumably influenced by evidence and experience, *Caring for People* took account of the choices open to potential carers: 'The deci-sion to take on a caring role is never an easy one' (DoH 1989: para. 1.9). This implicitly views the caring role as one which was a positive choice rather than a given or inevitable duty derived from relationships and social norms.

Formulation

It is possible to see the elements in *Caring for People* (DoH 1989) as part of an 'official plan' and to argue that carers were formally considered in the policy making process. The mid to late 1990s later witnessed a reworking of official action as part of the dynamic process of social problem con-struction. Carers' organizations and policy makers who observed the early implementation of the full community care reforms from 1993 argued that the 'fine words' of the policy documents were making little significant difference. The conception of and consensus building around the Carers (Recognition and Services) Act 1995, were further attempts to develop an 'action plan' for carers: this time with greater specificity.

As described by Carers National Association (1997a) this Act was 'the first piece of legislation to recognise fully the role of the carer' (p. 3). It gives carers who provide 'regular and substantial' care the right to ask for an assessment of their ability to care and puts a duty on local authorities to take any such assessment into account when formulating the service package or plan for the person receiving care. In contrast to the explicitly adult focus of *Caring for People* (DoH 1989), this Act includes not only those adults who provide care for other adults but also those adults who care for children who are sick or disabled, and young people (under 18 years old) who provide care for a relative. This is an important development from the stereotype of spouse or adult child as carer. As we shall see later the position of children as carers has been a recent, albeit professionally led, focus of attention.

However, it is important to recall that the Carers Act 1995 was not government inspired or mainstream government policy, although parliamentary time was found for its discussions. The Act was the result of the chance success of the Members of Parliament (MPs) special ballot for private members' bills. MP Malcolm Wicks' selection in this lottery permitted parliamentary discussion of the matter: his work was assisted by the Carers National Association and a variety of pressure and interest groups, together with the Associations of Directors of Social Services (England and Wales) and Social Work Services (Scotland) who provided professional and local authority impetus. The Carers Act can therefore be seen as 'official', but in terms of the overall plan for community care it is clear that the government thought good practice with carers was a matter more for encouragement than legislation.

Implementation

Finally we move to discuss the implementation of both the community care reforms and the Carers Act 1995 on carers. Box 6.2 reports findings from a survey of carers one year after the Carers Act was implemented. A further survey (Carers National Association 1997b) of local authorities

---

Box 6.2 The impact of the Carers Act 1995

One year on from the Act a survey of carers who were in touch with the Carers National Association found that:

- carers only asked for an assessment when they felt they were reaching breaking point;
- half had not been informed of their rights to an assessment;
- half did not know how an assessment could help them;
- one-third did not know they were entitled to an assessment (almost all performed substantial and time-consuming tasks);
- one in six found it was already too difficult to obtain services – this was ascribed to financial pressures on social services.

Of those who had received an assessment:

- half had seen an increase in services;
- nearly two-thirds were happy with the process of assessment;
- just over half were content with the outcome of the assessment.

The survey, conducted with people already in touch with the Carers National Association, found only one-fifth had been assessed but most were spending much time in caring for relatives.

Source: Carers National Association (1997a).

across the UK (including Northern Ireland's Trusts) found great diversity between the levels of support provided and many differences in practice related to carers' assessments. Many referred to their own financial problems as constricting their abilities to provide support. Even so not all had informed carers of their rights extensively, and some were not able to confirm that carers had received copies of the care plans or knew when they were being assessed.

This picture of carers' assessment in practice is closely related to the impact of the community care reforms more generally on carers. The promises of legislation, policy and ministerial guidance were considerable: to what extent were the questions raised by the titles of the Carers National Association's (*Community Care: Just a Fairy Tale?* (1994) and *Better Tomorrows?* (1995)) justified? In the next section we look at the impact of reforms.

Evaluating the community care reforms

In *Caring for People* (DoH 1989) great stock was placed on the notion that the reforms would enhance services for carers. The White Paper put it unambiguously: '... a key responsibility of statutory service providers should be to do all they can to assist and support carers.' (para. 2.3). Among its positive suggestions of how to translate this into reality were strategic changes married to improvements in individual working practices.

First, at the level of strategy, users and carers alike were seen to benefit from greater clarity about the responsibilities of each agency encountered. Notable in many studies of caring has been the confusion between local authority and health services. Second, strategic planning through the process of consultation around community care plans was to consider services for carers and to take on board their views. Finally the establishment of inspection units for residential care aimed to both raise the quality of care provided and implicitly offer reassurance to the public that vulnerable residents' interests would be protected. Carers naturally are among those most likely to require reassurance since they may face most disquiet at the prospect of 'letting go'.

At the personal level, *Caring for People* brought the concept of care manager centre stage. For carers the notion of an identified, contactable, accountable coordinator of care, perhaps with time and interest to work with them in partnership, held out great promise. Much research had argued the potential of such an approach – from Glendenning's (1985) study of families caring for their disabled children to the influential findings of the Kent Care Management Studies (e.g. Challis and Davies 1986). Both of these examples argued that carers could benefit in a number of practical but also emotional ways from one skilled professional who had the time and resources to offer meaningful support.

What we have seen is a concentration on the problems of carers. These have been identified and quantified and they have also been reported more subjectively as 'burden'. The word 'burden' has been frequently employed to cover a range of experiences, bringing with it notions of 'unfairness', lack of balance and hardship. A burden is to be carried or endured and is overwhelmingly negative. In looking for the dimensions of burden many researchers have debated whether it is more keenly felt by specific types of carers or alternatively whether certain characteristics of the individual being cared for create burdens or exacerbate difficulties.

If we look for difficulties we are very likely to find them and perhaps to ignore other aspects of relationships. For services the focus of carers' problems may equally have been a one-sided response but one which is understandable since welfare services exist to meet need. The next section explores aspects of carers' needs.

Taking a break

One relatively common form of service provision for carers is the provision of support to enable them to take a break from caring. Frequently referred to as *respite*, this term has been criticized as being unhelpfully generalized and simplistic, and, moreover, as a term it carried with it negative connotations of seeing the disabled person receiving such care as a 'burden' which needs to be put aside for temporary relief. Stalker (1996) noted that the Social Services Inspectorate has deliberately avoided using the term 'respite care', preferring instead the phrase 'short-term breaks' in its guidance to good practice.

The origins of short-term care lie scattered through welfare services with hospitals (long-stay and convalescent), local authorities (old people's homes, other residential homes and hostels), private individuals (through fostering or boarding out in respect of children and adults), educational establishments and charitable bodies all providing breaks of some kind. In many instances respite has been seen as involving a period of time away from home but it is also currently used to describe other much shorter services: day care, sitting services or flexible services in which the common denominator is that the caring tasks and responsibilities pass to another person. In some instances that person may be a professional or trained worker; in others volunteers or a mixture of staff and helpers may be involved. Finally, just to add to the complexity, such services may be free (e.g. a place in a day hospital) or subject to charges or fees.

In the past and to an extent today, respite or shared care has been one of the few resources specific to carers. Much effort has been put into developing a break that is reliable and yet flexible. Key problems have been identified, from carers' perspectives. We shall see later that for those 'placed' in respite other serious problems surface and often overlap.

The quality of care

Hubert's (1991) study – of the views of parents of severely disabled young people about the respite care provided for their children – identified the distress felt by parents. One mother described the lack of attention given to her son: 'Each time he comes home with little things wrong, and they're minor things to other people . . . but it just aggravates me and I feel I'm doing him down by sending him back there' (p. 40).

Other research findings are less negative though relatively low numbers of families with disabled children make use of short-term care lasting overnight or taking the child away from home. The importance of educational services in providing a break from caring responsibilities may account for this, as may breaks for parents provided informally by members of their extended families, notably grandparents.

Quality of care arguments still persist however, and concerns about physical care may extend to concerns about a lack of emotional or environmental support: a child-centred respite service may need to provide sophisticated medical or nursing support within a building open to visitors, 'ordinary' messy children's activities and within a budget restricting one-to-one attention.

Russell (1996b) has identified a number of quality indicators for short-term care among parents of disabled children (see Box 6.3). Many of these indicators (and there are others) could be translated into services for other ages or with other disabilities. The research of Levin *et al.* (1994), for example, highlights a number of *policy* and *practice* issues. Among policy were questions of *availability* and *variation* between areas: as with many aspects of welfare provision there are wide geographical differences and while these might be perceived as local responses to need they can also be viewed as frustrating local inequalities.

Box 6.3   Russell's quality indicators

- Being local and accessible
- Providing good care – not medicalized but not ignoring special needs
- Availability on demand
- More support for first-time users
- Responsiveness to the age of the child
- Being integrated with other support
- Providing information and choice

Source: Russell (1996).

The research of Levin *et al.* (1994) explored the views of carers of older people with significant mental confusion. They found that many agencies and professionals were involved with the families concerned and thus another policy problem – *overlap* and *duplication* – arose. Similarly, while relief care was targeted at those with the most severe physical and mental problems and those who expressed the most stress in providing care, it was perhaps not enough to make an appreciable difference either by being sufficient in quality or timely enough to prevent stress. As with other features of community care, there exists a potential tension between the requirements to support carers while simultaneously focusing resources on those in most need, since these almost by definition may have no one to provide support.

This tension is manifest in a number of carers' suggestions about improvements to short-term care. For care to be offered at an early stage more will need to be available. For choice about amount and frequency (if an increase is sought), more again will have to be provided. While some of Levin *et al.*'s (1994) practice points could be accomplished within existing resources (see Box 6.4) they acknowledged that extensions to services and an improvement in quality would require extra funding.

Box 6.4 Good practice for short-term care

- Publicity and information for carers on the range of services
- Efficient referral
- Choice about aspects of the service
- Written information on specific services
- Opportunities to visit and to be visited by those who are to provide the care
- Knowledge of staff names and service routines
- Invitations to reviews
- Encouragement to seek advice
- Information about transport problems
- Referral to other services if there are problems

Source: Levin *et al.* (1994).

A small piece of research by Healy and Yarrow (1997) illustrated some of these deficiencies. Although only a minority of older people live with their children, the figure rises to one in ten of women aged over 80 years. In this study most carers received formal services (they were recruited through contact with services). Despite this a number said they were not informed or were misinformed about social security matters as well as care services: a commonly reported view was that 'nobody tells you'.

In common with other research findings and at a time when the community care changes could have been expected to have been fully absorbed, the families in Healy and Yarrow's (1997) study (mostly daughters) made a number of almost predictable points (Box 6.5).

In relation to their own circumstances of providing care for their older relative (typically the carer's mother) in their own homes, these carers

---

Box 6.5 Carers' needs

- They needed information about benefits and services
- They needed realistic choices
- They needed an income to cover the costs of caring
- They needed workplace support
- Services should be adequate and responsive
- Choice was needed in respect of respite
- Housing should meet the needs of extended families
- Services should be affordable

Source: Healy and Yarrow (1997).

asked for information about the practicalities and consequences of taking on this course of action.

Carers and copers

The literature on caring has generally focused on carers' difficulties. These have been conceived to lie in the inherent difference in their situations from ordinary experiences. Most of us however will experience some forms of care-giving or care-receiving ourselves. It is increasingly part of ordinary life for individuals to be involved in care but how this is experienced depends to a considerable extent on social factors such as gender, economic status and age.

Gender

In this section we explore what factors assist individuals to cope and the necessity for helping professionals to be aware of the diversity of carers' needs. *Gender* has for many years determined how carers are perceived, from being a taken-for-granted aspect of female relationships to new visions of women as trapped in a 'sandwich generation' – pulled between the needs of their ageing parents and the demands of spouse, children and employment. But this is a stereotype – women's roles in community care may be affected by a whole number of major social changes (see Box 6.6).

Box 6.6   Social changes influencing care needs

- The growing numbers of older people
- The increased proportion of older people among the population
- Women's increased participation in the labour market (full- and part-time)
- Decreased family size
- Higher rates of single parenting
- Increased geographical mobility
- Survivorship of many individuals with disabilities

As women generally live longer it is they who may receive care in old age or provide it until very late in life. To speak of women carers however can overlook the varied experiences between, for example, those who are providing care late in life, perhaps for a partner, and those who give birth to babies with multiple disabilities. However, both may by affected by assumptions which see their caring as extensions of their 'natural' role as wives or mothers (see Gilligan 1993). This perspective argues that women have innate abilities as carers and that caring is a feminine role requiring the virtues of loyalty, duty and patience, accompanied by household management skills. Feminists have argued that this is simplistic and that care-giving is not integral to relationships; indeed it can damage or change them into less valued states. Lonsdale (1990) for example, pointed out that receiving personal care from a partner may affect the relationship detrimentally, turning it into work or an embarrassing encounter.

However, Parker's exploration of the experiences of younger people who became disabled after their marriage, and of their spouses who provided care, discussed this element of emotion more critically. The carers (both men and women) interviewed by Parker (1993: 118–20) spoke of caring for their partners as:

- challenging normal expectations;
- embarrassing for both parties;
- producing an apparent loss of adult or equal status for the person receiving care;
- distressing when witnessing pain;
- physically and emotionally inescapable;
- hard to share.

Coping with caring tasks was bound up with the *relationship*. Although formal services were important to the carers interviewed, Parker argued that, arising from her own experience and that of those she interviewed, matters of feeling and emotion are central to informal care.

Coping, then, has to be seen as more than adequate and high-quality service provision: it has to be acceptable, and either support or enhance relationships. For women, services are frequently said to be inappropriate in that they are not flexible enough to meet women's needs by sustaining their abilities to carry out tasks they enjoy or to provide assistance in areas of difficulty. Most practitioners will recognize the difficulty of getting help with matters such as gardening or household maintenance which older women at times may require. However, such women may be willing and able to carry on with housework activities such as preparing meals and not welcome assistance in this area – for example, the bulk delivery of frozen meals.

Gender, then, has to be viewed as a useful tool in analysing policy, service delivery and interpersonal relationships. In an early analysis of community care the phrase 'for community read family, for family read women' (Finch 1984: 44) came to assume a self-evident truth. So much was this so that the General Household Survey's findings (Green 1988) of considerable male involvement in informal care were greeted with surprise. The era of the discovery of *male carers* had begun.

'Male carers' as a subject for policy and practice expanded our understanding of the diversity of carers and the differences between carers. While research often observed the numerical superiority of women carers it could no longer ignore men's roles. So, for example, when Levin *et al.* (1994: 5) referred to three times the number of women caring for relatives with dementia as men, the position of the male minority required explanation. This is particularly relevant to service planning and expenditure since studies have shown that characteristics of users (e.g. their degree of disability) are less significant than carers' circumstances and attitudes in relation to the potential for the user being supported at home. Davies (1998: 89) pointed out that carers' circumstances will also reflect the labour market and housing provision as well as social trends such as marital and household arrangements.

While all of these factors are gender related they point to the importance of seeing male and female relationships across the life course as well as in a 'snapshot'. Using a **life course perspective** helps when exploring why patterns of female kin providing care persist in some families or communities, or why some individuals may provide care while those in similar circumstances do not. Finch and Masons' (1993) description of the efforts and commitment of relatives to support family members – for example, through long and arduous travel to provide practical assistance and emotional care – held that negotiation was important and should be seen as bound up with long-standing relationships. While some individuals in their research argued that taking on a caring role was too difficult because of employment, distance, family commitments, lack of competence and lack of resources (Finch and Mason 1993: 112) others overcame such problems. This was not because they were female, or daughters, but because their structural position within families contributed to the likelihood of reciprocal commitments to family members. In one of their examples, the Simpson family had negotiated the roles of carers over two decades (Finch and Mason 1993: 81–93).

Gender is a complex factor in caring relationships though it has been a dominant theme in line with feminist critiques of household structures and patriarchy. Its influence now extends to analysis (rather belatedly) of relationships in later life (Arber and Ginn 1990) and of abusive relationships within formal and informal care (Whittaker 1995; Aitken and Griffin 1996).

Socioeconomic factors

Some authors, however, have maintained that informal care is inevitably situated in socioeconomic contexts and that gender is not the only variable of interest. Graham (1991), for example, has pointed to the similarity in experiences between poorer women providing care within their own families and low-paid women providing care to others in settings such as residential or nursing homes. She has observed that in many areas of the UK women in this position are more likely to be from minority ethnic backgrounds.

Poverty among carers and the difficulties this causes often lies beneath the surface and Glendinning (1992) has drawn together material demonstrating the impact of caring for individuals' current financial status and also their future levels of savings and pensions. While caring there may be higher levels of expenditure – for example, on heating, special diets or equipment (such as special chairs, creams, clothing and so on). There may also be reduced opportunities to 'shop around' for cheaper items or to buy in bulk. Such findings have fuelled campaigns by carers for increased acknowledgement of the costs of caring. Many carers contrast the benefit available to those providing a 'week's work' of care (the invalid care allowance (ICA)) with the amounts paid by social services departments in respect of residential or nursing home care. The ICA has itself been criticized for its partiality as well as its parsimony: it is not available to individuals over 65 years and is only available for those providing 35 hours of care each week. Notoriously, until 1986, it was not available to 'housewives' who were presumed to care as part of their domestic role.

Recent moves to permit disabled people to receive cash instead of services (under the Community Care (Direct Payments) Act 1996) will be discussed more fully in the following section. Carers' groups have pointed to the exclusion of these sums from payments to those who are closely related. Clearly there is still a policy tension around encouraging and replacing income loss among family carers (e.g. through the ICA) and beliefs that such carers might pressure or take advantage of their disabled relatives if direct payments were available within families. Such conflict around care is not confined to the level of policy.

Differing perspectives

Different perspectives exist between carers and those receiving care (whom, for readability's sake will now be referred to as service users, although services may be rather thin on the ground or non-existent). Rogers and Pilgrim (1989), for example, referred to two influential mental health pressure groups as examples of conflicting values. They conceived of MIND (the National Association for Mental Health) as the 'progressive view of citizenship' while they viewed the National Schizophrenia Fellowship (NSF) as promoting the interests of relatives (carers in some instances) who construct NSF policy which they perceived to be paternalistic and conservative. In the opinion of Rogers and Pilgrim the rights of patients are superseded by the views of relatives accompanied by much of the psychiatric profession.

While carers' groups can undoubtedly be mutually supportive and empowering, there is, none the less, potential for conflict with service professionals and service users. Carers' groups however are seen as part of coping strategies and many professionals initiate and sustain such groups. Some groups are time limited and have an educational focus, covering for example benefits, methods of lifting people safely and stress reduction. Others, by contrast, are less formally structured and provide opportunities for general discussion and mutual support, with the premise that no one other than a carer can empathize or proffer advice grounded in experience. Still others embark on advocacy roles for carers or on behalf of service users. In the UK such groups have often merged into the voluntary sector, for example, MENCAP, Scope and the Alzheimer's Disease Society. Carers providing assistance to those with comparatively rare medical conditions are now often put in touch with national or even international groupings of other families or self-help groups by professional advisers. Increased communication in respect of medical conditions may be helpful to carers but for some this level of information may be difficult technically or even in emotional terms. Coping as an activity and also as a 'state of mind' has been particularly developed by Beresford (1994) in her study of parents looking after a child with disabilities. Beresford pointed to parents' abilities in managing the emotions involved and the many extra tasks, and their attempts to sustain patterns of ordinary family life. One of the parents interviewed by Beresford provided an illustration of this:

> One night a week I always feed the children early. Penny (sibling) is a bit too big to be rushed off to bed but I make her go and do something by herself, and I put Jenny (disabled child) to bed. Then we have a meal on our own, quite often have a bottle of wine with it and just spend some good time together at least once a week. It sounds a bit clinical scheduling it into the diary but I find I have to do that otherwise the time just gets eroded away.
>
> (Beresford 1994: 89)

Other parents, interviewed as part of a study of families with an adult child with learning difficulties (Heyman et al. 1998), identified ways in which they coped with risk – in this case the perceived dangers of the neighbourhood or outside world. Using this perspective 'the sharply contrasting views' (Heyman et al. 1998: 206) of family carers and service professionals were investigated to explore a perennial – and only at times understated – view that parents could be overprotective or stifling. In this study professionals were more optimistic about the abilities of people with learning disabilities to learn from mistakes. Parents, however, perceived that they would be left to 'pick up the pieces' of failure or harmful events. One parent, for example, considered that professionals were being exploitative of people with learning difficulties: 'I think to a certain extent they are being used, aren't they? Maybe I am being nasty, but I supposed they are being used in an experimental way' (Heyman et al. 1998: 213).

Coping, therefore, among parents, other relatives or carers is often situated in examples of daily life and needs to be viewed in the context of individual dynamics as well as policies and professional practices. Even an extensive, and expensive, care package probably constitutes a small percentage of time spent with the service user compared with that spent with a co-resident carer, or even carers who do not live with the person receiving care.

The rewards of care

Finally in this section we consider the important focus on the *positives of care* developed by Nolan et al. (1996) whose research has identified the pleasure and positive feelings accompanying many care-giving relationships. While these have been implicit in many studies, professional focus has generally been on problems, needs and deficiencies. Part of Nolan et al.'s argument is that such positives may vary between individuals and that some are not immediately obvious. Using their framework, a person providing care for a relative with dementia, for example, may experience positives in respect of seeing the person receiving care looking happy or at least contented. They provided these examples from their large-scale survey, which asked people to report aspects of their care that they found satisfying: 'When my mother gets pleasure from something I've planned and when I manage to turn her unhappiness to happiness'; and 'When my husband can remember something about where he has been or what we have done. This means he has enjoyed himself and that makes all the hard work worthwhile' (Nolan *et al.* 1996: 88).

In identifying satisfactions for carers, Nolan *et al.* (1996) developed ideas about the types of possible benefits: first in the form of interpersonal gains (e.g. feeling appreciated); second in the form of interpersonal satisfactions (e.g. feeling needed or challenged); and third as outcomes of caring (e.g. developing interests or skills). Such is the impact of a focus on satisfaction that Nolan *et al.* referred to this as necessitating a need 'to break the mould' in the way that care-giving is conceptualized (p. 159).

Distinctions and difficulties

In their reworking of the GHS data of 1985, Parker and Lawton (1994) pointed to the need for a **longitudinal approach** to reflect carers' experiences over time and the ways in which care-giving relationships may follow different courses. Such perspectives may also assist in charting the ways in which care-giving may evolve out of informal helping relationships and the move, in either direction, from physical to personal assistance and to activities involving both types of assistance. Parker and Lawton suggested that evidence shows that those at the 'heavy end' of caring – often older carers and women providing care for a generally older group of people with illnesses or disabilities – have increased numerically from 1.76 million individuals in 1985 to 1.94 million in 1990. This is a group, on the face of it, under considerable pressure, particularly as overall service provision appeared to these researchers to be biased against co-resident carers and against those whose relatives provided care (Parker and Lawton 1994: 88). The targeting of services on those in most need may perforce exclude individuals with carers.

The homogeneity of carers is further challenged by one other element which entered professional discussions in the early 1990s and attracted policy attention more latterly. The position of children who provide care for relatives, mainly parents, was 'discovered' through local studies in the UK in Tameside, Sandwell and Liverpool, and the term 'young carers' has been used to distinguish these children from other carers and indeed other children or young people. While in most discussion and studies the experience of young carers has been seen in relation to their experience of being the main or central carer, researchers such as Gilliard (1997) have also addressed the needs of children affected by close contact with other relatives who are ill or disabled. Her studies focus on the situation of children whose older relative, generally grandparents, have dementia. In one example, 12-year-old Clare described to Gilliard her sense of injustice at having to share a bedroom now their grandmother had come to live with them. Gilliard comments 'Clare bitterly resents this intrusion into her privacy, just at a time when she particularly wants some personal space . . . Clare has turned almost overnight from being a happy young girl into a touchy, argumentative adolescent' (Gilliard 1997: 19).

Much of the research on young carers has pointed to similarities in their position with other carers, in that caring was often taken on without preparation, the individuals concerned felt there was no other option and their tasks could be many and varied (Newton and Becker 1996). None the less their position as children means that a range of other helping professionals and services may be involved, particularly education, since problems and stresses may be identified in connection with school work or attendance. Being identified as a child 'in need' through the Children Act 1989 (Section 17) may mean that appropriate assistance and support can be provided, though child care services can be perceived as threatening and stigmatizing. In striving to abide by the principle that young carers are 'children first and carers second' (Newton and Becker 1996: 37) efforts have to be made to reassure children and parents alike that professional intervention will be positive.

The challenge to carers

The National Institute for Social Work study of quality in services (Harding and Beresford 1996: 1) showed that both users and carers value:

> courtesy and respect, being treated as equals, as individuals, and as people who make their own decisions . . . workers who are experienced, well informed and reliable, able to explain things clearly and without condescension, and who 'really listen'; and . . . workers who are able to act effectively and make practical things happen.

In this respect both carers and users appear to have relatively modest demands and it would seem on the surface that good interpersonal skills alone should contribute to general achievement of high-quality services.

Why then does research and the reported experience of carers present such a generally negative picture? This section considers major challenges to providing high-quality services for carers in its portrayal of the mismatch between carers' aspirations and practitioners' interventions.

Ethnicity issues

A small number of local studies about informal care within minority ethnic communities have begun to explore the meaning of caring and the experiences of individuals. Many of them, as a critical overview of research in this area demonstrated (Butt and Mizra 1996), have pointed to similarities between carers from all backgrounds – general reports of feeling unsupported, isolated and invisible. However, out of these studies come a range of challenges to service planners because it seems that the needs of ethnic minority carers are various and 'compounded by both discrimination and the continuation of service provision geared towards meeting the needs of the white majority' (Butt and Mizra 1996: 105). The variety of needs identified include education, health promotion, information and access to services.

Many studies have referred to the impact of inadequate housing, low-paid or lack of employment, and poor incomes as adding to the stresses of caring generally. The greater likelihood of such disadvantages among ethnic minority communities means that carers' activities and emotions can be bound up with the challenges of day-to-day existence, made particularly severe if racism is perpetrated.

The **ethnocentric** nature of service provision and professional cultures has been subject to considerable scrutiny in the 1990s. A number of services have developed strategies to meet carers' needs – for example, through the provision of information, outreach services and training for staff at all levels. Specific services for families from different cultural or ethnic backgrounds have been established, particularly within the voluntary sector, often building on religious groupings' activities. Examples exist in areas of provision such as day care, luncheon clubs and meals services. In order to help access community care services, other funds have been directed to advocacy, interpreting and consultation groups. Such small-scale initiatives need to be evaluated and professional education has its part to play in challenging stereotypes and eradicating the barriers to fair and quality services. The power of stereotypes persists with three main threads commonly reported (see Box 6.7).

Box 6.7 Main stereotypes of ethnic minority carers

1 Numbers of ethnic minority carers are few. However, evidence shows that they are as prevalent, if not more so because of higher rates of illness and disability in poorer communities (Butt and Mizra, 1996).
2 Ethnic communities 'look after their own'. However, patterns of demography vary between groups; while some extended families exist, others may be nuclear and not have wide support systems (see Atkin and Rollings 1993).
3 People from ethnic minorities do not *want* services. Some may not, but the reasons for this can be that services are unresponsive, over-stretched or of low quality.

Shah (1998) provided an illustration of the impact of stereotyping in professionals' responses to Asian families who had children with learning difficulties. She reported that many workers held preconceived notions of Asian culture and beliefs which determined their responses. Misunderstandings existed and assumptions carried great weight: '. . . it is not surprising that Asian parents feel judged even before they have had their first visit' (p. 188). In Shah's experience discrimination can be overt but is more commonly concealed, subtle or a result of ignorance. Whatever the cause, the consequences can be that:

• services are unavailable or withheld;
• help is trivial or tokenistic (Shah 1998: 184).

We are only just beginning to look for the effects of different health-belief systems on the ways in which people manage their own illnesses or disabilities, or provide care to relatives. Hill and Machin (1998), for example, have argued that an understanding of 'traditional' medicine among Asian communities needs to be considered in the context of Western medicine, but that both these types of medicine are changing. For patients and professionals, but also for carers, Hill and Machin's point that 'different world views can generate intercultural incomprehension' (p. 117) is helpful in addressing the issue of differing perspectives but it may also be the case, of course, that carers and their relatives or service users hold differing views. One example, given by Hill and Machin, is that of parents who express negative views about the relevance of normalization in respect of their children with disabilities.

Communication issues

While problems regarding communication with carers are a lasting theme in the research literature, developments in work with people from minority groups illustrate the complexities of communication. More is involved than the provision of information, the availability of written material or the professional explanation. Communication with carers is a process which involves implicit decision making about the carer's place in the service professional-patient/client relationship. This is particularly challenging when the person receiving care is an adult, for here principles of autonomy and confidentiality come into play, although many young people would also argue that these are relevant to their situations.

In the UK the issue of confidentiality has assumed prominence in two areas of informal care: the rights of people with learning disabilities to sexual relationships and their protection from exploitation, and the rights of adults with severe mental health problems to confidentiality in respect of their care in the community. Both are high-risk areas: the first involving people with learning disabilities bringing in its wake concerns about vulnerability, promiscuity and eugenic threats. The second, in mental health, has recently been the focus of a series of influential inquiries into homicides committed by individuals who have been receiving psychiatric services or care in the community – for example, those involving the homicide of a carer include the Hampshire Report (Mischon 1996) and the report into the care and treatment of Norman Dunn (Keating 1997).

Common to both these areas of individual, service and public anxiety are issues about the claims of carers for information and decision making powers. In the case of men or women who wish to have sexual relationships, carers, particularly parents, have concerns about the potential for the individuals involved to be coerced into harmful or distressing relationships. From the carers' point of view professionals may use the principle of confidentiality to hide information such as the start of sexual relationships or may encourage, through adherence to 'ordinary life' principles, activities or involvement that parents find objectionable or inappropriate. While these perspectives may often be stereotyped in relation to parents in particular, the issue of confidentiality lies in competition with demands for parents to be involved and informed, consulted and communicated with in relation to aspects of daily life and major decision making. The proposals of the Law Commission (1995) – for courts to be able to appoint individuals to make decisions in respect of health care and welfare for those lacking mental capacity – look set to keep this tension alive.

Russell (1996a) has drawn attention to the needs for the parent movement, which has been particularly influential in campaigning for quality services in respect of people with learning difficulties, to work together more with groupings of people with disabilities to construct a common agenda. As she notes, parents often have high expectations and services need to negotiate with parents in order to make community care viable and effective. This will involve addressing dilemmas and conflicting views in a spirit of partnership – a term more frequently encountered in relation to the care of children than in relation to provision for adults. This idea was illustrated by one of the parents Russell interviewed: 'Parents are partners in the care of their child, they deserve respect, sensitivity. No one chooses to have a disabled child . . . you shouldn't have to break down in order to get services (1996a: 78).

Russell observed that: 'Changes in legislation and public policy only produce positive changes if they take account of the reality of family life when a child has a disability or special need and the impact that the child has on the everyday lives of those in the family (1996a: 78). Principles of confidentiality and communication become key to understanding how carers themselves negotiate with services but also with those on the receiving end of care or personal attention.

In relation to services for people with severe mental health problems, communication between professionals and welfare agencies has been centrally prescribed (for example, the *care programme approach* provides a formal structure for the exchange of information). The position of family members is more complicated. In contrast to other adult relationships within caring, relatives of individuals with severe mental health problems have rights by virtue of this relationship (see Twigg 1994) in respect of receiving information and over admission to and discharge from detention. In this context relatives have called for more involvement in the care plans or treatment of family members and, indeed, a number of professional interventions (see, for example, the initiatives described by Lefley 1996) place great importance on involving family members and addressing family interactions in order to reduce symptoms of distress.

Confidentiality and patient autonomy can sit uncomfortably with these ideas and it is no surprise that carers and professionals can be confused about the boundaries distinguishing good communication from attention to the principles of confidentiality. As one parent noted in interviews carried out to explore the differing views of carers, service users and professionals:

> it would have helped if I had been involved at an early stage when schizophrenia was diagnosed, particularly on the day when he was given the diagnosis itself. I was only told some while later when he had really retreated from talking about it. If I had known I could have said 'come on XXX, it's not the end of the world' and worked with him to find a good life. I know he's an adult, I know there is confidentiality, but he lives with me and has done for his 31 years, he is my son and I care for him . . . I could care better if I was in the know.
>
> (Shepherd *et al*. 1994: 49)

There can be, as Shepherd *et al.* observed, tension between protecting patient confidentiality and relatives' needs to know.

To what extent should family members be given details of their relatives' diagnosis and potential for harm or self-harm? Currently, the climate of concern around mental health services has provided, in the form of inquiries, accounts of professionals' actions and their thinking behind their practices. It is clear that professionals seek to maintain a balancing act between competing principles but also that these are determined by variabilities in relationships, the capacity or mental states of the individual patient or service user and perceptions of carers as actively involved in providing care. For example, in the case of Mr Francis Hampshire, who killed his wife Mrs Catherine Hampshire at their home in 1994 while he was mentally disturbed, the consultant psychiatrist's letter to the family's GP (reported in the Inquiry) after his visit to the family home said: 'I have not had the opportunity to speak to his wife, who has stated firmly that we should not ring the house because he [Mr Hampshire] believes that she is conspiring against him. Presumably her position is extremely vulnerable' (Mischon 1996: 15).

The complexities of communication and determining the needs of carers and those receiving care and treatment are part of the wider debate in policy and practice about the proper recognition of the needs and interests of those labelled 'carers'. We conclude this section with a final reference to theoretical discussion about carers and their place within service provision.

From their study of 90 carers, Twigg and Atkin (1994) argued that carers' ambiguous position within the service system – being part of the caring relationship and yet not the direct focus of service providers – led to distinctive responses by service professionals or agencies. First, they identified ideal types of carers and resources. The most commonly encountered model was where professionals saw carers as resources – they looked after their relatives well. In this model: 'Concern with carer welfare . . . is marginal or non-existent: and the potential conflict of interest between the carer and cared-for person is ignored (Twigg and Atkin 1994: 12). For services, this notion of carers as resources conveys a sense of carers reducing demand on services and the almost tangible relief of hard-pressed purchasers or providers on finding that an individual has capable, willing and accessible relatives, neighbours or friends.

Twigg and Atkin's (1994) second model of carers as co-workers moves to construct the well-being of the carer as instrumental in achieving the well-being of the disabled person. Providing assistance to the carer to enable him or her to continue this role is familiar among service-providing agencies and much debate has taken place within services about the balance of care – for example, whether a person with dementia should be greatly encouraged to enter day care in order to provide both carer and cared-for with a break. For professionals in such circumstances, devising an acceptable solution for both parties may be an important aim of their work.

The third model formulated by Twigg and Atkin (1994) considered carers as co-clients; as individuals in need of services in their own right. Here, as in the example given above of encouragement of an older confused person to take up day care, the service focus is on the carer more explicitly. The care manager may seek to reduce the carer's feelings of distress or of guilt and may enrol other professionals or carers to counsel or advise on the boundaries that can be drawn. Dimensions of the debates about carers being over-protective because of their own needs have echoes here.

Lastly, Twigg and Atkin (1994) developed a model of superseded carers in which carers' status can also be seen as that of relatives since they may reduce certain aspects of their caring roles or pass these on to others. As an example, a disabled person might move from being cared for at home by parents (carers) to more independent (of carers) accommodation with support from services at various levels. While the disabled person's parents might be involved in support in this new living arrangement, in many eyes their status may have moved from carers to relatives or parents. The fluidity of terms however is notorious but the essence of this model is that independence from carers may be seen by some professionals and agencies (as well as by disabled individuals) as a legitimate service aim that resonates with official policy targets of ordinary life and social inclusion.

Learning from carers

Finally, we draw attention to the potential for service professionals to go beyond discussions about carers' worlds to talk directly to carers. In doing so local variations in services and the maps of local resources can be given greater attention than is the case in more generalized accounts. There is, for example, likely to be substantial variation in the service world and the informal environment between rural communities and urban areas. One strategy for increasing purposive communication with carers has been to seek their contribution to skills training and to the updating of practitioners' knowledge.

Involvement in professional education was reported by members of the County Durham Service Users and Carers Forum (Town 1997) where users and carers worked collaboratively to improve and develop services. Town outlined the belief of Forum members that professionals were not all 'bad' but needed help in acquiring understanding:

> We people were also saying that if a real understanding of the needs and feelings of carers and users was ever to be appreciated by those whose job it was to make provision, these people themselves should be the ones to talk to the professionals and, surely, to participate in their training . . . we established ourselves as trainers so that we could become part of the structure within which professionals are made.
>
> (Town 1997: 140)

This approach focused on both education of current practitioners and those in training. It reflected the view that while users and carers might benefit from improved services themselves they felt an onus to act altruistically for users and carers of the future. Town (1997) also reported that their optimism about the potential for change among professionals was not universally shared by users or carers, such had been their disappointment in encounters with representatives of services in the past.

Conclusion

This chapter has explored carers' worlds and the efforts made to place these in the context of practice in community care. It is clear that carers' experiences vary and there are many distinctions between their expectations, their socioeconomic status and their relationships with people receiving care. Emphasis on carers' abilities to cope and their positive experiences has to some extent revised the problem-centred approach to carers and has required rethinking of commonplace terms such as burden and stress. The concluding discussion about practitioners' potential for learning from carers suggests that we may now be entering a period when policy makers will increasingly be challenged by carers who have reached accommodation with disabled people about shared interests and agendas. The new language of citizenship and inclusion has potential for addressing the joint needs and wishes of many carers and disabled people.

Summary

- Carers are not homogeneous. They have unique relationships, needs and resources. They have only recently been recognized by services and planners. Some argue that this recognition is only because they are cheap and committed.

- Research has often focused on carers' problems rather than their experiences in the round. Those providing community care services need to acknowledge carers' skills and experience but also have to be aware that carers may hold conflicting views from service users.

- Feminism has played an important part in understanding informal care. Attention to issues of gender needs to be accompanied by understandings of class, sexuality, ethnicity and age.

- Learning from carers can be valuable for professionals. Many are involved in efforts to develop quality services. They have useful insights into the impact of disability and illness. Professional support has the potential to assist carers who wish to continue and those who are no longer willing or able to so do.

Further reading

Beresford, B. (1994) *Positively Parents: Caring for a Severely Disabled Child*. London: Social Policy Research Unit/HMSO.

Parker, G. (1993) *With this Body: Caring and Disability in Marriage*. Buckingham: Open University Press.

Twigg, J. and Atkin, K. (1996) *Carers Perceived*. Buckingham: Open University Press.

References

Aitken, L. and Griffin, G. (1996) *Gender Issues in Elder Abuse*. London: Sage.

Arber, S. and Ginn, J. (1990) The meaning of informal care: gender and the contribution of elderly people. *Ageing and Society*, 10: 429–54.

Atkin, K. and Rollings, J. (1993) *Community Care in a Multi-Racial Britain: A Critical Review of the Literature*. London: HMSO.

Beresford, B. (1994) *Positively Parents: Caring for a Severely Disabled Child*. London: Social Policy Research Unit/HMSO.

Blumer, H. (1971) Social problems as collective behaviour. *Social Problems*, 18 (3): 298–306.

Briggs, A. and Oliver, J. (eds) (1985) *Caring: Experiences of Looking After Disabled Relatives*. London: Routledge and Kegan Paul.

Butt, J. and Mirza, K. (1996) *Social Care and Black Communities*. London: HMSO.

Carers National Association (1994) *Community Care: Just a Fairy Tale?* London: Carers National Association.

Carers National Association (1995) *Better Tomorrows?* London: Carers National Association.

Carers National Association (1997a) *Still Battling? The Carers Act One Year On*. London: Carers National Association.

Carers National Association (1997b) *In on the Act: Social Services' Experience of the First Year of the Carers Act*. London: Carers National Association.

Challis, D. and Davies, B. (1986) *Case Management in Community Care*. Aldershot: Gower.

Davies, B. (1998) Shelter-with-care and the community care reforms, in R. Jack (ed.) *Residential versus Community Care*. London: Macmillan.

DoH (Department of Health) (1989) *Caring for People: Community Care in the Next Decade and Beyond*, Cm. 849. London: HMSO.

Equal Opportunities Commission (1982a) *Who Cares for the Carers?* Manchester: EOC.

Equal Opportunities Commission (1982b) *Caring for the Elderly and Handicapped: Community Care Policies and Women's Lives*. Manchester: EOC.

Finch, J. (1984) Community care: developing non-sexist alternatives. *Critical Social Policy*, 9: 6–18.

Finch, J. and Mason, J. (1993) *Negotiating Family Responsibilities*. London: Routledge.

Gilliard, J. (1997) Between a rock and a hard place: the impact of dementia on young carers, in M. Marshall (ed.) *State of the Art in Dementia Care*. London: Centre for Policy and Ageing.

Gilligan, C. (1993) *In a Different Voice*. Cambridge, MA: Harvard University Press.

Glendinning, C. (1985) *A Single Door*. London: George Allen & Unwin.

Glendinning, C. (1992) *The Costs of Informal Care: Looking Inside the Household*. London: HMSO.

Graham, H. (1991) The concept of caring in feminist research: the case of domestic service. *Sociology*, 25 (1): 61–78.

Green, H. (1988) *General Household Survey 1985: Informal Carers*. London: HMSO.

Harding, T. and Beresford, P. (1996) *The Standards We Expect*. London: National Institute for Social Work.

Healy, J. and Yarrow, S. (1997) *Family Matters: Parents Living with Children in Old Age*. Bristol: Policy Press.

Heyman, B., Huckle, S. and Handyside, E. (1998) Freedom of the locality for people with learning difficulties, in B. Heyman (ed.) *Risk, Health and Health Care*. London: Edward Arnold.

Hill, M. and Machin, T. (1998) Race, health and risk, in B. Heyman (ed.) *Risk, Health and Health Care*. London: Edward Arnold.

Hubert, J. (1991) *Home Bound: Crisis in the Care of Young People with Severe Learning Disabilities*. London: King's Fund Centre.

Keating, D. (1997) *Report of the Independent Inquiry into the Treatment and Care of Norman Dunn*. Newcastle: Newcastle and North Tyneside Health Authority.

Law Commission (1995) *Mental Incapacity*. London: HMSO.

Lefley, H. (1996) *Family Care-giving in Mental Illness*. London: Sage.

Levin, E., Moriarty, J. and Gorbach, P. (1994) *Better for the Break*. London: National Institute for Social Work Research Unit.

Lonsdale, S. (1990) *Women and Disability*. London: Macmillan.

Manthorpe, J. (1999) Putting elder abuse on the agenda: achievements of a campaign, in M. Eastman and P. Slater (eds) *Elder Abuse: Critical Issues in Policy and Practice*. London: Age Concern.

Mischon, J. (1996) *The Hampshire Report*. London: Redbridge and Waltham Forest Health Authority.

Newton, B. and Becker, S. (1996) *Young Carers in Southwark: The Hidden Face of Community Care*. Loughborough: Young Carer Research Group, Loughborough University.

Nolan, M., Grant, G. and Keady, J. (1996) *Understanding Family Care*. Buckingham: Open University Press.

Parker, G. (1993) *With this Body: Caring and Disability in Marriage*. Buckingham: Open University Press.

Parker, G. and Lawton, D. (1994) *Different Types of Care, Different Types of Carer: Evidence from the General Household Survey*. London: HMSO.

Parker, R. (1981) Tending and social policy, in E. Goldberg and S. Hatch (eds) *A New Look at the Personal Social Services*. London: Policy Studies Institute.

Penhale, B. and Kingston, P. (1995) Social perspectives on elder abuse, in P. Kingston and B. Penhale (eds) *Family Violence and the Caring Professions*. London: Macmillan.

Rogers, A. and Pilgrim, D. (1989) Mental health and citizenship. *Critical Social Policy*, 26: 44–55.

Rose, H. and Bruce, E. (1995) Mutual care but different esteem: caring between older couples, in S. Arber and J. Ginn (eds) *Connecting Gender and Ageing*. Buckingham: Open University Press.

Russell, P. (1996a) Parents' voices: developing new approaches to family support and community development, in P. Mittler and V. Sinason (eds) *Changing Policy and Practice for People with Learning Disabilities*. London: Cassell.

Russell, P. (1996b) Short-term Care: parental perspectives, in K. Stalker (ed.) *Developments in Short-Term Care*. London: Jessica Kingsley.

Shah, R. (1998) 'He's our child and we shall always love him': mental handicap – the parents' response, in M. Allott and M. Robb (eds) *Understanding Health and Social Care*. London: Sage.

Shepherd, M., Murray, A. and Muijen, M. (1994) *Relative Values*. London: Sainsbury Centre for Mental Health.

Stalker, K. (1996) Principles, policy and practice in short-term care, in K. Stalker (ed.) *Developments in Short-Term Care*. London: Jessica Kingsley.

Town, N. (1997) The County Durham Service Users and Carers Forum. *Journal of Interpersonal Care*, 11 (2): 139–48.

Twigg, J. (1994) Carers, families, relatives: socio-legal conceptions of care-giving. *Journal of Social and Family Law*, 3: 279–98.

Twigg, J. and Atkin, K. (1996) *Carers Perceived*. Buckingham: Open University Press.

Walmsley, J. (1997) Caring in families: a case study, in M. Allott and M. Robb (eds) *Understanding Health and Social Care*. London: Sage.

Whittaker, T. (1995) Violence, gender and elder abuse: towards a feminist analysis and practice. *Journal of Gender Studies*, 4 (1): 35–45.

PROFESSIONAL DIRECTIONS

PROFESSIONS IN COMMUNITY CARE

Introduction

The history of the professions involved in health and social care is a history of change, sometimes as slow movement, sometimes as abrupt bursts; and these changes are often precipitated by changes in the machinery of provision. The 1990 National Health Service and Community Care Act (and more concretely, its implementation in 1993), constituted such a change, and may well be seen as resulting in major shifts in the roles of the professional groups involved.

In this chapter I intend to focus on the position of three professions whose work has been affected in important ways by the development of community care, and to consider what implications community care has for the continued professional functioning and identity of those three groups. The three concerned are *social work*, *nursing* and *general practice medicine*. First though I shall consider something of the present position of these professionals in social and health care, and contrast this with their historical position.

The professionals

GPs

Professional power in health care has always been located with the medical profession: 'In the health field medical dominance is a necessary feature of the professional power and superiority of the medical practitioner in relation to other occupations' (Turner 1995: 138). Medicine secured its dominance through the exercise of considerable political skill during the nineteenth century (Witz 1992) and has sustained that dominance for most of this century; certainly up to and beyond the foundation of the NHS in 1948, the final shape of which represented another success for the political skills of the medical profession (Klein 1995).

The traditional power structure in medicine and in the machinery of health care has tended to favour the hospital and the hospital-based doctor against the doctor based in the community or in other kinds of institution. In Turner's words 'the hospital is . . . symbolic of the social power of the medical profession' (1995: 153). The role of the consultant, in particular, has for many decades been one of disproportionate power and authority.

GPs have tended to see themselves as the least powerful part of the profession, despite their pivotal position in the actual delivery of health care. Prior to the 1990 reforms, primary health care and general practice medicine were the central components of the health care system, and were recognized as having been underresourced and undervalued throughout the history of the NHS. Attempts to rectify this ran up against the entrenched power of the secondary health care sector in the form of hospital-based consultants and their allies among health department officials (Klein 1995). This was compounded by the fact that prestigious technical developments in medicine during the post-war period, involving highly technology-dependent treatment and care, tended to be hospital-based and consultant controlled. Such developments inevitably emphasized an image of general practice as uninspired and unimportant by comparison.

A change of direction began in the 1960s and gained momentum with the **Alma-Ata Conference** in 1978, which shifted the emphasis back towards community health, health promotion and primary care. Also, an awareness of the effectiveness of GPs as efficient **gatekeepers** in an increasingly costly health service began to inform thinking about health care. Allsop (1995) comments that by the 1980s GPs' provision of primary care was high on the government's policy agenda. Both of these developments led to a greater appreciation of the potential importance of general practice.

Social workers

Throughout its history as a formal occupational category, social work has experienced some *ambiguity* in terms of its professional status because of the absence of an independent professional regulating body, and the consequent power of employers to define professional standards and impose these on professionals.

Social work only became a unified profession in terms of training in the early 1970s, and the pressure of the employers' agenda continued to overshadow the development of a clear professional agenda in the following decades (Sibeon 1990). For nearly all the time since the 1970s, low public esteem has been a problem for social workers, though, as Langan (1993) describes, the cause of that low esteem has been a series of widely publicized failures on the child care/child protection side of the social work remit.

Social work's negative image has not been associated to anything like the same degree with failures with the user groups who are most likely to be receiving community care. In fact, these groups – the elderly, disabled, chronically ill, those with learning disabilities and those with mental health problems – have, prior to the reforms of 1990, consistently had low priority both within social work itself (Hugman 1995) and apparently within the public sphere as a whole.

In the 1970s and 1980s social workers were less likely to specialize in working with these groups than in areas such as child protection, and much of the work of social care with these groups fell within the remit of social services employees who were not qualified social workers but had a range of backgrounds and skills.

Nurses

Nurses have, like doctors (and unlike social workers) a distinct professional boundary policed by an independent professional regulating and registration body. However, nurses are similar to social workers in that they are overwhelmingly employees rather than independent contractors like GPs. The employers most relevant to our purposes are mainly, though not exclusively, community health care trusts and GP practices.

In recent years, community nursing as a specialism has emerged from community-based nursing specialisms such as district nursing, health visiting and community psychiatric nursing, and is gaining in importance in relation to the rest of the profession, although according to Twinn *et al.* (1996) community nursing has not yet established a clear and cohesive identity.

The history of nursing has been characterized by a struggle for decades to mark out a role which does not consist of being a doctor's assistant, or an attendant (Dingwall *et al.* 1988). At different times nurses have sought to develop their role by enhancing the technical and technological demands of their work on the one hand, and the interactional and person-centred nature of their work on the other (Smith 1993). The history of the last three decades in nursing has been of movement away from a relatively hierarchical group with formalized procedures and relationships, towards a profession consisting of autonomous and self-responsible practitioners. This process has been particularly identifiable in community nursing where the practical autonomy of practitioners is less likely to be compromised than in the hospital setting (Nettleton 1995). However, the enhanced role of GPs during this period means that medical power remains a major factor – perhaps the major factor – in the politics of community nursing.

The impact of community care

Nursing

It is clear that the impact of community care has been different on each profession, in that the three professions have had to adapt to the internal market, but in rather different ways.

The arrival of the community care reforms alongside the NHS internal market served to make the community nurse's position in the care system somewhat less secure than it had been beforehand (Owens and Petch 1995). Nurses have experienced in a particularly acute way the ambiguity of the health/social care boundary, as they have had to negotiate a demarcation of tasks with social services employees whose role is in some cases not professionalized to anything like the same degree (Higgins *et al.* 1994).

There is some reason to suppose that nurses have found their role somewhat threatened by the development of the internal market in community care (see McDonald *et al.* 1997) and according to Twinn *et al.* (1996), nurses are still unsure that they have a significant contribution to make. Their professional environment has also been affected by the increasing role of fundholding GPs as purchasers of community nursing services and in some situations as employers of nurses. Nurses have tended to remain in a position where their services are being purchased, rather than where they are the purchaser, and this may be seen as perpetuating a situation where nurses are placed in a relatively passive role in relation to other professionals, and to the organizations involved.

However, this situation may well change. The Labour government elected in 1997 has expressed a clear intention of involving community nurses in the newly-created primary care groups, thereby involving them directly and extensively in commissioning alongside GPs. This holds the possibility of a significant shift towards a more active and empowered role for community nurses (Department of Health 1997).

General practice

The introduction of the internal market into the health service, creating the role of **GP fundholder** seems to have succeeded in shifting the medical centre of gravity to primary care and in making real the power and importance of the GP which previously had been largely potential. On the positive side, GP fundholders have in many cases developed a very effective purchaser/provider relationship with the secondary sector of the NHS in purchasing health care for their patients, and some GPs have been able to negotiate an improved service with NHS trusts (Glennerster 1994). However this has created some problems and strains for GPs. Two of these are especially worthy of mention.

First, the changes have produced two kinds of GP practice: fundholding and non-fundholding. There is evidence that fundholders have an advantage in accessing the resources of the rest of the NHS because of their purchaser role, creating a potentially two-tier system for patients (Bain 1994). Second, there is evidence that some GPs are very unhappy about this situation, and also about the responsibility involved in resource distribution implied in the fundholding role (Robinson and Hayter 1995; Ayres 1996). However, this situation will probably change. Proposals by the Labour government to replace fundholding with group commissioning by primary care groups, introduced in the White Paper *The New NHS* (Department of Health 1997) are evidently intended to address the problem of a two-tier system by involving all GPs in commissioning.

It is part of the fundholder's role also to purchase services from other providers where there is medical need – for example, providers of community social care, including local authorities. This presents the GP with a more complex set of interprofessional transactions – with local authorities, private providers and so on – which are less established and therefore more difficult and unpredictable than purchaser/provider transactions within the NHS. The management of these transactions to the best advantage of the user is a major challenge for GPs as a professional group.

Social work

The introduction of the '**purchaser/provider split**' system has presented challenges for social workers also. The culture of social work has in its three decades of unified existence developed largely in the context of large unitary employing organizations which have sometimes been framed as supportive to social work goals, sometimes as inimical, but always providing the context for professional practice. The move in departments towards internal purchaser/provider differentiation and the requirement to make use of the private sector outside the local authority compass have created a different relationship between social worker and the organizational context which has led to real strains in social work professional identity (Aldridge 1996).

The functions required by community care have in some cases been distributed in such a way that social workers experience a process of *deskilling* (Hadley and Clough 1996; Lewis *et al.* 1997). At the same time, many of those performing key functions in community care provision within local authorities are not members of the social work profession, and there is evidence that the ways of working characteristic of social workers and those of other social services staff show some real differences, despite a shared organizational culture (Twigg and Atkin 1994). The uncertain status and boundaries of social work have therefore been confirmed and exacerbated by community care and there is a real question as to what kind of shape practice in community care will take in the long run – whether it will reflect the values and culture of the social services department as it has developed in recent years, or the values and culture of the social work profession.

Interprofessional collaboration

Some of the demands of community care have already been identified. The most central demand, however, for members of the professions discussed, and of others, is one of collaboration. Community care by virtue of its structures and processes requires, more urgently than previous systems, that sustained and effective interprofessional collaboration and teamwork become the norm of health and social care. So nurses, social workers and GPs are required to work together in a number of different combinations, and with a number of other groups.

The requirement for this kind of work has often been referred to as 'interprofessional teamwork', though the meaning of the concept of 'team' is problematic here, and varies a good deal in accordance with context. It is generally the case that increased contact of one identifiable group with another group will impact on the culture of both groups. Experience of alternative norms offers a threat to the group's coherence which may produce a response of greater determination to maintain the cohesion of the group – accompanied perhaps by an increase in negative feelings towards the other group (Baron *et al.* 1992). However, where a group includes a distinctive minority, the presence of such a minority can enhance the performance of the group (Nemeth 1986), and may allow a greater openness to the alternative world view offered by the other group.

The kind of contact involved will have a considerable effect on the outcome of this process, as will the power relations of the groups involved and the circumstances in which the contact takes place. I shall say more about the issues of interprofessional teamwork in Chapter 8. At this point, however, I shall focus on two key aspects of professional identity that are likely to impact on interprofessional collaboration: professional knowledge-base and professional values.

Professional knowledge-base and collaboration

General practice

One of the trade marks of a profession is an identifiable knowledge-base which is transmitted through training and education, and developed and adapted through research and other modes of reflection on practice. The knowledge-base of general practice medicine has long straddled both the physical and the social domains.

Nettleton (1995) describes the GP's focus as biographic and **holistic**. However, it is rooted in the knowledge-base of the medical profession as a whole, in that all medical practitioners undertake an extensive immersion in medicine's knowledge-base before coming to focus on knowledge and skills relevant to general practice. On the other hand, the core knowledge-base of medicine is at some distance from some of the skills which GPs need to use most frequently (Turner 1995). Hence, the rooting of the general medical knowledge-base in the physical sciences (Taylor 1993) does not sit easily with the demands of general practice, involving as they do an important measure of interpersonal and social skills, and psychological, social, political and organizational knowledge.

The arrival of the internal market has placed yet greater emphasis on social knowledge, and also on managerial and economic knowledge. The skills required by all professional workers in the internal market of health care and community care – skills of negotiation and resource prioritization – are likewise distant from the skills which traditionally constitute the core of medicine. The recent changes in the legal framework of primary care create more possibilities for innovation for general practice medicine, and as part of this create more demand for reskilling and adaptation. It is not surprising that one of the most persistent concerns expressed by GPs is the inadequacy of their training for the demands of fundholding, commissioning and the internal market. There is real concern as to whether GPs are sufficiently enabled to develop their knowledge and skills in these domains.

Nursing

The knowledge-base of the nursing profession has also traditionally had a foot in both the physical and the social/psychological camps (Marriner-Tomey 1989), but the latter area has been more comprehensively developed, explored and internalized by its members than is the case with GPs. One feature of the nursing knowledge-base seems particularly important in the context of community care: a conscious emphasis on an holistic approach to user needs, which permeates a good deal of professional literature and education and impinges in a real sense on the culture of practice. This has an important ideological function as a counterweight to the **reductionism** which has traditionally been characteristic of medicine. (Taylor 1993).

The holistic approach seems appropriate to the provision of community care, which aims above all to be comprehensive. However, holism in nursing tends to be partial, in that it is individualistic. Those aspects of the individual that can be understood in the immediate context of physical and psychological existence are strongly responded to, but the wider social and political dimensions of the person are less strongly represented in nursing theory and method (Sheppard 1990). It may be that the nursing knowledge-base needs to evolve more explicitly towards the social and the political in order to equip community nurses to develop the full potential of their increasing role in community care.

Social work

The knowledge-base of social work has always been characterized by a tension between the social and the personal: knowledge derived from the social sciences – particularly sociology and social policy – on the one hand, and knowledge derived from psychology and social psychology on the other. Social work theory has sought to develop in a way that brought together the social and the individual, though most models of social work show a bias towards one or the other. Practice skills have shown a similar tension between the skills of the individual caseworker – which are derived to some extent from counselling skills – on the one hand, and the skills of the mobilizer of resources – the implementer and influencer of policy – on the other.

Before the changes of the early 1990s and the new community care policy Howe (1987) divided social work theorists into four types: the revolutionaries, the consciousness-raisers, the seekers after meaning, and the fixers (see Box 7.1). These positions involve different degrees of emphasis on the individual and the social dimensions, as well as differing positions on the political and moral agenda of social work (between ameliorating individual circumstances at one pole, and changing society at the other). The arrival of the internal market and the new community care policy raised a number of difficult questions about the social work knowledge-base. Several commentators have characterized the internal market as a manifestation of a post-modern social order which does not allow for commitment to absolute principles of any sort (Howe 1994; Parton 1994). It has been argued that relativism is the dominant mode of thinking in social work in this context (Piele and McCouat 1997), and it could be argued that a de-centring of social work theory is necessary to allow the flexibility to accommodate the unpredictable demands of the new situation, while retaining the ability to theorize. There may be a danger, however, of a non-reflective bureaucratization of practitioners in community care, already described in embryo by Lewis *et al.* (1997).

Box 7.1   Howe's four types of social work theorist

- The revolutionary
- The consciousness-raiser
- The seeker after meaning
- The fixer

Possible realignments

The significance and ownership of a knowledge-base is part of professionalism, but leads to something of a problem of professional identity in this context, as the kind of knowledge relevant to community care is characterized by overlaps and blurred boundaries between the identified territories of different professions (Nocon 1994). This raises a question as to whether there is any prospect of a realignment of professions as knowledge, skill and practice become demarcated by new boundaries.

Beattie (1995) imagines a new alignment in health care based on models of health. Many GPs would find common ground with many nurses on that basis, and may wish to part company with hospital-based colleagues. Nocon (1994), with reference to work with elderly users, comments on merging knowledge, and implies the possibility of user-group-based professional alignments.

It could be argued that there has been plenty of time during the past century for such professionals to emerge, yet they have not. In social work the opposite has happened. But then, organizational boundaries have in the past kept workers with the same user-group in separate bureaucracies, in a way that is now much less the case. Or it could be that a new professional alignment will be based on the skills and knowledge necessary for the commissioner/purchaser role, particularly initial assessment. The primary care groups envisaged by the 1997 White Paper (Department of Health 1997) may offer an opportunity for community nurses and GPs to move closer together in that respect. In all, it may be that Howe's (1994) analysis of post-modern decentring is particularly useful in reminding us that classifications of knowledge and skill should be viewed as **social constructs**. All three professions have histories of changing their knowledge-base in significant ways during their lifetime, and it may be that the social and political durability of these professions as institutions will prevail.

The demands of working together

The strains of interprofessional practice show themselves actually or potentially in all areas of professional functioning: in relation to the use of knowledge and skill; in relation to power, authority and status; in relation to political and moral values. I propose now to focus mainly on the interprofessional issues that may be identified or predicted in the last of these three areas. Community care is a redefinition of skills and necessary knowledge, and an exercise in the redistribution of power and resources, but above all it is a moral and political enterprise.

Professional values and ethics

A shared body of values and moral priorities is one of the indices of a profession, and in many respects it is these which mould the culture of the profession and its response to the demands of change in the working environment. GPs, nurses and social workers carry specific collections of moral values in their theory, practice and organizations which are likely to create conflict both between professional groups and between members of those groups and others involved in community care – for instance, managers (Wall 1995).

I have considered elsewhere the differences between the codes of ethics and knowledge-bases of social work and nursing (Wilmot 1995). A number of differences were identified, and the values of social work seemed on this evidence to be more *collectivist* and rights-based, and those of nursing more *individualist*, and based around values of care and obligation. Social work values are strongly suffused with a concern for perceived social injustices, particularly those arising from inequality of power and social value (Dominelli 1996). The machinery of state provision is seen as potentially or actually inimical to the interests of users in some situations, and a high value is placed on an activist response on the part of social workers to state bodies in that context (British Association of Social Workers 1986).

Nursing values are more concerned with valuing the position of the individual in terms of care, autonomy and rights. Nursing on the whole does not have in its code or in its literature an agenda of scepticism in relation to the political machinery of provision, or of political action. The values of general practice medicine seem to be ultimately *individually focused*, with a strong concern for the well-being of individuals and the preservation of life, and an emphasis also on the centrality of the doctor's duty to the patient (Smith and Morrissey 1994).

There is some evidence that GPs also value family obligations to patients on the part of relatives more highly than social workers or nurses (Dalley 1993; Twigg and Atkin 1994). At the same time there is a strong awareness of collective issues on the part of many GPs and a high valuation of the collectively sustained right of the citizen to free health care. In this respect GPs seem more similar to social workers in their acceptance of a political agenda as central for their professional practice.

Values of community care

The principle of community care as it has been understood for many decades is predicated on a number of broad propositions concerning duty and obligation between fellow citizens, between members of the same community and between people in a number of more specific relationships (Qureshi 1990; Spicker 1993). The policy of community care as it has taken shape since the late 1980s is also predicated on implicit or explicit moral propositions, though not always the same propositions as those of community care in the 1970s and 1980s. The language of *Caring for People* (Department of Health 1989: 4) values what is 'normal' and 'homely', speaks of people 'achieving their full potential' and having a 'greater individual say in how they live' but also implicitly values economy and family responsibility. The practice of community care is likewise based on a set of broad values concerning human good – specifically, those features that give value to daily life (Skidmore 1994).

There is a degree of diversity, even contradiction, in the moral propositions embedded in policy and practice, and in particular there is a tension between concepts of public and private responsibility (Wilmot 1997). It is not surprising, then, that implementing the policy of community care raises a number of value dilemmas which are likely to intrude into the practical business of delivering services. I shall now consider four value dilemmas that seem to be significant for community care, as follows:

1 Who has the responsibility to provide what?
2 What is the legitimate focus of professional obligation?
3 How should resources be distributed and prioritized?
4 What should be the role of the professional in this context?

Who has the responsibility to provide what?

The location and distribution of responsibility to provide care constitutes one of the major areas of potential contention in the community care system. It is clear that the expectation of the policy makers is that care commissioned by the local authority will constitute only a part of the total of care provided in the community. Most care will continue to be provided informally within the community, by neighbours and above all by families, and 'it is right that they should be able to play their part in looking after those close to them' (Department of Health 1989: 4).

The local authority has an enabling responsibility with regard to all care provided, in the sense that it is required to encourage, support and facilitate informal care arrangements as well as the provision of care from formal agencies. The policy operates in a context where, on the one hand, there is a long history of erosion of the traditional notion of family responsibility (especially the responsibility of female relatives) for the care of the needy. On the other hand, there was a clear agenda on the part of the government which introduced the policy to encourage and promote the revival of *family norms*, and *community responsibility* towards its members (Finch 1990). The distribution of responsibility between the agency of the state (in this context the local authority) and the family and community is impossible to specify because we are dealing with different kinds of responsibility, with different moral bases. However in principle the overall thrust of policy has been towards pushing as much responsibility as possible onto the family and community, and limiting that taken on by the state (Twigg and Atkin 1994).

The practical ramification of this is likely to show in situations where there is pressure on the family to provide care and that pressure cannot be eased by the professionals and may indeed be exacerbated by their intervention – where formal care is not available. This situation will create dilemmas for the professionals involved, and these will place pressure on their value systems, both professional and personal.

On this issue we can identify differences of perspective between professions, though these do not always follow a coherent pattern in terms of the responses of different individuals. There is some evidence that perspectives on family responsibility vary and that the continuum of variation represents different positions on how far it is legitimately a family responsibility to care for dependent relatives. Some evidence exists of more patterned differences, particularly in Dalley's (1993) study of professional attitudes to family care. This showed that GPs were more likely to believe that families ought to provide care, social workers were more likely to believe that the state should provide care rather than the family, and district nurses and health visitors held intermediate positions. There is a good deal of common ground between these findings and those of Twigg and Atkin (1994).

What is the legitimate focus of professional obligation?

How should professionals working in community care divide and focus their professional obligation, and the service, priority and commitment that accompanies that obligation? There are clearly a number of issues here, some of which are basic to human services in our system, others which are specifically characteristic of community care.

In the first category are questions of conflicting obligations between employer and user. Situations where the professional's sense of obligation to the user conflicts with duties as an employee are familiar in many settings and are certainly not new. However, the obligations of the professional can now be argued to be drawn in a number of other directions also. Carers have a distinct position in the structure of professional obligation – partly resulting from the development of policy, partly from the development of social and moral norms, and partly from specific legislation detailing particular rights on the part of the carer, especially in the 1995 Carers (Recognition and Services) Act. This is in itself heavily overshadowed by the extent of legal obligation to the user, but in terms of the political and moral contours of the situation, it can be argued that the carer has a legitimate claim on the professional in a number of ways (Twigg and Atkin 1994).

Another possible focus of obligation is the community. Clearly 'the community' could be a number of different things and in professional terms its definitions could stretch between a neighbourhood (and resident neighbours) at one end, to an entire town or district at the other. It could indeed be that 'community' comprises the entire population. But there is a sense in which professionals may quite reasonably see themselves as having some obligations to *a* community. If the community's participation is to be sought in the provision of care, there is a reasonable argument for a degree of reciprocity in this. A relationship between professional and community may seem a desirable thing, and such a relationship is certain to involve some expectations and obligations.

Different professions work within rather different traditions in this respect. Medicine has a strong tradition of placing obligation to the individual patient in a special category where it is protected from conflict with the claims of others – relatives or other members of the community in particular (Dalley 1993; Twigg and Atkin 1994; Dombeck 1997). Social work by contrast has a tradition of differently distributed obligations with relatives, carers and community members clearly in the frame as foci of obligation. This tradition is expressed in the often-posed question 'who is the client?' and represented in a concrete form most recently in the 1995 Carers (Recognition and Services) Act, and in practice in Twigg and Atkin's (1994) findings.

Nursing seems to stand in an intermediate position on this issue. An emphasis on cooperative and equal relationships with relatives is clearly expressed in the United Kingdom Central Council for Nursing, Midwifery and Health Visiting (UKCC) code of professional conduct (UKCC 1992), and also expresses itself in the nursing literature and in nursing practice (Wilmot 1995). But the distinction between the patient and others is generally maintained.

These differences between professions may connect with the different positions on the obligations of relatives as reported by Dalley (1993). The expectation that relatives should be seen as having a substantial responsibility perhaps sits more comfortably with a view that one's own obligation is primarily or exclusively to the patient.

Perspectives on the professional relationship to the community are less clear. Each profession encompasses a tradition of community-oriented practice. In the case of medicine, community medicine and public health medicine both focus the professional obligation with the community as an entity. In nursing, community-oriented health promotion likewise focuses the professional's obligation specifically on the collectivity of the community. In social work there is a community-oriented tradition of community social work that inhabits its boundary with community work, though according to Hillman and Mackenzie (1993) it is now somewhat marginalized. It is not clear, however, how far any of these traditions of thinking have penetrated community care practice.

How should resources be distributed and prioritized?

This is a major issue with many ramifications. Some of these are entirely under the control of higher managerial levels which are not easily influenced by individual professional practitioners. However, the policy, and resulting machinery of community care purport to have shifted the level of resource allocation decisions downwards towards the practitioner level (Meredith 1995) and this presents the professional with some dilemmas which arguably were less acutely experienced, or even not experienced at all, under the pre-1990 system.

The resource allocation role exists because there is not enough to meet all needs, and therefore something akin to rationing is necessary. On that basis there is a need to agree on a response to the rationing situation (Wall 1995). There is an issue, first, about acceptance of the situation where rationing is made necessary by a particular distribution of state (and possibly public) priorities. The need for rationing is defined and argued within the overlapping frameworks of demographics, economics, culture and politics. These definitions and arguments, though strong, are not to be confused with 'facts', in that they ultimately involve a *choice* on the part of governments and citizens and are based finally on cultural and moral priorities. Professionals whose role involves the implementing of these priorities at service delivery level may need to clarify their position on those arguments, or establish a rationale for not doing so.

Within the framework of an agreed need to ration, the criteria for rationing remain a problem. A shared and sustainable definition of need is required, with some gradations (Lightfoot 1995). A common understanding of distributive justice is required, with particular relevance to the defining and ensuring of equality of access, based on a shared definition of rights (Ungerson 1993). The importance of the prospect of effectiveness in the provision of a service needs also to be defined, and the uneven development of services where new approaches are being developed needs to be matched against the need for equality of provision. In addition, a balance needs to be agreed where these principles come into conflict with one another. This might be addressed through a formula of agreed weightings of different factors (need, utility, equality etc.), though such weightings would always be open to dispute. Or it may be addressed through the developing of a decision making algorithm which guides the *process* of decision making rather than its *content*.

The allocation of resources is a major aspect of the operation of community care, and the difficulties raised by the process of allocation are likely to evoke rather differing responses from different professions. Nursing may be the least positively oriented towards taking a role in the distribution and rationing of resources. Purchasing in the NHS, as Cole and Perides (1995) point out, is at authority level rather than practitioner level (except for fundholding GPs) and this has limited nurses' accumulation of experience in purchasing (although, as suggested earlier, this may soon change). Also, the advocate role of the nurse conflicts in a substantial way with the performance of a rationing role, and the relatively low profile of resource allocation in the traditional nursing repertoire has tended to reinforce this distancing.

The response of GPs is rather different, though in some respects also negative. It is clear that the medical profession has traditionally made decisions with a rationing element in them – particularly where treatments are seen as being insufficiently likely to be effective and therefore to be a waste of resources. However, it is also clear from discussion in recent years that the introduction of an explicit rationing role in fundholding general practice has been experienced by many GPs in a negative way because it has produced a forced and undesired change in their relationship with the patient, from unalloyed individual obligation to the maximizing of well-being of the patient population through the optimal allocation of resources (Smith and Morissey 1994; Toon 1994). It is not yet clear how, if at all, GPs are implementing a rationing role, but it is fair to say that a commitment to rationing will involve for many GPs a future change of some significance. The Labour government's proposed new arrangements will not remove this pressure, though it will redistribute it. Evidence as to what sort of principles GPs use or might use in rationing is sparse. Ayres (1996) found that GPs are concerned about efficiency, but tended to cite this as a way of *avoiding* rationing, rather than as a principle used to *apply* rationing.

Social work and the agencies of social care have a rather different history, in that the front line worker has always been involved in making assessments for services and deciding on the need for resources. Since 1993 this situation has been built upon in that some purchasing responsibilities are located at practitioner level (Cole and Perides 1995), so the rationing function is very much a part of the social work task. However, rationing takes place in a rather different context from that of medicine or nursing, in that social work agencies have a direct relationship with the local electorate which does not exist in health care. This may make it easier and more acceptable to take on a rationing role. On the other hand the political tradition in social work is more radical than in medicine or nursing, with a more explicit agenda relating to social justice and the addressing of social inequality and disadvantage, and a special remit towards disadvantaged groups in society (British Association of Social Workers 1986). As rationing invariably raises issues of justice, social workers are likely to be subject to conflicting principles on this issue.

What should be the role and status of the professional in this context?

The meaning of professional role and professional status in community care is clearly open to a good deal of discussion and review, though this is in part a continuation of the discussions on this issue that have gone on for several decades in the case of some of the professions involved, particularly nursing and social work (Wilding 1982; Abbot and Wallace 1990). Many professional characteristics serve to distance the professional from the user, carer and community, and create a disparity of power and status. This is in conflict with one of the declared principles of community care: user empowerment. It also creates dilemmas in relation to the professional values of the professional involved, all of which declare a commitment to relationships of cooperative equality with service users. The way in which professionals see themselves as responding to that disparity presents one of the most interesting professional dilemmas in community care.

Medicine, with the longest history and highest profile in the public mind, is both advantaged and disadvantaged by its position. The tradition of medicine is the most individualized and patient-centred of all three professions under consideration, and again this may create a problem in a situation where the ability to respond to context is crucial.

While nursing does not have the resource power of the fundholding GP, it also has a less proactive, critical and politically reflective stance towards the organization of care (and specifically the organizations that provide care) than social work does. Against this must be set the tradition in nursing of patient advocacy which implies a degree of distancing from employing and care-giving organizations.

The position of the professional is interesting in the community care context. A large part of what is distinctively professional – that part which depends on the exercise of special expertise and a special moral commitment – must focus on the business of assessment, and the delineation of boundaries between what can only be provided by specific practitioners and what must be provided collaboratively. There is clearly a requirement for professional expertise of various sorts in assessing need. There is also a need for adherence to a set of ethical and political principles which can render the business of assessment not only valid and reliable but also fair and humane. There is clearly an advantage in this being undertaken by professionals who are subject to a code of ethics – preferably a code which is enforceable by a professional body. The key assessors, social workers, are not in that position.

Principles for interprofessional collaboration

The final part of my discussion focuses on the way in which the different characteristics of the professional groups involved in community care might be put to best use, and in particular how differences, even conflicts, may be made sources of energy and advantage, rather than of disruption and dislocation. We may be dealing with differences of principle which concern beliefs about personal obligation; role-centred obligation (as with the obligations of family members); professional obligation; beliefs about the limitation or expansion of the role of the state; beliefs about the legitimacy or otherwise of community involvement in the lives of individuals; beliefs about individual autonomy and privacy; beliefs about justice and necessity. The management of those differences in a way that does not deny them or conceal them from the user is important.

It is not appropriate to take a completely moral relativist view of differences of opinion about conflicting professional priorities in relation to community care. Community care is among other things a political and moral enterprise, and though its goals are not agreed, there is no doubt that the policy is intended to do good in a moral sense as well as in a political and practical sense. It does matter what community care is *for*. Although it may not be possible to achieve a consensus about the goods that community care could or should achieve, it should be possible to establish an agreed sense of obligation to the user, and agreed priorities for the user's benefit.

It may be possible to achieve consensus on other commitments also. One such would be a commitment to work towards a clearer shared understanding of the goals of community care. This would imply that those involved – those who are subject to that obligation – should act in such a way that such a shared understanding is brought nearer. This both logically and practically implies certain behaviours, not least of which is a willingness to be fully cognizant of the other person's view and fully committed to understanding that view. This immediately has implications for the way in which interprofessional dialogue is conducted, and implies a set of ground rules for this process. There are situations where such ground rules could usefully be made explicit – for instance, in the context of a multi-professional team.

Having argued that complete **moral relativism** is not appropriate, there is a good argument for adopting a framework of pluralism around the issues we are dealing with (by pluralism I mean a view that differences of perspective should be accepted, but that it is worth attempting to find some shared principles). The shared principle which I am suggesting rests on differences of perspective between professionals, and states that the achievement of a consensus about the desirable goods of community care is not necessarily in itself a desirable good. There are strong arguments in favour of *not* insisting on consensus, certainly not consensus for its own sake. Areas of disgreement bring a number of benefits. They allow a diversity of views and therefore allow for adaptation and creativity. They enhance autonomy. In particular, a diversity of perspectives among professionals, where properly managed, enhances the autonomy of the user. Users who are faced with a monolithic unity of perspective from all the professionals involved run the risk of being disempowered and alienated. In a situation where professional practices reflect differing perspectives and world views the user has a better prospect of experiencing some validation for their own perspective.

There are identifiable principles that underpin such a relationship of interprofessional pluralism. One set of principles is presented by Dombeck

(1997), who argues for the development of a shared culture and mythology based on the exchanging of 'stories' between members of different professions. The importance of such a shared culture is not that it creates consensus but that it provides an agreed way of dealing with disagreement. What particular ways might be adopted will depend on circumstances.

Habermas (1991) provides a rationale and a set of principles by which communication between people adhering to differing values can be conducted in a way that accepts real moral difference while containing the relationship in an over-arching structure. On a more detailed level, Schreier and Groeben (1996) offer a set of principles for dealing with difference in a way that preserves both the integrity of participants and the integrity of the social structure containing the differences. These and other collaborative models can easily be dismissed as extolling virtues which are easy to recognize in theory but impossible to practise. Any collaborative model which has a real effect on the way professionals interact will clearly make demands on the people concerned, and require the development of new skills. New skills require training, and training requires time and resources. So the management of interprofessional difference must take its place in the queue for resources. The danger, and perhaps the likelihood, is that it will go to the back of the queue.

Conclusion

The professions under discussion have recent histories characterized by change – in the main, change imposed from without, generally by government. The ability to influence and steer those changes varies from profession to profession, but all three have in different ways experienced a sense of being marginalized in relation to more powerful groups. The arrival of post-1990 community care has presented both dangers and opportunities to all three professions. The greatest opportunities have probably been experienced by GPs, and the greatest dangers by nurses. The ability to adapt to the changes resulting from the reform of community care is as important as the ability to influence those changes, and an important part of adaptation is the ability to collaborate. The skills of collaboration are in many ways very similar to the skills of adaptation, and the flexibility and creativity required for both are thereby crucial parts of the professional repertoire. It is clear from the plans of the post-1997 Labour government that further threats and opportunities await, possibly rather differently distributed, but requiring the same skills and qualities in response.

Summary

- This chapter introduced the three professions under discussion – nursing, social work and general practice medicine – and considered their position and recent history.

- The implications of community care for each of these professions was explored, and it was suggested that nurses have the most uncertain position in the present situation, though this may well change in the context of planned changes in the NHS.

- Issues of interprofessional collaboration were considered, and the implications of differences in professional knowledge-base and values were explored between the three professions under discussion.

- Four value issues of potential disagreement between the professions were explored. These relate to responsibility for provision, the legitimate focus of professional obligation, the distribution and prioritization of resources, and the role and power of the professional.

- Possible principles for interprofessional collaboration were considered. These relate particularly to the management of interprofessional differences and disagreements which, it was suggested, can be positive and helpful if appropriately managed.

Further reading

Owens, P., Carrier, J. and Horder, J. (1995) *Interprofessional Issues in Community and Primary Health Care.* London: Macmillan.
Soothill, K., Mackay, L. and Webb, C. (1995) *Interprofessional Relations in Health Care.* London: Edward Arnold.

References

Abbott, P. and Wallace, C. (1990) *The Sociology of the Caring Professions.* London: Falmer Press.
Aldridge, M. (1996) Dragged to market: being a professional in the postmodern world. *British Journal of Social Work*, 26: 177–94.
Allsop, J. (1995) Shifting spheres of opportunity: the professional powers of general practitioners within the British National Health Service, in T. Johnson, G. Larkin and M. Saks (eds) *Health Professions and the State in Europe.* London: Routledge.
Ayres, P. (1996) Rationing health care: views from general practice. *Social Science and Medicine*, 42: 1021–5.
Bain, J. (1994) Fundholding: a two tier system? *British Medical Journal*, 309: 396–9.
Baron, R., Kerr, N. and Miller, N. (1992) *Group Process, Group Decision, Group Action.* Buckingham: Open University Press.
Beattie, A. (1995) War and peace among the health tribes, in K. Soothill, L. Mackay and C. Webb (eds) *Interprofessional Relations in Health Care.* London: Edward Arnold.
British Association of Social Workers (1986) *A Code of Ethics for Social Work.* Birmingham: BASW.
Cole, R. and Perides, M. (1995) Managing values and organisational climate in an interprofessional setting, in K. Soothill, L. Mackay and C. Webb (eds) *Interprofessional Relations in Health Care.* London: Edward Arnold.
Dalley, G. (1993) Professional ideology or organisational tribalism? The health service-social work divide, in J. Walmsley (ed.) *Health, Welfare and Practice.* London: Sage.

Department of Health (1989) *Caring for People: Community Care in the Next Decade and Beyond*, Cm. 849. London: HMSO.

Department of Health (1997) *The New NHS: Modern, Dependable*. London: HMSO.

Dingwall, R., Rafferty, A. and Webster, C. (1988) *An Introduction to the Social History of Nursing*. London: Routledge.

Dombeck, M-T. (1997) Professional personhood: training, territoriality and tolerance. *Journal of Interprofessional Care*, 11: 9–21.

Dominelli, L. (1996) Deprofessionalising social work: anti-oppressive practice, competencies and postmodernism. *British Journal of Social Work*, 26: 153–76.

Finch, J. (1990) The politics of community care in Britain, in C. Ungerson (ed.) *Gender and Caring*. London: Harvester Wheatsheaf.

Glennerster, H. (1994) *Implementing GP Fundholding: Wild Card or Winning Hand?* Buckingham: Open University Press.

Habermas, J. (1991) *Communication and the Evolution of Society*. Cambridge: Polity Press.

Hadley, R. and Clough, R. (1996) *Care in Chaos: Frustration and Challenge in Community Care*. London: Cassell.

Higgins, R., Oldman, C. and Hunter, D. (1994) Working together: lessons for collaboration between health and social services. *Health and Social Care in the Community*, 2: 269–77.

Hillman, J. and Mackenzie, M. (1993) *Understanding Field Social Work*. Birmingham: Venture.

Howe, D. (1987) *An Introduction to Social Work Theory*. Aldershot: Wildwood House.

Howe, D. (1994) Modernity, postmodernity and social work. *British Journal of Social Work*, 24: 513–32.

Hugman, R. (1995) Contested territory and community services: interprofessional boundaries in health and social care, in K. Soothill, L. Mackay and C. Webb (eds) *Interprofessional Relations in Health Care*. London: Edward Arnold.

Klein, R. (1995) *The New Politics of the NHS*, 2nd edn. London: Longman.

Langan, M. (1993) New directions in social work, in J.A. Clarke (ed.) *Crisis in Care?* London: Sage.

Lewis, J., Bernstock, P., Bovell, V. and Wookey, F. (1997) Implementing care management: issues in relation to the new community care. *British Journal of Social Work*, 27: 5–24.

Lightfoot, J. (1995) Identifying need and setting priorities: issues of theory, policy and practice. *Health and Social Care in the Community*, 3: 105–14.

McDonald, A., Langford, I. and Boldero, N. (1997) The future of community nursing in the United Kingdom. *Journal of Advanced Nursing*, 26: 257–65.

Marriner-Tomey, A. (1989) *Nursing Theorists and their Work*. St Louis, MI: Mosby.

Meredith, B. (1995) *The Community Care Handbook: The Reformed System Explained*, 2nd edn. London: Age Concern.

Nemeth, C.J. (1986) Differential contributions of majority and minority influence. *Psychological Review*, 93: 23–32.

Nettleton, S. (1995) *The Sociology of Health and Illness*. Cambridge: Polity Press.

Nocon, A. (1994) *Collaboration in Community Care in the 1990s*. Sunderland: Business Education Publishers Ltd.

Owens, P. and Petch, H. (1995) Professionals and management, in P. Owens, J. Carrier and J. Horder (eds) *Interprofessional Issues in Community and Primary Health Care*. London: Macmillan.

Parton, N. (1994) Problematics of government, (post)modernity and social work. *British Journal of Social Work*, 24: 9–32.

Piele, C. and McCouat, M. (1997) The rise of relativism: the future of theory and knowledge development in social work. *British Journal of Social Work*, 27: 343–60.

Qureshi, H. (1990) Boundaries between formal and informal care-giving work, in C. Ungerson (ed.) *Gender and Caring*. London: Harvester Wheatsheaf.

Robinson, R. and Hayter, P. (1995) Reluctance of general practitioners to become fundholders. *British Medical Journal*, 311: 166.

Schreier, M. and Groeben, N. (1996) Ethical guidelines for the conduct in argumentative discussions: an exploratory study. *Human Relations*, 49: 123–32.

Sheppard, M. (1990) Social work and community psychiatric nursing, in P. Abbott and C. Wallace (eds) *The Sociology of the Caring Professions*. London: Falmer Press.

Sibeon, R. (1990) Social work knowledge, social actors, and de-professionalisation, in P. Abbott and C. Wallace (eds) *The Sociology of the Caring Professions*. London: Falmer Press.

Skidmore, D. (1994) *The Ideology of Community Care*. London: Chapman & Hall.

Smith, L. and Morrissey, J. (1994) Ethical dilemmas for general practitioners under the UK new contract. *Journal of Medical Ethics*, 20: 175–80.

Smith, P. (1993) Nursing as an occupation, in S. Taylor and D. Field (eds) *Sociology of Health and Health Care*. Oxford: Blackwell.

Spicker, P. (1993) Needs as claims. *Social Policy and Administration*, 27: 7–17.

Taylor, S. (1993) Approaches to health and health care, in S. Taylor and D. Field (eds) *Sociology of Health and Health Care*. Oxford: Blackwell.

Toon, P. (1994) Justice for gatekeepers. *Lancet*, 343: 585–7.

Turner, B. (1995) *Medical Power and Social Knowledge*. London: Sage.

Twigg, J. and Atkin, K. (1994) *Carers Perceived: Policy and Practice in Informal Care*. Buckingham: Open University Press.

Twinn, S., Roberts, B. and Andrews, S. (1996) *Community Health Care Nursing*. Oxford: Butterworth Heinemann.

Ungerson, C. (1993) Caring and citizenship: a complex relationship, in J. Bornat, C. Pereira, D. Pilgrim and F. Williams (eds) *Community Care: A Reader*. Basingstoke: Macmillan.

United Kingdom Central Council for Nursing, Midwifery and Health Visiting (1992) *Code of Professional Conduct for the Nurse, Midwife and Health Visitor*, 3rd edn. London: UKCC.

Wall, A. (1995) Ethical and resource issues in health and social care, in P. Owens, J. Carrier and J. Horder (eds) *Interprofessional Issues in Community and Primary Health Care*. London: Macmillan.

Wilding, P. (1982) *Professional Power and Social Welfare*. London: Routledge and Kegan Paul.

Wilmot, S. (1995) Professional values and interprofessional dialogue. *Journal of Interprofessional Care*, 9: 257–66.

Wilmot, S. (1997) *The Ethics of Community Care*. London: Cassell.

Witz, A. (1992) *Professions and Patriarchy*. London: Routledge.

TEAMS IN COMMUNITY CARE

Introduction

If the distinctive characteristics of different professions in community
care are to be combined in the most effective way, the context in which
that combination will be achieved is the team. The team constitutes the
smallest unit of coordinated service delivery in which the combined social
and health care needs of users can have some prospect of being met. It is
also the unit of delivery which has enjoyed the greatest concentration of
attention and aspiration in the literature on community care in recent
years. The government which introduced the legislation creating the present
system of community care clearly saw the team as a crucial component in
the planned system – and that importance has not diminished. 'Working
together' is a phrase which has come to express an almost unquestioned
good in the culture of the caring professions engaged in community care,
and the importance given to the team idea is probably not unrealistic.
The management of service delivery at higher levels in organizations such
as social services departments and NHS trusts cannot be effective if the
team is not effective. Much is hoped of the team. Can it deliver?

What is a team?

The first requirement in exploring this issue is a working definition of the team. This is not entirely straightforward as Engel (1994) points out. WHO's definition of a health team (quoted by Engel) places some emphasis on the proposition that the team is among other things a group, and arguably the dynamics of the team can be understood in large part in group terms. However, other views provide a very different perspective.

If we look at Øvretveit's (1993) discussion of team structures, we see a rather different picture. The range of team structures runs from the established, traditional working group – operating in physical proximity to one another and with a consistent and inclusive management structure – at one end of the spectrum, to the 'client team' – a temporary assembly of workers involved in helping one user – at the other. The latter situation may not require any communication involving the whole team, or any face-to-face interaction involving all members. As a social and organizational unit it is clearly very far removed indeed from the traditional team, and it fails also on many definitions of a group.

So, can a team still be a team if it is not a group? If it cannot, we are left with something of a problem in defining and understanding working arrangements of the sort discussed by Øvretveit (1993). If it is not a team, what is it? The problem is compounded by the fact that Øvretveit's discussion covers a spectrum of different combinations of people – the two models of the traditional team and the 'client team' are in fact the extremes of a spectrum of closely graduated variations. The problem is not only one of deciding whether the 'client team' is a team, but also of deciding where on that spectrum we can place a line that divides the team from the non-team.

One approach to the problem is to be more precise about the meaning of the term 'group' than I have been so far. There are clearly different ways of using the term. I can use 'group' as a collective noun, merely indicating that I am talking about more than two individuals within one frame of reference, and not asserting or implying anything about their interaction or relationship. Or I can use the term to refer to a social unit of great complexity, and imply a good deal about interactions and relationships. More specifically, the social unit I am referring to is likely (though not certain) to be the **'small group'** with an even more specific constellation of characteristics, reviewed comprehensively by many writers, including Baron *et al.* (1992) and Johnson and Johnson (1987).

There is no problem in saying that the team is a group in the first sense of 'group' or 'small group'. Clearly a team consists of several people. The problem arises if we try to equate the team with the definition of 'small group' as a well-specified social unit. There is a point on Øvretveit's (1993) spectrum of different team arrangements where the team ceases to be a group of that sort. It is certainly hard to see how some client teams can function as social units of the 'small group' kind.

However, the client team is more than a collective noun. It is considerably more than a collective way of referring to those people who have a direct delivery role in the community care provision for one user. The client team is characterized also by coordination and complementarity. This is to some degree a characteristic of small groups, though their coordination may be of an informal kind, and may be a completely unconscious pattern of their members' behaviour. Team coordination is likely to be more explicit and conscious, even though the team may be very ungrouplike in other ways. If I employ a 'team' of craftsmen to work on my house, but they have no contact with one another and no opportunity to coordinate their work other than through my instructions, those craftsmen none the less constitute a team by that definition.

This does not mean that coordination can be equated exclusively with team-ness. Coordination is clearly important in community care as in many other activities, but it is also a characteristic of *most* human activities. In terms of the factors that regulate the output of individual contributors, there is not one single intellectual framework that allows us to understand all coordinated activity. Economics, politics, organization theory, individual and social psychology all provide frameworks for understanding coordinated activity. 'Teamwork' as an intellectual framework can apply to any of these areas, but it will only effectively explain parts, often small parts, of what we see. We cannot just define the team as coordinated people and leave it at that. Such a definition stretches the word 'team' until it becomes useless.

In fact, teams in community care generally have *some* of the characteristics of groups (more often than not, small groups) even where they do not have *all* their characteristics. For instance in Øvretveit's (1993) classification, even in the client team coordination for each individual member is accompanied by communication with at least one other team member, and also by awareness that a team exists, and that one has a role in it, and of who the other members are. This is clearly a very weak version of the 'small group' of social psychology, but it bears a family resemblance to that small group. It is perhaps no accident that some of those who seek to identify what makes teams effective tend to highlight small group-like characteristics very prominently. This is apparent in the case of Belbin (1993). So I suggest that the small group provides a framework for understanding much of that form of coordinated activity known as teamwork. As a framework it does not explain all coordinated activities involving small collections of people, but it explains a good deal. I propose therefore to consider the relevance of small group theory to the functioning of the interprofessional team.

Small groups working

There is clearly a practical rationale in combining a range of different kinds of expertise in a complementary social system. However there is still a question as to whether people actually work more effectively in small groups than they work in other arrangements. One of the most basic arguments in favour of teamwork of any description is that people function better in a group: they perform better as individuals when they are accountable to a group, and they make better decisions when making them as part of a group. This has been variously explained by the stimulant effect of the proximity of members of our own species (Zajonc 1965); by the anxiety created by being observed (Cottrell 1972); and by conflict between desire to attend to the task and desire to attend to the other members (Baron *et al.* 1992).

In fact, the research evidence suggests that group membership only enhances performance in certain kinds of tasks – generally simpler tasks. There is some evidence that group membership depresses performance in more complex tasks (Bond and Titus 1983). This is not surprising. If we are aroused by the presence of our team-mates, the degree of that arousal will determine whether it enhances or depresses our performance. We know that while arousal up to a given level has an enhancing effect on performance, beyond that level its effect is depressive. A number of factors have been identified which slow down the performance of the group in performing tasks that many or all the group's members are individually well capable of performing. So the group is not an unmixed blessing. We can be sure only that the group will have an impact on the behaviour of its members, but we cannot be sure whether that will be positive or negative in terms of quality of task performance.

Key features of groups which affect teamwork

There are several areas where the dynamic of the group is likely to be relevant to the team. One is that of group norms. Every group that interacts becomes a small social sub-system in its own right, and as part of that process it develops its own norms of behaviour which may be slightly, or significantly, at variance with the social norms in the group's environment. The group's norms will mould the behaviour of its members while they are in contact with one another. In the team context this clearly has a good deal of significance for the way the team operates. However much team members stimulate one another by their presence, if team norms are inimical to effective practice, the stimulant effect will be counterbalanced by the team's norms. This is illustrated by one of the pioneers of small group research, Sherif (1936), who found that group pressure can lead a group member to literally deny the evidence of their senses and agree (with apparent sincerity) to propositions which they would normally see as palpably untrue. In the context of the interprofessional team, the team's norms with regard to interactions between members of different professions will be a crucial aspect of the functioning of the team.

Another main feature of small groups which seems to be sufficiently fundamental to apply generally to teams is the predisposition for group members to perform complementary roles, and the impact of these roles on group functioning. One of the earliest investigators to identify specific functional roles in small groups was Bales (1950), whose system included such roles as information seeker and active listener. Hare (1994) reviews a number of different collections of roles subsequently identified by different researchers. In many cases these role systems show some similarity to each other, though others are more distinctive. It seems that groups tend to propel their members into several kinds of role complementarity, and that a wide and flexible distribution of roles enhances group performance. The distribution of group roles among individual members becomes particularly relevant when we consider the interprofessional team, where the professional role might have some effect on the roles performed by an individual in the team. That, of course, would depend also on group norms, and the kind of pattern of expectations that the team creates.

The interaction of norms and roles also helps to shape the functioning of the group in a number of other ways. Power distribution in the group reflects both norms and roles. Johnson and Johnson (1987) have identified a number of distinctive sources of power and kinds of power in the group context: reward power, coercive power, referent power (based on personal ability to gain the respect and compliance of other members), expert power, information power, and legitimate power (based on the 'legitimacy' in the wider society of that individual's power). The importance of power distribution in teamwork clearly cannot be underestimated – even more so when applied to interprofessional teamwork.

The differing sources of power identifiable in a team may bear some relationship to the skills and status of different professions. There is some evidence of a power differential between different professions which shows itself in some ways in the team. This is illustrated by Dombeck (1997: 12) who says that 'very often in team situations the physician assumes the responsibility for leadership and other team members collude with this decision'. We might suspect that the physician's behaviour in this context is often an exercise of 'legitimate' power – power based on the status of that group member in the world outside the group. The response of the other members might suggest the same. The distribution of different sources of power between the members of an interprofessional team is a promising area of study.

However, there are more fundamental power issues in society at large which show themselves within the team – for instance, gender-based inequality. West and Field (1995) refer to evidence of male team members ignoring the contributions of female members in the team context, thereby importing an external power differential into the team process. It is clear from small group research over several decades, and from team research over a shorter period, that effectiveness in task performance is closely associated with an equal distribution of power in the group (Johnson and Johnson 1987; Brooks 1994; Sessa and Jackson 1995). Though power clearly can have many sources, there is a strong accumulation of evidence that skewed unequal distribution will depress a group's performance.

The norms of communication in the group – who transmits what information to whom; how information is dealt with by the group – are likely to be of central importance in the team context. It is clear that patterns of communication in small groups are shaped by complex processes. Stasser and Titus (1985) found that information held by particular group members may or may not be shared with the rest of the group, depending on how that information relates to the emerging preferences of the group. The supposition that all information relevant to the group's tasks will automatically be exchanged seems to be overoptimistic. Despite the power potential of useful information, group members may well not share it. This is clearly of fundamental importance to teamwork, where a free flow of information seems to be essential.

The flow of information must clearly also be affected by the norms that influence which group members exchange information when all members are not accessible, as outlined by Handy (1993). How far information is routed through one individual and disseminated by that individual (Handy's 'wheel' system), and how far it is transmitted person to person (Handy's 'circle'), or in an open exchange connecting all members with one another (Handy's 'web') again has a considerable influence on the team's shared information base, as well as on the team's ability to deal with particular problems. Handy reports, for instance, that the 'wheel' is quicker and more efficient than the 'circle' or the 'web', but that the web is better at solving complex, open-ended problems.

Decision making in groups

The group's norms of power distribution and information distribution come together in the group's norms of decision making, which are clearly going to be of importance to the quality of the group's **output**. The group's ability to make use of all available information and expertise, including minority as well as majority views is part of what makes group decision making potentially more effective than individual decision making (Nemeth 1986; Van Dyne and Saavedra 1996).

However, this depends on the group's ability to value appropriately the contributions of group members to the decision making process, and this is in turn affected by issues of power and status within the group. Unsurprisingly, disagreements tend to be resolved on the basis that those with most power prevail, but this is not exclusively the case. Where the group is divided between minority and majority, minorities have a better prospect of influencing members of the majority in those members' private individual thoughts than in their public behaviour and statements. Where minorities are able to express their position consistently, they are often able to sway a group decision (Gebhardt and Meyers 1995). This may speak optimistically of group capacities to produce good-quality decisions. However, other factors may work in the opposite direction.

The phenomenon of 'groupthink', identified by Janis (1968), appears to propel groups towards risky and ill-considered decisions based on partial attention to facts and analysis in situations where all members of such a group would be capable of making much better-quality decisions as individuals. Groupthink involves the development of risk-taking norms in the group, alongside a collusive exclusion of evidence or arguments that might place the group's preferred course of action into question. High-risk decisions result from this process. There is evidence to support the existence of groupthink – though other factors such as leadership, time pressure and decision making procedures seem to have an effect also (Neck and Moorhead 1995; Mohamed and Wiebe 1996) – and it must be seen as a question mark over the advantages of group decision making.

Teams working

The study of the team in its own right, as a distinct entity (as against the small group as a more general category) presents some specific challenges in terms of research. The most salient of these, arguably, is the question as to what aspects of team functioning can most usefully be measured. Zeiss *et al.* (1997) argue that there is a tension between focus on team output, team process and team structure. Accurate observation and measurement of team process is clearly not easy, but, they argue, instruments have been developed to do aspects of this.

In health and social care, *output* is not easy to measure either, because health and social care are concerned primarily with issues of well-being and empowerment. Two major studies of the team in the past 20 years have chosen different types of output as their focus: task performance in the case of Belbin (1981, 1993), and innovation in the case of West and his various collaborators (e.g. West and Altink 1996). Each has sought to relate aspects of team structure and process to the chosen output. In Belbin's case the distribution of team roles was the focus; in West's case, the team climate.

Belbin's (1981, 1993) work sought to identify specific complementary team roles, the performance of which enhances the team's output. He identified these roles through the use of team exercises and the factor analysis of team members' perceptions of their own and other team members' performance. The roles – nine in the most recent version – are: coordinator, plant, resource investigator, shaper, monitor-evaluator, teamworker, completer-finisher, implementer and specialist. These have been widely adopted in management practice, along with Belbin's assessment instrument. Belbin suggests that the achievement of a full repertoire of roles by the team may depend on the kind of people who are included in the team.

The performance of the identified roles is not something that is necessarily completely exchangeable, as it is in, for instance, Bales' (1950) roles, where the important thing is that somebody performs each role. In Belbin's system different individuals are better suited to specific roles, and therefore the most effective team is one that includes individuals with the full range of role predispositions. The validity of Belbin's methods in identifying roles has been questioned by several writers (e.g. Dulewicz 1995) but he has also received validation from other researchers (e.g. Senior 1997). Other workers in the field have also come up with lists of team roles (e.g. Woodcock 1989) but none, as yet, as influential as Belbin.

Factors which influence performance

Anderson and West (1996) developed a list of team and organizational characteristics which, if present, should maximize performance and, particularly, should maximize the team's ability to be innovative. The list is constructed around five superordinate scales: participative safety, support for innovation, vision, task orientation and social desirability. These have been subjected to testing in several countries, a process which is ongoing at the time of writing. This work is particularly relevant to community care in that West and his various collaborators have done much of their work in health care, and are especially interested in teams in primary health care, involving personnel and activities closely allied to those of community care. As part of this work, West has recently taken account of the relationship between professional groups in the team context, and identified a number of processes and issues around this – most saliently that professional difference interacts with gender difference to create a major obstacle to team effectiveness. West also gives extensive attention to the organizational context of the team, and identifies a number of factors in the team-organization relationship which impact on the team's performance (West and Altink 1996; West 1997).

Other investigators have variously focused on roles or norms, in some cases both. Many of the instruments used in measuring team functioning are adaptations of those developed originally for the study of small groups (e.g. Bales 1950). However, there has been a good deal of effort devoted to developing a wider range of instruments for measuring team performance and explaining variations therein. Zeiss *et al.* (1997) reviewed the instruments of team evaluation identifiable in the literature and concluded that, while a range of instruments have been developed, focusing variously on team process, team structure and team task achievement, there is still a dearth of evaluation instruments in certain areas, particularly in relation to team-organization interaction, and in terms of task achievement.

Teams in community care

The team in community care has specific characteristics which make it distinctive. First, it is very likely to be interprofessional, and to include within its processes a range of interprofessional issues. Second, it may well be interorganizational, and be affected by issues arising between the organizations who employ its members. Third, its structure may limit its functioning as a group, in that it may have a very short life span, and may also not involve much face-to-face contact between team members (Øvretveit 1993).

Interprofessional teams

The first issue for the team, of interprofessionality, inevitably involves our discussion overlapping with that of Chapter 7. Professions differ in their cultures in a number of ways, and these differences are likely to have some impact on the behaviour of team members. It is clear from the work of West (1997) that interprofessional differences can present a major difficulty to the team. It is also clear from other sources that the cultures and histories of nursing and social work, for instance, are distinctively different, and that this will have an effect on values, priorities and models of working (Beattie 1995). There is evidence of differences in moral priorities and values between the two professions – for instance, in relation to family responsibilities and state involvement (Dalley 1993). Nursing and social work also have different ideologies regarding the role of the professional in relation to society, to formal organizations and to the user.

Social work is more context oriented, and also more inclined to frame the political and social order as problematic (Wilmot 1995). This may have implications for the team members preferred relationship with employing organizations, and for their response to a number of other issues. There are also differences in knowledge-base, and in the language and perspectives that go with different theoretical underpinnings. There are different norms in relation to organizational relationships, particularly to managerial authority and power. Some of these present real challenges to the ability of the team to function effectively. In another sense, however, it is precisely these differences which make teamwork worthwhile. Some differences are necessary to the team if they can be appropriately mobilized. It is likely that diversity, and specifically multidisciplinarity, will enhance the performance of the team, if Nemeth's thesis that the presence of a minority in a group can improve performance by encouraging divergent thinking is correct (Nemeth 1986; Hellkamp 1996). It appears from West's (1997) evidence that the positive potential presented by difference is not always realized in primary care, and it is unlikely that community care will be any better in this respect.

We need, then, to consider what kind of relationships and processes in the team might optimize interprofessional working. Allport (1954) argued that relationships will benefit from contact; where members of different groups are working together, in regular close interdependent contact with one another, there will be a tendency for each group's perception of the other to become more positive. However, contact on its own is not sufficient. Specific conditions need to obtain before the contact has a positive effect. The conditions are: that power relationships between members of two groups should be roughly equal; that egalitarian norms prevail; and that groups should be engaged in shared activities that involve a valued output. So, unequal power will not help to develop positive interprofessional relationships.

Iles and Auluck (1990) applied this principle to interprofessional relationships in health and social care. We may suspect a link here to West's (1997) finding in relation to interprofessional problems complicated by gender issues. We know from the history of professions involved in health and social care that power and gender are closely linked to interprofessional conflict (Witz 1992). However, this cannot always be the case. The profession which most often has an unequal allocation of power – the medical profession – is certainly male dominated but, in general practice in particular, that numerical domination is diminishing so a simple gender/ power analysis of interprofessional problems will not work in all cases. It can be argued that the norms, values and practices of different professions reflect gender differences when these are not completely reflected in numbers – e.g. that medicine is more 'masculine' in its *norms* than nursing or social work – but the degree to which that necessarily produces conflict rather than complementarity is less clear. Allport's third condition for positive contact – for professionals to work together on real, non-trivial goals – makes sense in relation to the building of relationships of mutual respect, though there is clearly also the potential for real conflict as well as real achievement in those situations. What is clear is that the 'luncheon club' kind of interaction where members of different professions meet in a semi-social way to 'get to know each other' is not effective in achieving what is required.

The interprofessional dimension is not the only one of significance in the community care team. Equally characteristic of the team is that it often includes members who do not identify with any professional group, whose skills have not been either acquired or sanctioned by such identification. Workers in roles concerned with domiciliary services are not infrequently in this position. Clearly this must have a significant impact on the functioning of the team. As yet there is relatively little evidence concerning the contribution of people without a conventional professional designation to team functioning and team output.

However, some characteristics can be identified reasonably readily (Raelin 1994). First, team members without a specific professional designation are more likely to identify with the goals, values and norms of the organization which employs them. Their role as employee is likely to be a more important part of their identity, and a more important focus of commitment than will be case with people who were socialized into a professional identity before – and perhaps long before – they became involved in a particular care practice. What is less clear is how far workers in this position are likely to identify with the specific goals and culture of their team. What might the dynamics be here? There is some evidence that workers with a professional affiliation are more independent of the norms and goals of their employer than are those without (Raelin 1994). However, the goals and norms of the team may well not reflect those of the team members' employer. Teams are to some degree their own social system. It could be that professionals find it easier to identify with the goals of the team where these are not simply a reflection of the goals of the employing organization. It could be that workers without a professional identification find this more difficult. On the other hand intra-team conflict centring around conflicting professional norms, language or knowledge will presumably be less engaging for team members who do not identify with a profession (Twigg and Atkin 1994).

Teams and organizations

The relationship of the team to the organization is of crucial importance to its functioning as a unit of service delivery. Since the early days of team theory the organization's ability to provide an appropriate environment for the team to function, and at the same time to contain its functioning within the requirements of the organization, has been a major concern.

Homans (1951) offered a model of the team's position within the organization which highlights the potential for conflict between team and organization. The issue of the team's predisposition to express and implement the goals of the organization remains a major focus, but perspectives have moved somewhat and the relationship between team and organization is now seen by some writers as a dialectical one, involving appropriate tension and conflict. West (1997) argues that one indication of an effective team is that it can challenge the organization within which it operates. This does not imply that the team should disrupt the work of the organization, but rather that it should be a source of perspectives, behaviour and possibilities which constantly question the goals and operation of the organization, enabling the organization to respond to feedback and review its goals. The tension, in other words, is a creative one, and the relationship is dynamic.

In community care, there seem to be good arguments for encouraging teams to enter into this kind of relationship with the organizations that encompass them. The nature of community care as an activity, its professional, political and moral ambiguities and the economic and social agendas that run alongside it, all speak in favour of a culture where goals and methods are debated and reviewed, and where there is an open dialogue between the front line and the centre, involving real conflicts and contradictions of perspective.

Interorganizational teams

The nature of community care also injects another complication. Teams are often not only interprofessional but interorganizational: their affiliation and accountability connects them with more than one organization. This presents the team with a more complex task than that of questioning and evaluating the policies and practices of one organization. Their task will involve the reconciling of the goals and policies of the organizations involved into a workable team output. Beyond this, the team's perspective on those organizations will be comparative. It is clear from the limited evidence available that this process is an issue for interorganizational teams (Higgins *et al.* 1994).

An additional complexity arises where, as is increasingly typical in community care, organizations of different kinds are involved, including private and voluntary organizations as well as statutory bodies. Øvretveit's work (1993) shows the different ways in which teams can be constructed in this context, and different possible structures of leadership and decision making that might be appropriate for teams with different mixtures of organizational affiliation.

However, structural and procedural innovations, desirable as they are, may well not be enough to accommodate all relevant differences. Organizations differ in a range of ways that create complex issues for the team. Organizations have different priorities and definitions of need (Lightfoot 1995) and represent different constituencies (that is, their existence and activity is legitimized by different bodies). These constituencies range from central government in the case of health authorities and trusts, through central government plus local electorates in the case of local authorities, to memberships in the case of voluntary organizations, and shareholders/owners in the case of private organizations. Higgins *et al.* (1994) identify this issue as significant in relation to collaboration between health service and local authority employees. The wide difference in constituency means that the ultimate moral and social goals of these organizations, mandated to them by their constituency, will also probably differ. Central government and local electorates provide a mandate that tends to be universal in terms of service provision. Voluntary organizations usually have goals relating to service provision to the specified groups of users who are the concern of the membership, and private organizations also have goals involving the generation of profit and a return to shareholders where such are involved. Given these differences, it is clearly not going to be a simple matter to ensure that the agendas of the constituencies involved in the work of a particular team are consonant with one another. Although the discussion between collaborating organizations tends to be at management level, the reality is that issues of working detail can only be resolved at team level, and that teams will need the skills and capacities to do this. In addition, teams may come to identify their *own* constituency.

Other differences may well be of greater practical importance than formal goals, commitments and mandates, because they are less visible to the participants. Most salient of these are organizational culture and structure. Culture provides the background norms of organizational behaviour. As with culture generally, it is by its nature outside of conscious awareness most of the time. There is growing evidence that differences in organizational culture present real difficulties in interagency working generally (Higgins *et al.* 1994; Nocon 1994; Twigg and Atkin 1994). Structure, as a formal feature of the organization, is generally easier to focus on, and the problems created by differences of structure are perhaps easier to identify. Where structures do not easily match one another, it is possible to make arrangements which minimize the difficulties. Differences of culture are less manageable in this sense. One of the characteristics of effective groups is that they develop their own social norms which are to some degree, however subtly, distinct from those of the wider society outside of the group. Where the team functions effectively as a group, it will experience this development. Given that the team exists to provide a particular output, it is highly probable that the way in which the team understands and actions that output will be affected by the team's own norms. On one level this could be seen as a solution to the problem of a team being caught between two organizational cultures, in that it can develop its own culture, reflecting team personnel, structure and goals. However, this clearly depends on the employing organizations being willing to accept the consequences of this in terms of the team's relationship with managers in the respective organizations.

In any case, it is unrealistic to suppose that teams can be effective independently of the organizations that contribute to them. Teams perform best if their goals are part of the public domain rather than contained within the team (Weldon and Weingart 1993). This is most likely to work if there is clarity about goals at both team and organizational level. And it is clear from West's (1997) work that a crucial requirement for team effectiveness is feedback. Teams can review and evaluate their own output, but it is necessary for them to receive clear messages about the goals and priorities which apply to them, and to receive feedback from the larger bodies whose goals they are also there to pursue. And, while differences of emphasis can probably be accommodated, conflicting feedback is going to present a problem for teams; one which may threaten their ability to function effectively on their own terms, quite apart from being able to meet the requirements of the organizations encompassing them.

The organizational context of a team will also influence the way in which it functions. It is clear that teams in community care are not all cohesive, continuous groups with clear boundaries and identities. The range of structures available is set out by Øvretveit (1993), and two things are clear from his work: first that many of these structures are considerably looser than the traditional team; and second, that it is possible to be a member of several such structures at once. So, team membership is not an exclusive relationship for many people, but a network of involvements and loyalties.

Much can be gained for each team from this diversity of involvements. There is ample evidence that groups with insufficient internal variety of experience and perspective lose somewhat in terms of group performance (where this is measured by the performance of practical decision making tasks). Groups where members have alternative sources of information, experience and affiliation gain in some respects through the greater independence of members in relation to group norms. There is a greater willingness to risk conflict and question majorities. In this respect teams are strengthened by the fact that their members have other involvements also. But it is clear that teams which are heavily cross-cut with other networks will be less able to recruit their members into a partisan position where conflicts arise.

Sustaining the team from within

The contribution of the team to community care ultimately depends on several factors. One of these is the ability of community care organizations to collaborate in supporting and managing interorganizational and interprofessional teams. However, there is also a need for the people who make up those teams to have an appropriate repertoire to cope with the requirements of teamwork, in terms of attitudes, values and behaviours.

There is also a need for team members to have appropriate skills to make an optimal contribution to the functioning of the team. Certain skills seem particularly important in this context. Engel (1994) identifies a set of competences for collaboration in teams which includes adapting to change, participating in change, managing self, managing with others, and communication. The ability to understand contextual communication is particularly useful in group settings. The ability to recognize the needs of the group in terms of leadership likewise appears to be particularly important, and the ability to work with members of other professions is clearly of central importance in the context of community care. This involves among other things the ability to accommodate other perspectives which may be threatening to the perspectives one is applying to a situation. A degree of flexibility of thinking is important, as is the ability to cope with situations of unclarity and uncertainty.

However, there is also a question as to how the workings of teams should be regulated in terms of the legitimate expectations and obligations on their members. How far, for instance, is it legitimate for individual team members to compromise on personal or professional principles for the sake of team unity or interprofessional harmony? We can argue that teams seem to benefit from a certain degree of dissent, but it is clear that they also require a degree of consensus. Alongside this practical consideration, the team member needs to be aware also of obligations other than the team. It may be that however beneficial team functioning is to the quality of service received by users overall, a situation may arise where an individual worker disagrees with the rest of the team about the appropriate way forward with a particular user, and believes that their conviction about the benefit or rights of the user provides an adequate basis for refusal to accept the views of the rest of the team. A commitment to the usefulness of teams does not necessarily imply an unconditional commitment to the supremacy of team cohesion.

If disagreement is legitimate in these circumstances, it is also crucial that team members, and the team as a whole, have the capacity to manage the disagreement (as opposed to resolving it) without disabling the team in its legitimate functions. The ability to do this, for both team and individuals, is partly a matter of using the same skills which are relevant to a range of other team activities – communication, decision making, management of conflict, expression and acknowledgement of feelings.

Unfortunately, skill is not enough, as skills can be employed to inappropriate ends. The process also requires a commitment to particular principles and the ability to put those principles into practice. Among these might be: principles of equality of esteem and importance among team members (and by implication among different professionals); principles of care for the needs of other team members; principles of honesty and integrity in team communication; and principles of honesty and clarity about priorities where these conflict with one another. These principles are clearly demanding in their observance, and as a result of this, individual and team commitment to them is in constant danger of being overwhelmed by the demands and stresses of daily operation. There are a number of ways in which teams can be assisted to sustain commitment against these sorts of pressures.

One is to create a set of rules for team operation which embody and in effect enforce adherence to required principles. Clearly, such rules can only operate on the basis of consent, and ideally should be drawn up by the team. Their effectiveness depends mainly on their incorporation into the norms of the team. Janssens and Brett (1997) offer a set of requirements for the members of transnational teams which are transferable to interprofessional teams. These include equality of respect and importance, openness in acknowledging cultural differences, and explicit decision rules. Whatever rules are adopted, if they are experienced as in any sense external or marginal, they will not be observed. I have argued elsewhere that it may be necessary to seek to inculcate a commitment to appropriate principles upon individual members of the professions involved in community care teamwork, so that there is a predisposition to adhere to team rules from the outset (Wilmot and Jones 1997).

However, there is a danger that too much emphasis on getting the 'right kinds of people' into teams will lead to a psychologically determinist view of team functioning, and it is clear that there is also a need for teams to learn together to develop appropriate norms, and adhere to them.

Conclusion

It seems easier to agree that teams are a 'good thing' than to agree about what they *are* in the first place. The degree of consensus that teams are a 'good thing' is perhaps surprising. Teamworking is not easy, and where community care professionals are gathered together, an anecdotal impression is that 'bad team' experiences provide one of the commonest shared problems and readiest talking points. If that impression is accurate, it would not be surprising to find a high degree of disillusionment with teamwork.

However, important factors work against this. The 'small group' is a social unit of enormous importance and power for human beings. That importance may well be evolutionary as well as cultural, as small groups appear to have importance in most cultures. The small group can shape and sustain goal-oriented behaviour in human beings in the most adverse of circumstances.

So it is perhaps more appropriate to say that teams are 'a necessary thing' in community care – that they are unavoidable and it is incumbent on community care workers and managers to use them as effectively as possible. The special demands of teamwork in community care – interprofessional, interorganizational, multistructured teams – are being documented and investigated, and at the time of writing a body of knowledge is emerging which offers a reasonable prospect of providing a framework for the necessary skills to meet those demands.

Summary

- This chapter identified the importance of the team in the context of community care.

- The relationship between the team and the small group was considered, particularly in the context of team models which do not have all the characteristics of the small group as it is usually defined.

- Research evidence was offered on those characteristics of small groups in general, and teams in particular, which are associated with effectiveness.

- The demands of teamwork in community care were explored. In particular, the need for teams to include workers of different professional and occupational groups was considered. The team's relationship with the organization was also discussed, and the development of multi-agency teams in community care was considered in relation to the pressures on team functioning, and the ways in which the organization can support the team.

• The characteristics of team members needed to sustain teamwork were considered in relation to the development of appropriate skills, team norms and, possibly, rules or values.

Further reading

Handy, C. (1993) *Understanding Organizations,* 4th edn. London: Penguin.
Øvretveit, J. (1993) *Coordinating Community Care: Multidisciplinary Teams and Care Management.* Buckingham: Open University Press.

References

Allport, G. (1954) *The Nature of Prejudice.* Reading, MA: Addison Wesley.
Anderson, N. and West, M. (1996) The team climate inventory: development of the TCI and its applications in teambuilding for innovativeness. *European Journal of Work and Organizational Psychology,* 5 (1): 53–66.
Bales, R.F. (1950) *Interaction Process Analysis.* Reading, MA: Addison Wesley.
Baron, R., Kerr, N. and Miller, N. (1992) *Group Process, Group Decision, Group Action.* Buckingham: Open University Press.
Beattie, A. (1995) War and peace among the health tribes, in K. Soothill, L. Mackay and C. Webb (eds) *Interprofessional Relations in Health Care.* London: Edward Arnold.
Belbin, R.M. (1981) *Management Teams: Why They Succeed or Fail.* London: Heinemann.
Belbin, R.M. (1993) *Team Roles at Work.* Oxford: Butterworth Heinemann.
Bond, C. and Titus, L. (1983) Social facilitation: a meta-analysis of 241 studies. *Psychological Bulletin,* 94: 265–92.
Brooks, A. (1994) Power and the production of knowledge: collective team learning in work organizations. *Human Resource Development Quarterly,* 5: 213–35.
Cottrell, N.B. (1972) Social facilitation, in C.G. McClintock (ed.) *Experimental Social Psychology.* New York: Holt.
Dalley, G. (1993) Professional ideology or organisational tribalism? The health service-social work divide, in J. Walmesley (ed.) *Health, Welfare and Practice.* London: Sage.
Dombeck, M-T. (1997) Professional personhood: training, territoriality and tolerance. *Journal of Interprofessional Care,* 11: 9–21.
Dulewicz, V. (1995) A validation of Belbin's team roles from 16PF and OPQ using bosses rating of competence. *Journal of Occupational and Organisational Psychology,* 68: 81–99.
Engel, C. (1994) A functional anatomy of teamwork, in A. Leathard (ed.) *Going Inter-Professional: Working Together for Health and Welfare.* London: Routledge.
Gebhardt, L. and Meyers, R. (1995) Subgroup influence in decision-making groups. *Small Group Research,* 26: 147–68.
Handy, C. (1993) *Understanding Organisations,* 4th edn. London: Penguin.
Hare, A.P. (1994) Types of roles in small groups. *Small Group Research,* 25: 433–48.
Hellkamp, D. (1996) A multidisciplinary collaborative management and consulting model: the inner workings and future challenges. *Journal of Educational and Psychological Consultation,* 7: 79–85.

Higgins, R., Oldman, C. and Hunter, D. (1994) Working together: lessons for collaboration between health and social services. *Health and Social Care in the Community*, 2: 269–77.

Homans, G. (1951) *The Human Group*. London: Routledge and Kegan Paul.

Iles, P. and Auluck, R. (1990) From organisational to interorganisational development in nursing practice: improving the effectiveness of interdisciplinary teamwork and interagency collaboration. *Journal of Advanced Nursing*, 15: 50–8.

Janis, I.L. (1968) *Victims of Groupthink: A Psychological Study of Foreign Policy Decisions and Fiascos*. Boston, MA: Houghton Mifflin.

Janssens, M. and Brett, J. (1997) Meaningful participation in transnational teams. *European Journal of Work and Organizational Psychology*, 6 (2): 153–68.

Johnson, D. and Johnson, F. (1987) *Joining Together: Group Theory and Group Skills*, 3rd edn. London: Prentice Hall.

Lightfoot, J. (1995) Identifying needs and setting priorities: issues of theory, policy and practice. *Health & Social Care in the Community*, 3: 105–14.

Mohamed, A. and Wiebe, F. (1996) Toward a process theory of groupthink. *Small Group Research*, 27: 416–30.

Neck, C. and Moorhead, G. (1995) Groupthink remodeled: the importance of leadership, time pressure and methodical decision-making procedures. *Human Relations*, 48: 537–58.

Nemeth, C.J. (1986) Differential contributions of majority and minority influence. *Psychological Review*, 93: 23–32.

Nocon, A. (1994) *Collaboration in Community Care in the 1990s*. Sunderland: Business Education Publishers Ltd.

Øvretveit, J. (1993) *Coordinating Community Care: Multidisciplinary Teams and Care Management*. Buckingham: Open University Press.

Raelin, J. (1994) Three scales of professional deviance within organisations. *Journal of Organisational Behaviour*, 15: 483–501.

Senior, B. (1997) Team roles and team performance: is there really a link? *Journal of Occupational and Organisational Psychology*, 70: 241–58.

Sessa, V. and Jackson, S. (1995) Diversity in decision-making teams: all differences are not created equal, in M. Chemers, S. Oskamp and M. Constanzo (eds) *Diversity in Organisations: New Perspectives for a Changing Workplace*. Thousand Oaks, CA: Sage.

Sherif, M. (1936) *The Psychology of Group Norms*. New York: Harper & Rowe.

Stasser, G. and Titus, W. (1985) Pooling of unshared information in group decision making: biased information sampling during group discussion. *Journal of Personality and Social Psychology*, 48: 1467–8.

Twigg, J. and Atkin, K. (1994) *Carers Perceived: Policy and Practice in Informal Care*. Buckingham: Open University Press.

Van Dyne, L. and Saavedra, R. (1996) A naturalistic minority influence experiment: effects on divergent thinking, conflict and originality in work-groups. *British Journal of Social Psychology*, 35: 151–67.

Weldon, E. and Weingart, L. (1993) Group goals and group performance. *British Journal of Social Psychology*, 32: 307–34.

West, M. (1997) Collaboration improves the quality of care. Conference paper, *Journal of Interprofessional Care* conference 'All Together Better Health', London, 18 July.

West, M. and Altink, W. (1996) Innovation at work: individual, group, organizational and socio-historical perspectives. *European Journal of Work and Organizational Psychology*, 5 (1): 3–11.

West, M. and Field, R. (1995) Teamwork in primary health care 1: perspectives from organisational psychology. *Journal of Interprofessional Care*, 9: 117–22.

Wilmot, S. (1995) Professional values and interprofessional dialogue. *Journal of Interprofessional Care*, 9: 257–66.

Wilmot, S. and Jones, I.F. (1997) Rules, values and virtues for interprofessional education and practice. Conference paper, *Journal of Interprofessional Care* conference 'All Together Better Health', London, 18 July.

Witz, A. (1992) *Professions and Patriarchy*. London: Routledge.

Woodcock, M. (1989) *Team Development Manual*. Aldershot: Gower.

Zajonc, R.B. (1965) Social facilitation. *Science*, 149: 269–74.

Zeiss, A., Heinemann, G., Nichols, L. and Waite, M. (1997) Measurement of team performance and effectiveness: the veterans affairs interdisciplinary team training programme (ITTP) measures evaluation project. Conference paper, *Journal of Interprofessional Care* conference 'All Together Better Health', London, 18 July.

GLOSSARY

Advocacy: representing and promoting the needs and views of individuals or groups.

Ageism: prejudice or negative stereotypes about people based on chronological age.

Alma-Ata Conference: a conference organized by WHO in 1978. It culminated in the Alma-Ata Declaration, which emphasized the crucial role of primary health care, and the importance of social and economic measures in the optimization of health.

Assessment: a formal evaluation of an individual's needs, wishes, resources and strengths with the object of determining his or her eligibility for assistance in material terms.

Assumptions: usually unspoken, and often unconscious understandings of the reality or truth of a given phenomenon. May lead to actions as if the assumptions were true.

Audit Commission: a quango established in 1983 with a remit to monitor the efficiency and effectiveness of statutory health and social care providers and to advise on ways of improving their performance.

Beliefs: abstract concepts that an individual 'believes in' – i.e. believes to be 'true', despite there being no empirical proof; e.g. justice, god.

Care management: the process of assessing and meeting a service user's needs advocated in the 1990 NHS and Community Care Act. It includes the activities of: finding, referral and screening; assessing need; care planning and service packaging; monitoring and reassessment.

Carer: an individual providing assistance with activities of daily living and decision making for a person who is ill or disabled on an informal basis in the context of a relationship.

Charities: voluntary organizations recognized as meeting or promoting one of four objectives: religion, education, the relief of poverty or other purposes beneficial to the whole community.

Cold war: the period, roughly from the end of the Second World War to the early 1990s, of verbal and other non-military hostility between the 'communist bloc' of Eastern Europe and some other countries in that sphere of influence, and countries of Europe, the USA and elsewhere who described themselves as the 'free world'.

Community: a widely-used but complex and emotive concept with a multiplicity of meanings. It can refer to a defined locality or geographical area, a local set of relationships centred in a particular locality, or more broadly it signifies a sense of common identity based on shared interests or experiences not necessarily geographically-based.

Community care grant: a grant paid out of the social fund to allow the purchase of basic household items to enable someone to live in the community.

Consumer choice: this idea relates to users of welfare services having the opportunity to exercise choices over the type and nature of particular services they wish to receive; it does not imply users having direct control over the way the service is provided, managed or evaluated.

Contract culture: the dual process whereby the government grants method of funding public services is giving way to contracts and the delivery of welfare services is being transferred from public providers to voluntary and other organizations.

Culture: in the context of an organization or group, the patterns of behaviour and unstated assumptions that influence members of that organization or group.

Darwinism: derivations and further development from the original theory of Charles Darwin of the development of species by natural selection. Often popularized as the 'survival of the fittest'.

Decentralization: the process whereby services are devolved from central government to smaller localized units or to authorities and agencies closer to service users.

Deinstitutionalization: the resettlement and discharge of long-stay patients into the community.

Effectiveness: a measure of desired outcomes; the extent to which services are delivered to focused populations.

Empowerment: the processes involving users in identifying needs, engaging in policy making, service planning, management and assessment and having more direct control over service provision.

Enabling: the processes whereby statutory welfare agencies, rather than providing services, manage and plan provision purchased from alternative agencies.

Enlightenment: an eighteenth-century philosophical movement in Europe, characterized by scientific enquiry and the use of reason.

Ethnocentric: a focus on the needs and circumstances of a majority ethnic or racial group to the exclusion of minority(ies).

Eugenics: the study of human development through inheritance. Particularly at the end of the nineteenth century and the first half of the twentieth, eugenic ideas sought to influence which members of the population should be encouraged to breed, and which should not. They also had important effects on segregating certain groups of people in institutions.

Evidence based practice: a growing movement in the medical world where treatments are only applied if extensive research evidence exists for their effectiveness.

Existentialism: the philosophy that denies any external force in determining an individual's actions and beliefs. The individual will is thought by this philosophy to be the sole free and responsible agent in determining human destiny.

Externalism: a value position which regards input from *external* sources as more valid than a position derived from internal thought and analysis. Externalism stems from a lack of self-reliance (which enables people to form their own views) and this increasingly has people relying on external sources such as 'experts', 'gurus' and even 'famous' people such as TV personalities.

Gatekeeper: the individual or organization who is typically the first to be encountered by those seeking services, and who has the power to enable or block access to services provided to others.

Global economy: the phenomenon of the gradual breaking down of trade barriers across the world so that goods are sold increasingly freely between different countries. It also refers to the growth of multinational corporations without allegiance to any one country.

GP fundholder: A GP who has devolved budgets to provide and purchase medical care on behalf of his or her patients.

Green Paper: a consultative document produced by UK governments which interested groups and the wider public are invited to comment on as a prelude to the publication of proposals for legislation.

Holistic: an approach to the understanding of the human being which seeks to encompass all levels and perspectives into one overall framework.

Ideas: mentally constructed notions of how a phenomenon is, or might be. Often involving an original label or new use of an existing label to summarize them.

Ideology: a set of shared beliefs or understandings of reality which serve both as a basis for action and the means of legitimizing outcomes to actions; a way of thinking or body of ideas.

Inclusion: the value position that all people, by virtue of their rights as human beings and citizens, should be included in the facilities and privileges available in a given society. Inclusion has been especially applied to education, but is increasingly being used as a campaigning position for a whole range of services.

Independent sector: a term used to distinguish non-statutory from statutory welfare, and encompassing both commercial enterprises and voluntary organizations.

Individualism: a philosophy which has benefits to the individual, as opposed to the group, as its key tenet. Adherents claim that individuals striving to maximize their self-interest create the conditions, through market mechanisms, for the overall interests of society to be raised.

Informal care: this refers to the care undertaken within families, and by friends and relatives, of people within their homes or within the community. Informal care is viewed as different from voluntary services. It often involves devoting long periods of demanding personal care to an individual.

Inputs: expectations of the resources required to provide a service.

Inquiry report (mental health): the report of a team of experts into the care and treatment of current patients, or those who have had recent contact with specialist mental health services, which is commissioned by central government to report on lessons to be learned and matters of accountability. Generally commissioned after homicide or serious incident.

Learning difficulty (or learning disability): slow intellectual development.

Life course perspective: a perspective from which ageing is viewed as part of the totality of human life, understood as a successive series of stages, from infancy through to old age.

Longitudinal approach: one in which the same study individuals are followed over time.

Managerialism: the importation of the practices and ideology of commercial management into state welfare services.

Materialism: the belief that all phenomena consist of matter and the interactions and movements of it. This includes material processes in the brain being the sole determinants of human reason and behaviour.

Medical model: when applied to services, implies they are set up, staffed and organized on the basis of a process of expert diagnosis, treatment and care by medically trained personnel. Has been criticized by a number of groups, especially disabled groups, for its belief that all problems reside physically in the individual, rather than being a combination of some impairment and society's reaction to it.

Metanarrative: an over-arching discourse or position which organizes other positions and seeks to explain or to represent them.

Metaphysical: in the context of a being, something beyond the material or natural; a phenomenon which cannot be demonstrated by empirical evidence.

Mixed economy of care: the provision of care services by more than one sector – state, commercial, voluntary, informal.

Model: a description, often simplified and often symbolic or mathematical, of a phenomenon in order to examine the phenomenon or make predictions based upon it.

Moral relativism: a perspective which rejects the search for a single 'correct' moral analysis, and envisages a situation where different moralities are all equally valid.

Normalization: a set of ideas, originating in Scandinavia but developed extensively in North America and worldwide by Wolf Wolfensberger. The development has led to a range of definitions and interpretations. One used commonly is 'the use of culturally valued means to obtain culturally valued lives for people at risk of devaluation'. The ideas examine the way in which certain people are devalued or 'wounded' by society's response to an impairment or difference and suggest a reversal of that process being the goal of services. Reconceptualized by Wolfensberger as **social role valorization**.

Outcomes: the contribution the service makes to the users' well-being.

Outputs: the measurable units of service delivered to service users.

Post-modernism: originating in the arts and architecture, a school of thought that rejects 'modern' scientific theories of society and human behaviour, especially those that seek to explain phenomena on a large scale or by a single metatheory.

Poverty: severe deprivation, usually associated with inadequate resources, especially financial. (see also **relative poverty**).

Professionalism: a process through which members of an occupation build up control over its practice through laying claim to particular expertise, and resticting access through establishing entry, training and qualifying criteria.

Purchaser/provider split: the division of state welfare agencies into two separate units, one charged with planning and purchasing services on behalf of service users, the other with delivering individual or groups of services.

Quality: standards that ensure that a service conforms to a specification and other requirements.

Quality of life: the concept that it is possible to define and measure the degree to which life is worth living. A range of attempts have been made, some based on individual's opinions of what constitutes quality in their own lives, and others on criteria devised by academics, doctors or ethicists. Some measurements have been used to justify certain treatments for individuals, or the withholding of those treatments.

Rationalism: ideas, stemming from the period of the Enlightenment, that human affairs should be decided by rational human beings. Rationalism stands in contrast to decisions based on appeals to external sources of morality, such as a god. In rationalism, the power of the human intellect is seen as the supreme force.

Reductionism: an approach to the understanding of the human being which seeks to explain everything (or as much as possible) by the use of one level of analysis or one academic discipline. For instance, biological reductionism would seek to explain all human behaviour through biological processes.

Rights: entitlements or privileges allowed by a society to all or some of its citizens. Distinction is made between legal rights, which are enforceable by using the courts, and broader notions of human rights, which are believed by some to exist 'naturally' but have generally been arrived at by a political consensus on certain issues.

Sensualism: a value position which has the pursuit of sensual pleasures – food, sex, drugs, bodily comforts – as the main point of life. It is therefore resistant to features of life which detract from that pursuit. Sensualism goes beyond ordinary concerns for health and well-being.

Service based economies: economies where the *dominant* industries are services, as opposed to manufacturing or food production. Such economies are dominated by banking, insurance and other financial services, and have a prominent place for legal, educational, tourist based and similar services. Service based economies are becoming increasingly common in the West.

Small group: a small number of individuals (usually not more than 12) with sufficient contact with one another to develop a social structure and pattern of interaction.

Social problem: a problem which is seen to relate to society as a whole, or specific groups within it. Can be seen as a problem for society and/or a problem that has *social* as opposed to *individual* causes.

Social role valorization (SRV): a reformulation and reconceptualization by Wolf Wolfensberger of his earlier principle of normalization. Drawing on the same analysis of devaluation SRV emphasizes the importance of social roles in this process and the use of valued social roles as a defence against and a remedy for devaluation of both individuals and groups.

Social theory of disability: a theory, originating with disabled people, that sees disability as being created by society's reaction to impairment, in particular the difficulty that capitalist industrialized society has in dealing with people seen as non-productive. It emphasizes collective action by disabled people to reclaim their own identity and campaign against the discrimination imposed by society.

Theories: as used in Chapters 3 and 4, theories are defined as explanations for phenomena, either in the physical or the social world, which can be tested and therefore possibly refuted. In social science many theories are only testable at the probabilistic level – i.e. where a theory holds good in most or the majority of cases – rather than the deterministic level where a theory holds good in all cases.

Universals: the notion that phenomena can be ordered in a hierarchical way such that any individual phenomenon is only a subset of one of only relatively few universal laws. This has been applied to so-called laws of human behaviour as well as physical laws and the notion of universality implies that the law applies and explains phenomena across different geographical, physical and social areas.

User involvement: refers to the involvement of service users in the ongoing provision of services, where users have a primary role in the way services are provided, managed and evaluated.

User/service user: replacing 'patient', 'client' and terms now regarded as oppressive such as 'dependant'. Service user describes individuals in receipt of community care services, generally in the community rather than in residential settings.

Utilitarianism: a branch of philosophy where the gains of human actions are weighed against their costs, and are seen as justified if a net benefit accrues. The issue to be resolved is how gains and costs are measured, and utilitarianism has ultimately settled on a scale of happiness and misery or suffering.

Values: personal, moral stances, usually based on beliefs that lead to a judgement about what is 'right' and 'wrong' in any situation or set of circumstances. Can be applied to more general positions on particular issues.

White Paper: a UK central government document setting out the government's legislative proposals.

INDEX

PSYCHOLOGY FOR NURSES AND THE CARING PROFESSIONS

Sheila Payne and Jan Walker

- What is psychology and how is it relevant to health care practice?
- What influences do psychological factors have in determining outcomes in health care?
- What are the different approaches within psychology which can be used to understand normal human functioning?

Psychology for Nurses and the Caring Professions is one of a series of texts which provide coherent and multi-disciplinary support for all professional groups involved in the provision of health and social care. It introduces students to a range of psychological theories and research, supported by evidence from health psychology. Applications are offered within a variety of health care settings, with an emphasis on health promotion and preventive care.

The authors draw upon their clinical, teaching and research experience to engage the student's interest through the use of case examples, special research-based topics and exercises for group discussion or individual study. The text has been carefully designed with the student in mind: a comprehensive reference list is provided at the end of the book, together with a glossary of terms. The text is illustrated throughout with diagrams, tables and graphs and suggestions for further reading are given at the end of each chapter.

Psychology for Nurses and the Caring Professions is a key textbook for all students undertaking diploma or degree level courses in nursing, health and social care.

Contents

Introduction to psychology – Understanding health and illness – Self concept and body image – Theories of learning: developments and applications – Perception, memory and patient information-giving – Stress and coping: theory and applications in health care – Development and loss in social relationships – Pain – Social processes in health care delivery – Epilogue – Glossary – References – Index.

240pp   0 335 19410 9 (Paperback)   0 335 19411 7 (Hardback)

RESEARCH INTO PRACTICE (SECOND EDITION)
A READER FOR NURSES AND THE CARING PROFESSIONS

Pamela Abbott and Roger Sapsford (eds)

Praise for the first edition of Research into Practice and Research Methods for Nurses and the Caring Professions:

> These books provide a good introduction for the uninitiated to reading and doing research. Abbott and Sapsford provide a clearly written and accessible introduction to social research . . . One of their aims is to 'de-mystify' research, and in this they succeed admirably . . . After reading the text and the articles in the reader, and working through the various research exercises, readers should have a clear appreciation of how to evaluate other people's research and how to begin their own.
>
> David Field, *Journal of Palliative Medicine*

This is a thoroughly revised and updated edition of the bestselling reader for nurses and the caring professions. It offers carefully selected examples of research, all concerned in some way with nursing or the study of health and community care. It illustrates the kind of research that can be done by a small team or a single researcher, without large-scale research grants. The editors have chosen papers which show a great diversity of approaches: differing in emphasis on description or explanation, different degrees of structure in design and different appeals to the authority of science or the authenticity of emphatic exploration. They show the limitations typical of small-scale projects carried out with limited resources and the experience of applied research as it occurs in practice, as opposed to how it tends to look when discussed in textbooks. The chapters have been organized into three sections representing three distinct types of social science research: observing and participating, talking to people and asking questions, and controlled trials and comparisons. Each section is provided with an editorial introduction.

Contents
Introduction – Section A: Observing and participating – Labouring in the dark: limitations on the giving of information to enable patients to orient themselves to the likely events and timescale of labour – Portfolios: a developmental influence? – A postscript to nursing – Section B: Talking to people and asking questions – Leaving it to mum: community care for mentally handicapped children – Planning research: a case of heart disease – Home helps and district nurses: community care in the far South-west – Studying policy and practice: use of vignettes – Section C: Controlled trials and comparisons – Treatment of depressed women by nurses in Britain – The mortality of doctors in relation to their smoking habits: a preliminary report – Ethnic variation in the female labour force: a research note – Postscript – Author index – Subject index.

The Contributors
Pamela Abbott, Julia V. Cayne, Richard Doll, Verona Gordon, A. Bradford Hill, Nicky James, Mavis Kirkham, Roger Sapsford, Melissa Tyler.

184pp   0 335 19695 0 (Paperback)   0 335 19696 9 (Hardback)

RESEARCH METHODS FOR NURSES AND THE CARING PROFESSIONS (SECOND EDITION)

Pamela Abbott and Roger Sapsford

Praise for the first editions of *Research into Practice* and *Research Methods for Nurses and the Caring Professions:*

> These books provide a good introduction for the uninitiated to reading and doing research. Abbott and Sapsford provide a clearly written and accessible introduction to social research . . . One of their aims is to 'de-mystify' research, and in this they succeed admirably . . . After reading the text and the articles in the reader, and working through the various research exercises, readers should have a clear appreciation of how to evaluate other people's research and how to begin their own.
>
> David Field, *Journal of Palliative Medicine*

This book, now substantially revised in its second edition, is about the appreciation, evaluation and conduct of social research. Aimed at nurses, social workers, community workers and others in the caring professions, the book is particularly focused on research which evaluates and contributes to professional practice. The authors have provided many short, practical exercises in the text, and the examples are drawn mostly from projects carried out by one or two people rather than large research teams. The clear, accessible style will make this the ideal introductory text for those undertaking or studying research for the first time.

The book may be used in conjunction with *Research into Practice* (Open University Press), a reader of useful examples selected by the same authors.

Contents
Section 1: Introduction – Finding out and making sense – Section 2: Assessing research – Reading research reports – Reading open interview research – Reading observation research – Reading about controlled trials – Reading survey research – Reading secondary sources – Section 3: Doing research – Using secondary sources – Survey research: design and sampling – Experimental practice – Open interviewing – Analysing text – Participant observation – Section 4: In conclusion – Writing up – In conclusion: research into practice – Glossary – References – Author index – Subject index.

224pp   0 335 19697 7 (Paperback)   0 335 19698 5 (Hardback)

SOCIAL POLICY FOR NURSES AND THE CARING PROFESSIONS
Louise Ackers and Pamela Abbott

- What is the relationship between social policy and health?
- Who provides social welfare?
- How has the provision of welfare developed?

Social Policy for Nurses and the Caring Professions is one of a series of texts which provide coherent and multi-disciplinary support for all professional groups involved in the provision of health and social care. It provides the student with a lively, readable and well illustrated introduction to social policy. The authors take as a starting point the importance of the conceptual connection between health and illness. The stress throughout the book is on the significance of social policy in preventing ill health and disability as well as supporting the sick and disabled. A broad approach to social policy is taken, and the text is organized around the provision of welfare in the following contexts:

- public
- private
- voluntary
- informal

Consideration is given to competing ideologies of welfare and the development of welfare as well as contemporary provision.

Social Policy for Nurses and the Caring Professions is based on the authors' first-hand teaching and research experience. The text has been carefully designed with the student in mind: a comprehensive reference list is provided at the end of the book, together with a glossary of important terms. The text is illustrated with tables and graphs throughout, and there are suggestions for further reading at the end of each chapter.

Social Policy for Nurses and the Caring Professions is a key textbook for all students undertaking diploma or degree level courses in nursing, health and social care.

Contents
What is social policy? – The development of a welfare state – Health inequalities and state health policies – Poverty, inequality and social policy – State income maintenance and welfare benefits – Privatization and social welfare – The changing role of the voluntary sector in the provision of social welfare – The role of informal care – The mixed economy of care: welfare services for dependent people – Welfare pluralism in the 1990s: the changing role of the state – Glossary – References – Index.

288pp   0 335 19359 5 (Paperback)   0 335 19360 9 (Hardback)

8202

8202